The theory of growth in a
corporate economy

The theory of growth in a corporate economy

Management preference research and development and economic growth

HIROYUKI ODAGIRI

Institute of Socio-Economic Planning
University of Tsukuba, Japan

CAMBRIDGE UNIVERSITY PRESS

Cambridge
London   New York   New Rochelle
Melbourne   Sydney

Published by the Press Syndicate of the University of Cambridge
The Pitt Building, Trumpington Street, Cambridge CB2 1RP
32 East 57th Street, New York, NY 10022, USA
296 Beaconsfield Parade, Middle Park, Melbourne 3206, Australia

First published 1981

Printed in the United States of America
Typeset by Science Press, Ephrata, Pennsylvania
Printed and bound by The Murray Printing Company, Westford,
Massachusetts

Library of Congress Cataloging in Publication Data
Odagiri, Hiroyuki, 1946–
The theory of growth in a corporate economy.
Bibliography: p.
Includes index.
1. Economic development.   2. Corporations – Growth.
3. Economic policy.   I. Title.
HD75.03   338.9'001   80-23494
ISBN 0 521 23132 9

Contents

Preface   ix
List of variables   xii
Introduction   1

Part I. Microeconomics

1 Modern corporations and the management   15
   1.1 *Introduction*   15
   1.2 *Forms of business firms*   16
   1.3 *The importance of large corporations*   21
   1.4 *The separation of ownership from control*   25
   1.5 *The goal of the management: pecuniary motives*   31
   1.6 *The goal of the management: nonpecuniary motives*   37

2 Takeovers and managerial choice   43
   2.1 *Introduction*   43
   2.2 *The v-g frontier*   45
   2.3 *A model of takeovers*   48
   2.4 *Managerial decision making under uncertainty*   53
   2.5 *Summary and concluding remarks*   64

3 The value and growth of the firm   68
   3.1 *Introduction: Optimization in two stages*   68
   3.2 *The value of the firm*   69
   3.3 *Marris's model*   71
   3.4 *Uzawa's model*   75
   3.5 *Research activity and the growth of the firm*   80
   3.6 *Summary and concluding remarks*   84

Part II. Macroeconomics

4 The role of corporate shares in general equilibrium   89
   4.1 *Introduction*   89
   4.2 *Notation, definitions, and assumptions*   92

4.3	*The rate of return and valuation ratio*	96
4.4	*The steady-state equilibrium in a one-class economy*	99
4.5	*The steady-state equilibrium in a two-class economy*	103
4.6	*Summary and concluding remarks*	108
	Appendix: Propositions 4.1 and 4.2 compared	110

5   The model of economic growth   111
5.1	*Introduction*	111
5.2	*The model without research activity*	114
5.3	*The model with research activity*	116
5.4	*The v-g frontier revisited*	121
5.5	*Why steady-state growth?*	131
5.6	*Summary and concluding remarks*	133
	Appendix: The model with research activity:	
	comparative analysis	135

Part III. Why a new theory?

6   Theoretical relevance: growth models compared   139
6.1	*Models of economic growth*	139
6.2	*Four models: Marx, Solow, Robinson, and Kaldor*	141
6.3	*The model of the growth of a corporate economy*	146

7   Empirical relevance: Japan's economic growth   151
7.1	*The facts*	151
7.2	*Management preference in Japan: more growth*	
	than market value	154
7.3	*Application of the model and some qualifications*	160
7.4	*Summary and concluding remarks*	163

Part IV. Fiscal and monetary policy

8   Fiscal policy in a moneyless economy   169
8.1	*Introduction*	169
8.2	*The model of the firm*	170
8.3	*The macroequilibrium*	173
8.4	*The model of economic growth*	174
8.5	*Policy implications*	176

9   Economic policy in a monetary economy   178
| 9.1 | *Introduction* | 178 |
| 9.2 | *The model of the firm* | 181 |

9.3   The macroequilibrium   184
9.4   The model of economic growth   186
9.5   Policy implications and concluding remarks   190

Part V. Toward a dynamic theory of a multisector economy

10   The managerial sector versus the neoclassical sector   197
     10.1   Introduction   197
     10.2   Assumptions   199
     10.3   The stock market   203
     10.4   The firms   206
     10.5   The model of economic growth   208

Bibliography   211
Index   219

Preface

Every theory of economic growth mirrors the author's view of the economy in which he lives. *The Theory of Growth in a Corporate Economy* is no exception. Ours is that many phenomena in a modern capitalist economy are best understood by viewing it as "a corporate economy" where the greater part of economic activity is carried out by a limited number of big joint-stock corporations to which entry is difficult and of which the management possesses strong (although not unlimited) power to pursue its own goals, even against the owners' interests. This book attempts to analyze, mainly theoretically, the dynamic properties of such a corporate economy. The scope and method of this study as well as the precise definition of corporate economy are presented in the Introduction.

The book is chiefly addressed to professional economists and postgraduate students, presuming an understanding of microeconomics and macroeconomics at the graduate level. Two chapters are exceptions, however. Chapter 7 discusses Japan's experience as compared to that of the United States. Those who are concerned with business and economic growth in Japan will find the chapter interesting even if they do not have a background in economic theory or have not read the preceding chapters. Chapter 1 describes modern corporations and the goal of management. It also presumes no background in the field because the topic is of interest to a wider range of scholars and students and should be useful as supplementary reading for undergraduate courses on microeconomics, managerial economics, and industrial organization.

Much of the work for this study was done while I was at Northwestern University as a Fulbright recipient. In fact, Chapters 2 to 7 are based on my doctoral dissertation. Work on other chapters was accomplished while I was teaching at Oberlin College and the University of Tsukuba in Japan. Naturally and fortunately, of course, I received encouragement and suggestions from many people in these and other institutions, which I am pleased to acknowledge.

This research started as a term paper for Professor Dale Mortensen's macroeconomics course at Northwestern, although there remains

ix

little similarity between that paper and this edition. During the two years preceding my graduation, Professor Mortensen encouraged me to pursue my own ideas and gave me his deep insights and constructive advice during our innumerable lengthy discussions. My debt to him is literally immeasurable. Professor John Ledyard made many theoretical comments and helped improve my writing; Professor Morton Kamien, despite his busy administrative schedule, provided several ideas that influenced this book. These three, my dissertation committee at Northwestern, spent considerable time at the dull and unpleasant task of reading my many preliminary papers. My sincerest thanks to all of them.

I had the benefit of presenting parts of this dissertation at several seminars at Northwestern in order to receive helpful comments from the participants. Among them, Professors Frank Brechling and Ronald Braeutigam, and Wayne Joerding, then a graduate student like myself, must be mentioned.

A year at Oberlin after Northwestern was a perfect setting to develop the research. Professor James Zinser, then the chairman of the Economics Department, took pains to let me concentrate on my research and also read a part of an earlier version of the book, making suggestions on both the theoretical aspects and on the language.

I am also deeply indebted to the late Professor Tsunehiko Watanabe and Professor Susumu Koizumi, both of Osaka University. Although neither has given any direct input to this study, it was their encouragement and advice during the years I was in Osaka (before Northwestern) that helped me to grasp Marris's model and realize its wide applicability.

During the preparation of this book, I received encouragement from Professor Robin Marris, who is now in Maryland. His interest in my work was a source of much pleasure and an honor because of my great intellectual debt to Professor Marris's many works on the managerial theory of the firm. Furthermore, he kindly read the entire earlier version and provided many constructive comments and suggestions that substantially improved the book.

None of these people are responsible for any errors, however, especially in that occasionally I stubbornly did not follow their suggestions.

Roseann Geyer, Vera Alferio, and Lynn Boone typed earlier versions and Sonia Hosono the final one. I owe much to their excellent skills.

Acknowledgement is made to the publishers of the following books and articles that kindly permitted quotations to be used in this book: Abegglen, J. C., *Management and Worker: The Japanese Solution* (Tokyo: Sophia University); Berle, A. A. and Means, G. C., *The Modern Corporation and Private Property* (New York: Macmillan); Friedman, M. "The Quantity Theory of Money – A Restatement," in *Studies in the Quantity Theory of Money*, ed. M. Friedman (Chicago: The University of Chicago Press); Galbraith, J. K., *The New Industrial State* and *Economics and the Public Purpose* (Boston: Houghton Mifflin; copyright in Great Britain, London: André Deutsch); Marris, R., "An Introduction to Theories of Corporate Growth," in *The Corporate Economy*, eds. R. Marris and A. Wood (Cambridge: Harvard University Press); Uzawa, H., "Time Preference and the Penrose Effect in a Two-Class Model of Economic Growth," *Journal of Political Economy* 77(4):628–52 (Chicago: The University of Chicago Press).

Last but not least my thanks go to my wife, Mari, who has always encouraged me in doing something on my own, and to my then little son Kosuke, who was tolerant enough not to complain whenever I said "Otōsan, oshigoto" (Daddy has work to do).

H.O.

List of variables

The following list presents all the variables and symbols that are used in this book (except those for Simon's model in section 2.4 and those used in the footnotes but not in the text). Each of them is followed by the section where it is first defined. ("A" refers to Appendix.)

A	index of labor productivity	3.5
B	total value of bonds	2.2
C	the transaction cost incurred in a takeover	2.3
	total consumption by the noncorporate sector	4.2
D	total dividends	2.2
E	total market value of shares	2.2
	government expenditure (in Part IV only)	8.2
$F(t)$	the probability that a takeover has taken place by time t (in Chapter 2 only)	2.4
F	production function	3.3
Fr	production function for research activity	3.5
G	total capital gains	4.2
H	Hamiltonian equation	5.5
I	the cost of investment	3.2
K	capital	2.2
L	labor (measured in efficiency units)	3.3
M	development expenditure (in Chapter 3)	3.3
	the quantity of money (in Chapter 9)	9.1
N	the number of shares	2.3
	labor (measured in physical units)	3.5
P	profit gross of capital cost	2.2
Q	output	3.3
R	input to research activity (in Chapter 3)	3.5
	retained profits (in Chapter 9)	9.2
S	sales (in Chapter 1 only)	1.5
	total saving by the noncorporate sector	4.2
T	the length of time needed to achieve v_{max}	2.3
U	intertemporal management utility function	2.4
V	the total market value of the firm(s) ($\equiv E + B$)	2.2

W	total wages	4.2
Y	total income of the noncorporate sector	4.2
Z	executive compensation	1.5
a	the rate of increase of labor productivity $(\equiv \dot{A}/A)$	3.5
c	constants (in Chapter 2 only)	2.5
e	government expenditure per unit of capital $(\equiv E/K)$	8.2
g	the rate of growth of capital $(\equiv \dot{K}/K)$	2.2
g_d	the rate of growth of dividend per share	3.2
g^{**}	the value of g that maximizes v	2.2
$\tilde{g}$	the value of g such that the optimal value of a equals ξ^e	5.4
$g^{\#}$	the value of g such that $\hat{v}(g) = \psi'(g)$	5.4
h	hazard rate	2.4
i	the rate of interest	2.2
l	labor–capital ratio (measured in efficiency units) $(\equiv L/K)$	3.3
n	the rate of growth of labor force (measured in physical units)	4.3
p	the rate of profit $(\equiv P/K)$	2.2
p_m	the price of money in terms of goods	9.1
q	stock price	3.2
r	retention rate	2.2
s	the propensity to save	4.2
$\bar{s}$	the average propensity to save of a two-class economy	4.5
t	time	2.4
	tax rates (in Part IV only)	8.2
u	instantaneous management utility function	2.4
v	valuation ratio $(\equiv V/K)$	2.2
$\bar{v}$	the minimum valuation ratio to prevent a takeover	2.2
$\hat{v}(g)$	the v-g frontier when there is no research activity	5.4
$\tilde{v}(g)$	the locus of (v, g) such that the optimal value of a equals ξ^e	5.4
w	wage rate	3.3
x	equity–value ratio $(\equiv E/V)$ (in Part I)	2.3
	the price of neoclassical sector's product (in Part V)	10.3
z	the index of management preference toward growth	3.4
Π	profit from a takeover	2.3
Φ	the function to determine $\bar{v}$	2.3
Ω	a determinant	5.A
α	the ratio of the desired stock of money of firms to the comprehensive profit	9.1

β	the maximum tolerable probability of a takeover (in Chapter 2)	2.4
	the ratio of the desired stock of money of individuals to the comprehensive income (in Chapter 9)	9.1
γ	the relative portion of capital gains recognized by a shareholder as his income	4.2
$\epsilon(C)$	the elasticity of C with respect to θE	2.3
θ	the weight for deflating Z, S, and P (in Chapter 1)	1.5
	the proportion of shares to be purchased by a raider (in Chapter 2)	2.3
λ	Hamiltonian multiplier	5.5
μ	Hamiltonian multiplier (in Chapter 5)	5.5
	the rate of increase of money supply ($\equiv \dot{M}/M$) (in Chapter 9)	9.1
ξ	the rate of wage increase ($\equiv \dot{w}/w$)	3.5
π	the probability of a takeover (in Chapter 2)	2.4
	the price of output (in Chapter 3)	3.3
	the rate of deflation ($\equiv \dot{p}_m/p_m$) (in Chapter 9)	9.1
ρ	the discount rate of management	2.4
ϕ	the cost of increasing labor productivity	3.5
χ	Kaldor's technical progress function	6.2
ψ	investment per unit of capital ($\equiv I/K$)	3.2

Subscripts

max	maximum value	2.2
0	initial value	2.2
c	capitalists	4.2
h	households	4.2
w	workers	4.2
p	corporate sector	8.2
m	managerial sector	10.2
n	neoclassical sector	10.2

Superscripts

*	the optimal value for a firm	Introduction
0	the equilibrium value for the economy	Introduction
e	expectation	3.5
c	comprehensive (income or profit)	9.2

Introduction

The main concern of this book is the growth of a national economy. In this respect, the book adds to the already abundant literature on economic growth. It is unlike others, however, in its emphasis on the analysis of the behavior of firms in the economy. The economy we are concerned with is one where the representative firm is a large-scale corporation and not a tiny firm as has been the case with the neoclassical theory of the firm. From this comes the title – *The Theory of Growth in a Corporate Economy.*

It is general knowledge today that production and other economic activities are substantially carried out by a limited number of big corporations. Wherever and whenever one goes shopping, for instance, one is surrounded by the products of nationally known corporations or the anonymous products of less well-known but equally far-reaching conglomerates. In fact, shopping itself usually requires the use of vehicles produced by giant manufacturers. Typically, such producers are not only big no matter how their size is measured but also are comprised of many plants and offices and diversified enough to extend into several industrial fields. In addition, with little exception they are joint-stock corporations with almost no one owning more than 10 percent of the ownership of each.

In spite of this enormous role played by big corporations in our economic activity, little effort has been made to analyze theoretically the dynamics of an economy composed of these corporations. True, there have been many theories of economic growth. However, all these theories are developed either by implicitly assuming tiny owner-controlled firms or without making a microeconomic analysis of the behavior of firms. Needless to say, this is an unfortunate situation. A macroeconomic growth theory without microeconomic foundation is like a house without foundations: The structure of the theory becomes obscure, as well as the presumptions and ideas behind the theory. The predictions made from such a theory necessarily lack the power to convince people of their accuracy and applicability. Likewise, a theory of economic growth based on the analysis of numerous tiny competitive owner-controlled firms loses predictive power once the corporate

1

reality is recognized. This consideration naturally leads us to conclude that a model of economic growth, if it is to describe the dynamic movement of real present-day economies, must be based on a detailed analysis of the behavior of large-scale corporations.

Several efforts have been made to analyze the behavior of modern corporations. Opposing the traditional neoclassical theory of the firm where decisions supposedly are made by the almighty manager who knows everything about the operation of the firm and his interest perfectly coincides with that of the owners, several authors have argued for the impossibility (or the substantial cost) of imposing full rationality, due to the complex and sometimes rigid organization within a firm and the costliness of collecting necessary information; others have argued for the divergence of interest between management and owners. According to the latter argument, to control the management of a large corporation where the ownership is widely diffused, that is, no owner possesses more than a tiny share of the ownership, involves such a large cost that the management can safely pursue its own goal even against the owners' interest. The names of Baumol, Marris, and O. Williamson come to mind of those who have proposed to reformulate the theory of the firm based on objectives other than profit maximization or value maximization. Their theories are usually combined under the name of *the managerial theory of the firm*.

This book adheres to their thinking. We believe that the managerial theory is a realistic description of the behavior of modern corporations – at least, more realistic than the traditional one – and can effectively replace the traditional theory to explain many phenomena of a modern economy. Specifically, we believe that it is possible and meaningful to develop a theory on the dynamics of an aggregate economy out of a managerial theory. This study is such an attempt. In this sense, one may call it a theory of economic growth based on a managerial theory of the firm. To develop such a theory, we consider what is to be called *a corporate economy* and discuss the behavior of firms and the dynamic properties of general equilibria in this corporate economy. The rest of the introduction gives the definition of a corporate economy, the methodology, applicability, and specifications of the theory, as well as the structure of the book.

A corporate economy

A corporate economy is defined as an economy with seven basic characteristics, some of them mutually related, which are assumed throughout the book, except in the last chapter where a more neoclassical sector is assumed to coexist with the sector having these characteristics.

First, all the firms are assumed to be corporations in the sense of joint-stock companies characterized by (1) limited liability of shareholders, (2) continuity in existence, and (3) easy transferability of ownership interests. An implication of this assumption is that there is no legal reason that the managers must be the owners themselves. Another implication is that corporate shares as financial assets must be explicitly taken into account in discussing the general equilibrium.

The second characteristic is the separation of ownership from control in these corporations; that is, it is assumed that in every corporation no shareholder possesses such a large share of the ownership as to be able singly or within a small group of shareholders to achieve the majority of the ownership.

The third is the costliness of devices used for owners to control management, that is, to force management to pursue policies it does not like or to oust management. Probably two of the most important control devices are proxy fights and takeovers. Both are costly, however, when the ownership of a corporation is widely diffused, as has been assumed, and this costliness gives the management discretionary power, namely, the power to pursue its own goals safely at the expense of shareholders' interests.

The fourth pertains to the preference of the management: It is assumed that the management prefers rapid growth of the firm or, more formally, it intends to maximize the rate of growth of the size of the firm as measured by the book-valued assets. Why this is so is the main topic of Chapter 1.

The fifth is the separation of the corporate sector (i.e., corporations) and the noncorporate sector (i.e., households) in the economy and the barriers to enter the corporate sector. Because the corporate sector is composed of large-scale corporations with large and complex organizations, managing them would require highly sophisticated and specialized skills that most shareholders lack. Hence it is assumed that even if the return from investing a dollar in physical capital and running a business (namely, entering the corporate sector) is greater than the return from investing a dollar in financial assets such as corporate shares, no investor in the noncorporate sector can opt for the first alternative. In other words, it is assumed that substantial barriers exist to enter the corporate sector and that arbitrage by the noncorporate sector between real capital and financial assets is impossible. Of course, this implies that the rate of return to real capital – the rate of profit – may deviate from the rate of return to financial assets – the rate of interest – and that the divergence may persist in the long run.

This consideration leads us to the sixth characteristic, the separation between the decision to invest in physical capital and the decision to purchase financial assets. The former is made by the management in the corporate sector and the latter by the households in the noncorporate sector. Nothing is assumed to guarantee the identity between the two and they may be balanced only at an equilibrium. In this respect, we are Keynesian.

The seventh and final characteristic pertains to research and development and the resulting technical progress. In a corporate economy the research and development efforts, if any, are made exclusively by the corporate sector that undertakes them to serve its own goals – to develop new products and expand demand and/or to improve production technique and reduce future costs. This assumption is not far from reality. The role of independent inventors in our modern economy, despite popular tales of imaginative inventions by geniuses, has declined substantially in the last several decades and most of the inputs toward research and development today are made by businesses.

These characteristics define a corporate economy and are maintained throughout the book unless stated otherwise. We will return to them in several places and discuss their reality and implications.

Methodology

In spite of the criticism against the neoclassical theory of the firm and the neoclassical theory of economic growth, our methodological approach is to employ the neoclassical analytical tools as much as possible. The examples are the production function, the demand function, the discounting of future returns and costs, and the maximization of an objective function subject to constraints. The objective function of the firm in the present study differs from the neoclassical one in that the rate of growth is one of the arguments; however, as we will see, the neoclassical objective function in which the value of the firm is the sole argument may be regarded as a special case of ours. In addition, we agree with the neoclassical theory in that wealth owners in the noncorporate sector are assumed to maximize their wealth.

The characteristics of the markets, except those peculiar to a corporate economy, are other examples in our agreement with the neoclassical theory. Every market is assumed competitive and homogeneous; hence, for example, workers are all alike and no worker or employer possesses monopolistic (monoponistic) power. Another, perhaps more important, assumption in agreement with the neoclassical theory (but not with the Marxian or Keynesian theory) is that a general equilibrium with full employment in every market is attained.

There are two reasons why we believe it is worth while to attempt to follow the neoclassical methodology. First, in terms of logical rigor, the neoclassical theory is thought to have unique strength not found in other theories. This should explain why it has survived as the mainstream economic theory despite frequent adverse criticism. Our approach is to recognize this strength and utilize it as much as possible.

Second, we want to avoid an unnecessary controversy. It seems that past controversies between neoclassicists and managerialists have not been fruitful, and without doubt the difference in the analytical tools employed by the two schools is one of the causes for this unfortunate situation. There seems to have been a tendency for the neoclassicists to blame the managerialists on the ground that managerial theories are based on ad hoc assumptions, whereas the managerialists blame the neoclassical theory for its unrealistic assumptions and predictions. In our opinion such a tendency has obscured the essential difference between the two types of theories and has prevented the true understanding of managerial theories and their wide use. A reformulation of a managerial theory by means of the neoclassical tools, therefore, should clarify the difference between the two types of theories and contribute to a better understanding of the managerial theory among economists and students.

Applicability

One of the results of this study is that a difference in management preference can affect the equilibrium; more specifically, a preference of every management inclined more toward growth than toward the market value of the firm results in faster growth of the aggregate economy provided that firms engage in research activity. This should add to a better understanding of the factors determining the rate of growth of a national economy. For example, the common argument, at least among nonacademicians, has been that Japan could grow very rapidly after World War II because the management of Japanese corporations has been aggressive. Although such an argument has not been given serious consideration among academic economists, perhaps because nobody has precisely defined what aggressive management means, our theory strongly supports it. According to this theory, the rather vulgar notion of aggressive management is redefined as management preference inclined more toward growth than toward market value, and it is proved that this preference in fact affects the rate of growth of a national economy in an affirmative fashion. A difference in the speed of economic growth among countries, therefore, may now be attributed to a difference in management preference as well as to other more well-known factors; this explanation appears relevant particularly in the case of the unusually rapid growth of the Japanese economy. Chapter 7 will discuss this subject in detail, including why management preference in Japan is more growth oriented than that in the United States.

Further assumptions

In order to facilitate the formulation of a model of economic growth along the lines discussed so far, we make several additional assumptions, some of them being trivial or for simplifying purposes only, whereas others, admittedly, adversely affect the generality of the model.

First, some assumptions are required in order to maintain the comparison with the neoclassical theory. For example, all the noneconomic – political, social, ethical, and so forth – aspects of a corporate economy, as discussed by institutionalist writers, such as J. K. Galbraith, are totally disregarded. We also disregard sales-promotion activity and advertising by the corporate sector, following the neoclassical assumption that consumer preference is given. In fact, because the goods market is assumed perfectly competitive, every firm is a price taker although the theory, we believe, can be extended to include the case where the demand curve for a firm slopes downward.

Second, all the firms in the economy are assumed identical in order to avoid difficulties with aggregation. Apparently, this is unrealistic: Real firms differ from one another and an analysis of the interaction among them is desired. One such attempt is made in the final chapter where firms are separated into two categories and the interaction between them is analyzed. Within each category, however, the firms are still assumed to be identical.

Third, the government is neglected and accordingly no money is assumed to be issued, except in Part IV. Bonds, whether issued by the government or the businesses, are also disregarded in our discussion of the macroeconomy. In considering the general equilibrium, therefore, corporate shares are the sole financial assets (except in Chapter 9).

Fourth, there is neither inventory of products in the firm nor the depreciation of capital.

Fifth, there are several additional assumptions on the nature of research and development and technical progress: (1) All technical progress takes the form of process innovation as opposed to product innovation; that is, all innovation is made to improve production efficiency and to reduce future production costs and not to develop new products and expand demand. This assumption, we should note, is not so unrealistic as it may appear, for many of the new products are intermediate and capital goods that, in terms of the effects to the economy as a whole, are indistinguishable from new processes (Mansfield, 1968, p. 15). (2) All the technical progress is purely labor augmenting, namely, Harrod-neutral. (3) No technical progress is embodied, that is, irreversibly associated with investments in specific capital goods. (4) Technical progress results only from the research and development efforts by the corporate sector and no learning by doing in the sense of Arrow (1962a) takes place. (5) No dissemination of new technological knowledge among firms occurs. This last assumption implies that a firm can enjoy technical progress only through its own research and development efforts and monopolizes all the benefits from them, giving ample incentive for the firm to undertake research and development.

Sixth, our discussion is mostly confined to a steady state where the rates of growth, relative prices, and the share of wealth among classes in the noncorporate sector are constant over time. Consequently, our propositions are such that if there exists a steady-state equilibrium, it must satisfy such and such conditions; and if such and such conditions are met, then it is an equilibrium in the sense that every agent in the economy is content. In other words, our propositions do not preclude the possibility of non-steady-state equilibria that do not satisfy our conditions. Likewise, it is not possible to discuss the stability of our equilibria although a comparative analysis between two steady-state equilibria is of course possible. This means that the results of this study are most useful to analyze the long-run tendency of an economy when the exogenous variables are invariant over time.

Seventh, except in section 2.4, no consideration is given to uncertainty and imperfect information; that is, every agent in the economy is assumed to possess perfect and certain information on every matter relevant to him. This assumption is closely related to the assumption of steady state; for how can one be uncertain of future events if one knows that a steady state persists?

These assumptions will be examined further as they are introduced, giving a more detailed discussion of the rationale and implications.

Structure

The book consists of five parts, each divided into one to three chapters. Parts I and II present the basic model of growth of a corporate economy, constituting the theoretical core of this study. Part III discusses the relevance of the model, and the remaining two parts attempt to extend the basic model.

Part I deals with the microeconomic analysis of a corporate economy and is divided into three chapters. Chapter 1 discusses the nature of modern corporations and their management. The topics discussed are the forms of business firms, the concentration of major economic activity in a limited number of large-scale corporations, the separation of ownership from control, and pecuniary and nonpecuniary motives of the management. Our conclusion is that most economic activities in modern capitalist countries such as the United States and Japan are carried out by a limited number of big corporations (in the sense of joint-stock companies), in which ownership is widely diffused and divorced from control and the chief goal of management is the growth of the corporation subject of course to its survival. The discussion in this chapter is basically explanatory so that any student in microeconomics or industrial organization should be able to follow it. Because the major purpose of the chapter is to justify the assumptions of a corporate economy, such as the objective function of the management, those familiar with these topics may skip the chapter.

Chapter 2 discusses how decisions are made by the management, which maximizes the rate of growth of the book-valued assets of the firm subject to the constraint that it should be free from outside interference – the only outside interference assumed to be a takeover by an outside raider. For this purpose, the nature of a takeover is first analyzed and then the optimal decision making by the management is discussed. The case where the threat of a takeover is uncertain for the incumbent management is also analyzed.

Chapter 3 presents models of the firm. First, Marris's model is given and criticized. Second, Uzawa's model is presented and it is argued that the model is theoretically more acceptable than Marris's and yet has the same properties as Marris's. Third, research activity by the firm is introduced into Uzawa's model. Throughout these discussions the decisions are assumed to be made as formulated in the previous chapter.

Chapters 4 and 5 compose Part II which presents the macro-economic analysis. Here the economy is assumed to consist of three markets – labor, goods, and stock – and the equilibrium in the goods and stock markets is analyzed in Chapter 4. The steady-state equilibrium condition is derived for each of four cases, depending on whether there is one class – households – or two classes – workers and capitalists – in the noncorporate sector and whether or not the shareholders are rational.

Using this condition and the results derived in Part I, we present models of economic growth and discuss their properties in Chapter 5. Here models are presented first for the case where no research activity is undertaken (section 5.2) and then for the case where it is (section 5.3). Sections 5.4 and 5.5 give theoretical discussions of the specific assumptions used in the models of economic growth and because they are rather technical, those not interested in such details may skip them.

Part III aims to answer the question: Why is it necessary to add a new theory to the already abundant literature on economic growth? First its theoretical aspect (Chapter 6) is discussed and then its empirical aspect (Chapter 7). In the former, our model is compared to four popular models of economic growth – those of Marx, Solow, Robinson, and Kaldor – and it is argued that our model synthesizes some important aspects of these models, owing to the assumption of a corporate economy. As for the empirical relevance, the model is claimed to provide a good theoretical framework to investigate international differences in the speed of economic growth; Chapter 7 demonstrates how the faster economic growth in Japan compared to that of the United States is explained consistently with our model. It is argued that the economic, social, and psychological environment surrounding the Japanese corporation is such as to make management preference more toward growth, which is why the growth of the Japanese national economy has been so rapid.

Part IV attempts to discuss economic policies in a corporate economy. First, the government is introduced to tax both corporations and households and to purchase goods, and the optimal fiscal policy for economic growth is discussed (Chapter 8). Second, the governmental issue of money is added to the model and the optimal fiscal and monetary policy is considered (Chapter 9). Because the analysis is still confined to that of a steady state, however, the discussion is focused on the long-run asymptotic tendency of the effect of a persistent policy rather than on the short-run effects of a policy.

The final part has only one chapter. Here the corporate sector is separated into two sectors – the managerial and the neoclassical. The managerial sector is defined as a sector with the characteristics of a corporate economy, and the neoclassical sector, a sector with more neoclassical characteristics. In particular, entry into the neoclassical sector is assumed free. It is shown that the equilibrium properties of such an economy could be quite similar to that of one-sector economy and that differences in the preference of the management of the managerial sector result in different rates of growth of national economy. The behavior of the neoclassical sector, on the contrary, cannot affect anything but the relative price between the products of the two sectors. Thus it may be said that such a multisector economy involves an unequal distribution of power in favor of the managerial sector.

A bibliography follows the final chapter. It should be noted that only those referred to in the book appear in the bibliography and there are several unlisted sources from which I have benefited and been influenced by.

Notation

Notation that is used throughout the book is summarized in the List of Variables.

Throughout the book, for any variabile, say X, X^* denotes the optimal value of X for a firm, whereas X^0 denotes the macroeconomic equilibrium value of X. Whenever a function of the form, $y = f(x)$, where both y and x are scalars, is defined, a prime and a double prime are used to denote, respectively, its first and second derivatives; that is,

$f'(x) \equiv dy/dx$ and $f''(x) \equiv d^2y/dx^2$. Whenever a function with multiple arguments of the form, $y = f(x_1, x_2, \ldots, x_n)$, is defined, f_i and f_{ij} are used to denote, respectively, its first partial derivative with respect to the ith argument and its cross or second partial derivative with respect to the ith and jth arguments; that is, $f_i(x_1, \ldots, x_n) \equiv \partial y/\partial x_i$ and $f_{ij}(x, \ldots, x_n) \equiv \partial^2 y/\partial x_i \partial x_j$.

Terminology

We conclude this introduction with a note on terminology. The words "firm" and "corporation" are used interchangeably to refer to those firms in a corporate economy as previously defined. An exception to this rule is found in Chapter 1 where "corporation" is used to indicate "joint-stock company" and "firm," to indicate any business unit – corporation, partnership, or proprietorship.

The words "shares" and "stocks" are likewise used interchangeably to refer to the certificates of ownership interests in a joint-stock company. Mostly, however, "shares" are used in preference to "stocks," except for such familiar compounds as "stock price" and "stock market." This usage of words, perhaps more common in Britain than in America, reflects the influence of British authors such as Marris on my thinking. Nowhere is "stock" used to mean "inventory," thus avoiding confusion.

PART I

Microeconomics

CHAPTER 1

Modern corporations and the management

1.1   Introduction

Perhaps the first economist to recognize potential conflict of interest between owners and corporate managers was Adam Smith. In *The Wealth of Nations,* 1776, he wrote

> The directors of [joint-stock] companies, however, being the managers rather of other people's money than of their own, it cannot well be expected, that they should watch over it with the same anxious vigilance with which the partners in a private copartnery frequently watch over their own. Like the stewards of a rich man, they are apt to consider attention to small matters as not for their master's honour, and very easily give themselves a dispensation from having it.[1]

In spite of this insight by the "father of economics," the astonishing fact is that the mainstream economic theory as discussed in most current textbooks in microeconomics has been regarding the firm as a single *unit,* as if there were a single person – an owner-manager – who makes all the decisions relevant to economists. This is all the more astonishing if one recalls the fact that since Adam Smith's time, corporations (joint-stock companies) have spread enormously – slowly admittedly in the first hundred years after 1776, but explosively in the next hundred – and many of them have now evolved to cause giant corporations. The hypothesis of profit maximization, or market value maximization in the context of dynamic analyses, is a necessary consequence of such a mainstream or *traditional* view of the firm. Those who postulate this hypothesis and derive some conclusions usually defend themselves on the ground that what is important is not whether the hypothesis is realistic but whether predictions made from it are consistent with actual observations. Can one not start, however, from a more detailed analysis of business firms and postulate a more

---

[1] Adam Smith, *The Wealth of Nations,* Cannan Edition (New York: Modern Library, 1937), p. 700; as quoted by Jensen and Meckling (1976, p. 305).

15

realistic hypothesis to obtain important conclusions that have hitherto been neglected but which add to a better understanding of our economy?

Because the aim of this book is just this, with emphasis on the dynamic aspect of what we call a corporate economy, it is only natural to start with a detailed analysis of business firms in our economy. First, we will discuss the legal forms of business firms to demonstrate how corporations, namely, joint-stock companies, are prevalent today. Then, we will observe the extent to which the concentration of economic power to a limited number of big corporations has proceeded. Third, we will turn to the inside of these big corporations and discuss their important characteristic, the separation of ownership from control. Finally, we will discuss the motives behind the behavior of management. This will be considered first as to the pecuniary motives and then, the nonpecuniary motives. The question as to what is meant by management and who manages will be raised during the discussions.

Fortunately, several studies on these topics have already been made so that we will be able to use their results. These studies have dealt mostly with the United States, and thus our discussion will be directed more to the United States than to any other country. We would like to emphasize, however, that the arguments set forth in this chapter should apply not only to the United States but also to any capitalist country with similar characteristics, such as Western European countries, Canada, and Japan. To substantiate this fact, we will attempt throughout the chapter to give evidence for Japan as well as for the United States.

1.2   Forms of business firms

In the United States there are three forms of business firms: single proprietorship, partnership, and corporation. In a single proprietorship there is a single owner who makes all decisions and receives all the profit but at the same time is solely liable for any loss from the business. It is easy to start a proprietorship and naturally we have numerous proprietorships, such as farmers and small stores and restaurants. According to Samuelson, "you simply wake up one morning and say 'Today, I am in business!' And you are" (Samuelson, 1976, p. 102).

In a partnership, there are two or more who invest. Either of them makes decisions and all share its profit (or loss). Single proprietorship and partnership are alike except for the number of owners. The number is small and the owners are readily identifiable in both. The manager is an owner himself and in most instances the major owner. Of particular importance is that both are characterized by unlimited liability; that is, each owner is fully liable for the entire debt of the business. Whatever the amount one invests in a partnership, he is liable for its debt not only by the exact amount invested but in its full amount. It is thus possible that with only a minority ownership one has to pay for the entire debt and/or that one has to sell his personal belongings such as homes, automobiles, and paintings to pay off that debt.

The third form, corporation, is completely different in this respect. It is characterized by limited liability which means that one is liable only to the extent he has invested. One buys a share of a corporation for, say, a dollar and if it goes bankrupt he loses the dollar but no more; one need not sell his home to pay off the debt of the corporation whatever the amount. This provision gives a great incentive to those who want to invest but do not want to risk their wealth. Thus corporations can more easily finance their investment and the ownership of corporations can be widely diffused.

Corporation has other advantages, too. It is legally regarded as an independent entity which is not affected by the death of the owners, unlike a proprietorship or a partnership where the death of the owner forces the firm to close down or to reestablish as a new firm. Corporations issue shares, most usually of common stocks, which are freely traded in a market among investors. Consequently, investing in a corporation, namely, holding its shares, is a more liquid means of holding wealth (in the sense of Keynes) than investing in a proprietorship or a partnership. This also explains why corporations have advantages over the other two in collecting money from investors.

These facts predict that because proprietorship is the easiest form to establish it is dominant in terms of the number of firms, but because it has definite shortcoming in raising funds, the corporation becomes more dominant among larger firms.[2] Table 1.1 verifies this. Among fourteen thousand firms in the United States in 1974, proprietorships accounted for some 78 percent in number but only less than 10 percent

---

[2] Chapter 6 of Samuelson's (1976) popular textbook illustrates this fact very well by presenting an imaginary history of a toothpaste-producing firm.

Table 1.1. *Distribution of firms by type of ownership: United States,* 1974

	Number (thousands)	Sales (billion dollars)	Profit (billion dollars)
All industries			
Proprietorship	10,874 (78.2)^a	28 (9.2)	46 (22.9)
Partnership	1,062 (7.6)	39 (3.9)	9 (4.5)
Corporation	1,066 (14.1)	3,090 (86.9)	146 (72.6)
Total	13,902 (100)	3,557 (100)	201 (100)
Manufacturing			
Proprietorship	213 (46.7)	9.1 (0.7)	1.1 (1.5)
Partnership	31 (6.8)	7.5 (0.6)	0.6 (0.8)
Corporation	212 (46.5)	1,252.4 (98.7)	72.5 (97.7)
Total	456 (100)	1,269.0 (100)	74.2 (100)

^{a}Numbers in parentheses are percentages.
Source: U.S. Internal Revenue Service, *Statistics of Income, 1974* (Washington, D.C.: Government Printing Office, 1976).

in terms of sales. Corporations, on the other hand, accounted for only 14 percent in number but more than 86 percent in sales. Because many proprietorships are founded in nonmanufacturing industries – agriculture, trade, and services, in particular – the figures for corporations are larger if one looks at the manufacturing industry only, where corporations accounted for more than 98 percent of the industry's sales.

The situation is slightly different but still quite similar in Japan. In Japan, besides proprietorship and corporation (joint-stock company), there are three categories: *gomei, goshi,* and *yugen.* In a gomei, all the owners assume unlimited liability; in goshi, some of the owners assume unlimited liability, whereas others assume only limited liability (only an owner with unlimited liability can be the manager); in yugen, all assume unlimited liability. In this respect, yugen resembles corporation. In yugen, however, the number of owners is limited to fifty at its maximum and the issue of common stocks to be traded in an open market is prohibited. Table 1.2 illustrates the distribution among types of ownership in Japan, in which partnership refers to the sum of gomei and goshi and "limited" is the English translation of yugen.

Table 1.2 shows the number of establishments instead of companies and for this reason a direct comparison of Tables 1.1 and 1.2 of the two countries is misleading. Specifically, the percentage distribution would

Table 1.2. *Distribution of private establishments[a] by type of ownership: Japan, 1975*

	No. of establishments (thousands)	Employees (thousands)
All industries[b]		
Proprietorship	3,764 (74.4)[c]	10,750 (33.7)
Partnership	56 (1.1)	724 (2.3)
Limited	402 (7.9)	2,256 (7.1)
Joint-stock	839 (16.6)	18,179 (57.0)
Total	5,061 (100)	31,909 (100)
Manufacturing		
Proprietorship	490 (58.8)	1,863 (16.4)
Partnership	11 (1.3)	104 (0.9)
Limited	97 (11.6)	739 (6.5)
Joint-stock	235 (28.2)	8,626 (76.1)
Total	834 (100)	11,332 (100)

[a]"Establishment" is defined as a certain physical location where either goods are produced or services are rendered on business.
[b]Excluding proprietorships in agriculture, forestry, and fisheries and establishments of domestic services.
[c]Numbers in parentheses are percentages.
Source: Japan, Office of the Prime Minister, Bureau of Statistics, *Establishment Census, 1975* (Tokyo: Printing Bureau of the Ministry of Finance, 1977).

be modified in favor of proprietorships over joint-stock companies if the number of firms had been used in place of the number of establishments in Table 1.2, for on the average each of the joint-stock companies has more establishments than a proprietorship. In addition, because proprietorships in agriculture, and so on, are excluded from the Japanese data for all industries, it is likely that the number of establishments is underestimated for proprietorships.

Still, the picture that emerges from Table 1.2 is very much like that of the United States: Proprietorships outweigh corporations (joint-stock companies) in number but corporations are dominant in terms of the number of employees. The conclusion is strengthened if one looks at the manufacturing industry, where corporations account for more than three quarters of all the employees in the industry; this again agrees with the American data.

We have already explained why proprietorship and partnership are unfavorable forms of business organization once a business prospers

Table 1.3. *Percentage distribution of business firms with sales of more than $500,000 by type of ownership: all industries, United States, 1974*

	Number	Sales
Proprietorship	9.9	1.9
Partnership	8.2	2.7
Corporation	81.9	95.4
Total	100	100

Source: U.S. Internal Revenue Service, *Statistics of Income, 1974* (Washington, D.C.: Government Printing Office, 1976).

Table 1.4. *Percentage distribution of business firms (excluding proprietorships) with employees of 1,000 or more by type of ownership: all industries, Japan, 1975*

	No. of companies	No. of establishments	Employees
Partnership	1.1	13.1	6.5
Limited	0.0	0.0	0.0
Joint-stock	98.9	86.9	93.5
Total	100	100	100

Source: Japan, Office of the Prime Minister, Bureau of Statistics, *Establishment Census, 1975* (Tokyo: Printing Bureau of the Ministry of Finance, 1977).

and requires more capital. It is expected, therefore, that among large firms, corporations become all the more dominant. Tables 1.3 and 1.4 verify this conjecture. In the United States in 1974, among the firms with sales of more than a half million dollars, 82 percent were corporations whose sales together accounted for more than 95 percent of the sales of all such firms. Likewise, in Japan in 1975, almost 99 percent of the firms (excluding proprietorships) with employees of a thousand or more were corporations.

The moral of this section is the simple fact: The weight of economic activity is now carried out by corporations that issue shares salable on the stock market, although there are numerous proprietorships and partnerships. This fact implies that there is no a priori legal reason to expect identity between management and ownership within those firms playing a dominant role in our economy, for unlike proprietor-

Table 1.5. *Distribution of corporations by asset size-class: all industries, United States, 1974*

Asset size-class	No. of corporations (thousands)	Percentage Number	Assets
$250 million and over	1.8	0.09	64.4
$100–$250 million	2.0 (3.8)^a	0.10 (0.19)	7.6 (72.0)
$ 50–$100 million	2.9 (6.7)	0.15 (0.34)	5.0 (77.0)
$ 10–$ 50 million	17.2 (23.9)	0.87 (1.21)	9.3 (86.3)
Under $10 million	1,942.0 (1,965.9)	98.79 (100)	13.8 (100)

^{a}Cumulative figures are in parentheses.
Source: U.S. Internal Revenue Service, *Statistics of Income, 1974* (Washington, D.C.: Government Printing Office, 1976).

ships and partnerships, corporations may be run by nonowners. This may not surprise the reader; however, it should be noted that neither the role of corporate shares nor the possible separation of ownership from control has been given sufficient attention in the mainstream economic theory, the theory of economic growth in particular.

1.3   The importance of large corporations[3]

The majority of business activity, whether measured by sales, owned assets, number of employees, or profits, is now carried out by a limited number of corporations. Tables 1.5 to 1.9 were compiled to illustrate this fact. Table 1.5 shows that for all industries in the United States in 1974, the 1,800 corporations with assets of $250 million or more accounted for less than 0.1 percent in terms of the number of corporations and yet accounted for more than 60 percent of the total assets. Those small corporations with assets of $10 million or less accounted for nearly 99 percent in number but their combined assets were only 13.8 percent of the total.

The situation is not much different in Japan as Table 1.6 reveals, in which corporations are classified in terms of the number of employees

---

[3] Because the points to be raised in this section are closely related to the discussion of aggregate or overall concentration in the literature on industrial organization, a brief exposition should suffice: See Scherer (1970, Chapter 3); Blair (1972, Chapter 4); and Reid (1976, Chapter 3).

Table 1.6. *Distribution of companies (excluding proprietorships) by employee size-class: all industries, Japan, 1975*

Employee size-class	No. of companies	Percentage		
		Number	Employees	Paid-in capital
5,000 and over	288	0.03	17.8	35.3
2,000–4,999	503 (791)[a]	0.06 (0.09)	7.2 (25.0)	11.5 (46.8)
1,000–1,999	912 (1,703)	0.10 (0.19)	5.9 (30.9)	7.1 (53.9)
500–999	2,113 (3,816)	0.24 (0.43)	6.8 (37.7)	6.6 (60.5)
300–499	3,210 (7,026)	0.36 (0.79)	5.8 (43.5)	3.8 (64.3)
200–299	4,489 (11,515)	0.51 (1.30)	5.1 (48.6)	3.0 (67.3)
100–199	14,476 (25,991)	1.64 (2.94)	9.4 (58.0)	5.7 (73.0)
20–99	123,376 (149,367)	14.01 (16.95)	22.9 (80.9)	12.5 (85.5)
Under 20	731,311 (880,678)	83.04 (100)	19.0 (100)	14.5 (100)

[a]Cumulative figures are in parentheses.
Source: Japan, Office of the Prime Minister, Bureau of Statistics, *Establishment Census, 1975* (Tokyo: Printing Bureau of the Ministry of Finance, 1977).

instead of assets. For instance, about half of the total employees were employed in 1972 by the corporations with employees of 200 or more, which in number accounted for only 1.3 percent. These corporations also accounted for 67 percent of the total paid-in capital.[4] Moreover, because affiliates are treated as separate entities here as well as in the American data, the true influence of big corporations is even stronger if their affiliates are included.

Perhaps more startling is Table 1.7, which shows that in the U.S. manufacturing industry in 1973 a mere 136 corporations, each with assets of a billion dollars or more, owned more than half of the total assets of the industry and earned more than half of the total profits. The table also shows that a little more than a thousand largest manufacturing corporations accounted for approximately 80 percent of the assets and profits of the industry. In contrast, more than two hundred thousand smaller corporations jointly owned only 12 percent of the total assets.

[4] Paid-in capital refers to the value of outstanding preferred and common stocks, usually evaluated at the par value. Obviously, it is an unsatisfactory measure of the size of a corporation because neither accumulated retained earnings nor debts are included. The common use of this measure in Japan, however, will be justified if it is closely correlated with the total value of assets. According to Baba's (1974, p. 17) cross-sectional study of 471 large manufacturing companies in Japan in 1963, the value of the correlation coefficient was in fact quite large (0.969).

Table 1.7. *Distribution of corporations[a] by asset size-class: manufacturing, United States, 1973*

Asset size-class	No. of corporations	Percentage Number	Assets	Profits
$1 (American) billion and over	136	0.07	53	54
$250 million–$1 billion	260 (396)[b]	0.13 (0.20)	17 (70)	17 (71)
$100–$250 million	338 (734)	0.16 (0.36)	7 (77)	6 (77)
$ 50–$100 million	425 (1,159)	0.21 (0.57)	4 (81)	4 (81)
$ 10–$ 50 million	2,235 (3,394)	1.08 (1.65)	7 (88)	6 (87)
Under $10 million	202,710[c] (206,104)	98.35 (100)	12 (100)	13 (100)

[a]Proprietorships and partnerships are excluded. "Their combined assets total only about one percent of the whole, or less than one-third of the assets of Exxon Corporation" (Reid, 1976, p. 31).
[b]Cumulative figures.
[c]Estimated.
Source: U.S. Federal Trade Commission and Securities and Exchange Commission, *Quarterly Financial Report for Manufacturing Corporations, 1973;* cited by Reid (1976, p. 31).

Table 1.8. *Distribution of establishments by employee size-class: manufacturing, United States, 1972*

Employee size-class	No. of establishments (thousands)	Percentage Number	Employees	Payroll	Value added
1,000 and over	2	0.6	28.7	35.7	34.9
250–999	12 (14)[a]	3.8 (4.4)	28.6 (57.3)	27.0 (62.7)	28.2 (63.1)
100–249	21 (35)	6.7 (11.1)	17.9 (75.2)	15.8 (78.5)	16.0 (79.1)
20–99	76 (111)	24.3 (35.4)	18.6 (93.8)	16.1 (94.6)	15.5 (94.6)
Under 20	203 (314)	64.9 (100)	6.2 (100)	5.4 (100)	5.4 (100)

[a]Cumulative figures are in parentheses.
Source: U.S. Bureau of the Census, *Census of Manufactures, 1972* (Washington, D.C.: Government Printing Office, 1974).

Tables 1.8 and 1.9 are provided to facilitate a comparison between the United States and Japan. Both illustrate the distribution of establishments (not corporations) in the manufacturing industry according to the number of employees. It appears that the United States is characterized by a slightly higher degree of concentration;

Table 1.9. *Distribution of establishments by employee size-class: manufacturing, Japan, 1973*

Employee size-class	No. of establishments	Percentage			
		Number	Employees	Payroll	Value added
1,000 and over	844	0.1	16.2	23.8	26.5
500–999	1,433 (2,277)[a]	0.2 (0.3)	8.3 (24.5)	10.4 (34.2)	11.3 (37.8)
300–499	2,043 (4,320)	0.3 (0.6)	6.5 (31.0)	7.8 (42.0)	8.1 (45.9)
200–299	2,796 (7,116)	0.4 (1.0)	5.7 (36.7)	6.3 (48.3)	6.5 (52.4)
100–199	8,959 (16,075)	1.3 (2.3)	10.3 (47.0)	10.4 (58.7)	10.3 (62.7)
20–99	71,441 (87,516)	10.1 (12.4)	24.6 (71.6)	22.8 (81.5)	20.4 (83.1)
Under 20	620,931 (708,447)	87.6 (100)	28.5 (100)	18.5 (100)	16.8 (100)

[a]Cumulative figures are in parentheses.
Source: Japan, Ministry of International Trade and Industry, *Census of Manufactures, 1973* (Tokyo: Printing Bureau of the Ministry of Finance, 1975).

without doubt, however, the more impressive fact is the dominance of a limited number of big corporations in both countries.

Now that we have demonstrated that only a limited number of large-scale corporations carry out most of the industrial activity in such countries as the United States and Japan, the immediate question should be: Do these big corporations behave as the traditional microeconomic theory predicts? Although this question is to be answered in the rest of this chapter, two points should be raised here. First, giant corporations require so much capital that extensive diffusion of their ownership among a large number of investors is inevitable. The control of such corporations by means of majority ownership is extremely difficult because hardly anyone is wealthy enough to finance its growth. The extent of this diffusion of ownership will be the topic of the following section.

Second, these corporations are so large that it is very often impossible for each of them to restrict its operation within the boundary of an industry. On its path of expansion, a corporation will sooner or later be constrained by the growth of demand for its present industry and will attempt to sustain faster growth by entering other industries. In short, the corporation cannot but diversify. This explains why most of these large corporations individually operate in more than one industry. H. F. Houghton's study, although somewhat outdated, gives a clear picture: Among the one thousand largest U.S. industrial corporations in 1962, 15 participated in more than 50 five-digit census product lines; 236, in from 16 to 50 lines; 477, in from 6 to 15 lines; 223, in from 2 to 5 lines; and only 49 corporations among the one thousand confined themselves to one line.[5] The author could not find comparable statistics for Japanese corporations; however, few will doubt that Japanese giant corporations are equally well diversified (think of Hitachi and Kanebo, for instance).

Each of these corporations, therefore, is characterized not only by its large scale – huge assets, many employees, and a large amount of sales – but also by diversification, namely, by a number of product lines. Obviously, it is not easy to manage such a corporation; it is well beyond the ability of any one person to look after all these product lines and employees. Decentralization is inevitable and advanced management methods are essential. Only those people trained through experience, on-the-job training, and/or formal education as in business schools can have the necessary skills. And even these people as individuals would be unable to manage effectively. Only with decentralization of authority and cooperation among them can the task be achieved. The concept of an almighty manager who can and does make all the decisions for his company is nothing more than a past dream.

1.4   The separation of ownership from control

As far as company law is concerned, shareholders are supposed to control their company: They elect the board of directors by a majority rule at the annual general meeting, and this board has the authority to make decisions. The shareholders are also supposed to be able to fire the incumbent executive if they are not satisfied with his performance. How the statute is carried out in reality is another story.

We have already argued that those corporations dominant in our economy are so large that the ownership is inevitably widely diffused. As a result, most of the shareholders own only a tiny, almost infinitesimal, fraction of the shares of one company. They may purchase common stocks to prepare for retirement, or as the means to hold their wealth, or they may own stocks simply because they inherited them. Whatever the reason, the concern of these numerous shareholders is with the return and risk. They usually try to avoid putting all their eggs in one basket by diversifying their investment; their investment in one company would therefore be necessarily small. These shareholders usually do not have knowledge of those nominated for the board of directors, nor do they intend to spend their precious

[5] The result is cited in Scherer (1970, p. 67).

money and time to inquire about the nominees. Furthermore, only a few would be concerned or curious enough to spend time attending the general meeting to see what is going on; most would prefer either docilely to give their signature to the proxy statements provided by the management or not bother to vote at all. Typically, therefore, the management, with these proxy statements and the help of several friendly shareholders, has no difficulty at the meeting in getting the accounts accepted and ensuring the election of favorable candidates to the board of directors.[6]

It is true that shareholders may try to exert their influence on the management if they are very dissatisfied at its performance – too small profits and dividends of the company, for example. Their power, however, is strictly limited unless there are major shareholders whose investment in the company is so large as to attempt the difficult task of ousting the incumbent management.[7] The question to be asked, therefore, is, if there are such major shareholders in big corporations. This is explicitly what Berle and Means sought to answer in their epoch-making study nearly a half century ago.

They selected two hundred American nonfinancial corporations with the largest assets and classified them into five categories: (1) privately owned, (2) majority ownership, (3) minority control, (4) controlled by means of legal device, and (5) management control. A firm is considered to be privately owned if an individual, a family, or a group of business associates holds 80 percent or more of its voting stock. It is considered under majority ownership if the percentage is between 50 to 80, and minority control if 20 to 50. If no shareholder holds 20 percent or more of the stock, the firm is regarded as management controlled.[8]

They found that sixty-five corporations out of the two hundred were management controlled in this sense in 1929. This, however, shows only the form of *immediate* control and Berle and Means found cases

---

[6] This fact is observed not only in the United States but also in Japan. In fact, the description in the text seems to fit Japanese corporations better where it is not unusual to observe general meetings closing in ten minutes or so.

[7] Another means for the shareholders to exert their influence is to sell their shares to takeover raiders. This possibility is to be discussed in detail in Chapter 2.

[8] For the other category and for further detail, see Berle and Means (1932, Chapter 5).

Table 1.10. *Ultimate control in the 200 largest nonfinancial corporations: United States, 1929 and 1963*

	Percentage of no. of companies (200)		Percentage of total assets of companies	
	1929	1963	1929	1963
Private ownership	6	0	4	0
Majority ownership	5	2.5	2	1
Minority control	23	9	14	11
Legal device	21	4	22	3
Management control	44	84.5	58	85

Source: Robert J. Larner (1966, Table 1).

where those owners classified as exercising minority control are themselves corporations under the control of management. Because these perhaps should be regarded as management controlled, the authors reclassified the corporations according to the form of *ultimate* control. The result is reproduced in Table 1.10, which shows that the percentage of management control has jumped to 44 percent from the 32.5 percent in the case of immediate control. Only 11 percent had private or majority owners. This result led Berle and Means to conclude that "it is apparent that, with the increasing dispersion of stock ownership in the largest American corporations, a new condition has developed with regard to their control. No longer are the individuals in control of most of these corporations, the dominant owners. Rather, there are no dominant owners, and control is maintained in large measure apart from ownership" (Berle and Means, 1932, p. 117).[9]

The reader may have been surprised at the extent management control prevailed in as early as 1929 and wonder what has happened during the intervening decades. This question was answered by Larner (1966) who found that management control has become

---

[9] Berle and Means defined "control" by the following: "Since direction over the activities of a corporation is exercised through the board of directors, we may say for practical purposes that control lies in the hands of the individual or group who have the actual power to select the board of directors, (or its majority), either by mobilizing the legal right to choose them . . . or by exerting pressure which influences their choice" (Berle and Means, 1932, p. 69, their parentheses).

substantially more widespread after thirty-four years since the inquiry by Berle and Means. He discovered that in spite of the fact that he decreased the lower limit of the requirement for minority control to 10 percent from the 20 percent of Berle and Means, management controlled 80 percent of the two hundred then largest corporations immediately and 84.5 percent ultimately, a substantial increase (by 37.5 and 40.5 percent, respectively), compared to the results of Berle and Means. In addition, there was no privately owned corporation and only 5 corporations were under majority ownership. The results, summarized in Table 1.10, show clearly how significant the change was between 1929 and 1963 and how extensive management control has become.

For Japanese corporations, one of the early studies was conducted by Hirose in 1959. He found that among the two hundred largest corporations, thirty-three were owner controlled, approximately forty that previously belonged to the *zaibatsu* lines were controlled by financial institutions, and the remaining one hundred seven were management controlled.[10] The percentage, 53.5, of management control may appear small compared to Larner's result; however, it is necessary to recognize that most of the financial institutions supposed to control the forty corporations were management controlled themselves. Hirose's study, unfortunately, does not teach the form of ultimate control.

More recently, Miyazaki (1976) studied both immediate and ultimate control of Japanese corporations.[11] He selected the three hundred largest companies in Japan as of the end of the fiscal year 1970 and investigated the form of ownership of each. The results, summarized in Table 1.11, indicate that 30.3 and 38.7 percent of the three hundred corporations were, respectively, immediately and ultimately controlled by management; the extent of management control being less than in Hirose's and the American studies. Readers should be warned, however, that the results probably underestimate the importance of management control in Japan. For one thing, a company is classified as nonmanagement control even if no owner holds 10 percent or more as long as there is a family or a corporate affiliate who holds 3 percent or more. Thus those ten (seven plus three) companies classified by

[10] Hirose (1963, p. 147); as cited by Noda (1966, p. 236).
[11] An earlier similar study by Miyazaki (1972) is partly cited by Caves and Uekusa (1976, p. 69).

Table 1.11. *Ownership and control of 300 largest joint-stock corporations: Japan, fiscal 1970*

Status	No. of companies controlled by outside owner (concentration of shareholding)					No. of companies controlled by management	Total no. of companies	Percentage of all companies
	Over 90%	50–90%	30–50%	10–30%	Under 10%			
Outside shareholder control								
Family	1 *2*[a]	1 *1*	1 *3*	5 *8*	7 *7*	—	15 *21*	5.0 *7.0*
Corporate affiliate	1 *1*	1 *2*	3 *2*	9 *7*	3 *3*	—	17 *15*	5.7 *5.0*
Single company	11 *5*	15 *4*	10 *7*	11 *8*	5 *0*	—	52 *18*	17.4 *6.0*
Domestic, nonfinancial	8 *0*	12 *0*	9 *0*	3 *0*	0 *0*	—	32 *0*	10.7 *0.0*
Banking	0 *0*	0 *0*	0 *0*	1 *0*	5 *0*	—	6 *0*	2.0 *0.0*
Insurance	0 *0*	0 *0*	0 *0*	6 *7*	0 *0*	—	6 *7*	2.0 *2.3*
Foreign	3 *5*	3 *4*	1 *1*	1 *1*	0 *0*	—	8 *11*	2.7 *3.7*
Multicompany group	10 *11*	17 *22*	13 *18*	77 *66*	3 *8*	—	120 *125*	40.0 *41.7*
Domestic	3 *4*	10 *15*	12 *17*	76 *65*	3 *8*	—	104 *109*	34.7 *36.3*
Foreign	0 *0*	2 *2*	0 *0*	1 *1*	0 *0*	—	3 *3*	1.0 *1.0*
Foreign and domestic	7 *7*	5 *5*	1 *1*	0 *0*	0 *0*	—	13 *13*	4.3 *4.3*
Central and local government	1 *1*	2 *2*	0 *0*	2 *2*	0 *0*	—	5 *5*	1.6 *1.6*
Management control	—	—	—	—	—	91 *116*	91 *116*	30.3 *38.7*
Total	24 *20*	36 *31*	27 *24*	104 *91*	18 *18*	91 *116*	300 *300*	100.0 *100.0*
Percentage of all companies	8.0 *6.6*	12.0 *10.3*	9.0 *8.0*	34.7 *30.4*	6.0 *6.0*	30.3 *38.7*	100.0 *100.0*	—

[a] Figures indicate immediate control and ultimate control (italicized), respectively.
Source: Miyazaki (1976, p. 287).

Miyazaki as controlled by families or corporate affiliates would have been classified as management controlled by Larner.

For another, there is a problem peculiar to Japan: extensive shareholding among member companies of business groupings, the modern counterpart to prewar trusts or *zaibatsu*. We will discuss these groupings more in Chapter 7, but for now it is important to realize that the groupings such as Mitsui, Mitsubishi, and Sumitomo include quite a few large corporations covered by Miyazaki's study and these corporations tend to hold shares mutually. In fact, in 1973, the number of shares mutually owned in a grouping as a percentage of the total number of outstanding shares of the grouping was 25.8 in Sumitomo, 25.0 in Mitsubishi, and 20.0 in Mitsui (Futatsugi, 1976, pp. 38–47). Thus each of the corporations in these groupings may have been classified as owned by one or more corporations outside the corporation but inside the grouping to which the corporation belongs. In fact, Miyazaki regarded as nonmanagement controlled those corporations that belonged to groupings and of which the shares were owned by more than 3 percent by individual companies or multicompany groups.

It seems more reasonable to me, however, to include these corporations in the category of management control because there is no one who controls a grouping effectively unlike the prewar years when zaibatsu were owned by families, and for this reason these groupings appear to be run collectively by the managers of member corporations.[12] If this is true, then eight corporations classified under the heading of "under-10-percent ultimate control" should be reclassified as management controlled and quite probably many of those under 10 to 30 percent control should be reclassified as well.

In sum, it appears that at least eighteen corporations should be reclassified as ultimately management controlled; hence management-controlled corporations should account for at least 44.7 percent of the total (18 plus 116 as a percentage of 300). This still may well be an underestimate in view of the high average rate of mutual shareholding within groupings.

Miyazaki's result may underestimate the extent of management control for yet another reason – the neglect of the influences of creditors and directors. If a firm is heavily dependent on the loan from a management-controlled bank and/or if it has, as an influential director, the manager of another firm under management control, then

---

[12] This is the viewpoint taken in my previous work (1975).

the case may arise that the firm had better be regarded as management controlled even if it has, say, a single owner with more than 10 percent of the share. Nishiyama (1975) investigated the 332 largest listed corporations in Japan in 1970 taking these influences into account, to find that, by his own criterion, 296 were ultimately management controlled, 23 were ultimately owner controlled, 7 were foreign controlled, and 2 were government controlled, with the remaining 4 unidentifiable.[13] Hence, surprisingly, he concluded that 89 percent of the corporations are management controlled, implying that management control is as widespread in Japan as it is in the United States.

The principle behind this lengthy discussion is what Berle and Means asserted almost a half century ago: the separation of ownership and control and the prevalence of management control. In the United States and in Japan the ownership of present-day corporations is so widely diffused that few of them are owned as much as 10 percent by single owners. Each of the shareholders is seldom powerful enough to oust the incumbent management by himself and most of them, with their small shareholdings, would not undertake the time-consuming and cumbersome task. Here rests an ample opportunity for management of discretion, namely, to pursue its own goal even at the sacrifice of shareholders' interest without jeopardizing the position as management. To discuss the behavior of corporations, therefore, the motives of management should be analyzed.

1.5   The goal of the management: pecuniary motives

In order to analyze the motives that govern the behavior of the management, let us first separate pecuniary motives from nonpecuniary motives.

If a firm is completely under the control of its top executive – the chairman or the president, most usually – and if he behaves so as to maximize his pecuniary gains, then how the pecuniary gains of a top executive is determined must solely determine the behavioral rule of the firm. It is for this reason that several authors have attempted to trace the factors affecting executive compensation.

An early study was made by Roberts (1956), who conducted a cross-section analysis over 410 to 939 American companies in 1948 to 1950. He regressed several equations and found that the effect of sales

---

[13] For the criterion, see Nishiyama (1975, Chapter 2; the cited result is on p. 210).

on the compensation (salary + bonus + company contributions to deferred compensation) was significant, but the effect of profits or profit rate was not. Furthermore, he found that the relation between the compensation and sales is better explained by a log-linear equation, with the elasticity of 0.72. The result quite clearly implies a high probability that a top executive makes decisions so as to pursue larger sales as opposed to larger profits, a proposition not in line with the traditional microeconomic theory but in harmony with the prediction made by Berle and Means twenty-four years earlier that "the interests of ownership and control are in large measure opposed if the interests of the latter grow primarily out of the desire for personal monetary gain" (Berle and Means, 1932, p. 123).

But why is executive compensation dependent on the size of the company? The explanation may well be, say, sociological. The larger a firm is, the taller the hierarchical pyramid will be. Also, quite understandably, the pay of a boss should be larger than that of his immediate subordinates. Insofar as the pay of the worker at the bottom of the pyramid is determined competitively at the labor market (a seemingly natural assumption to make), then, the pay to the executive at the top of the pyramid should be greater for a larger firm. Simon (1957), taking this fact into consideration, presented a model of the compensation of executives, which also explains why the compensation-sales relation should be logarithmic rather than linear.[14]

McGuire, Chiu, and Elbing (1962) followed Roberts's study and confirmed his findings. Their analysis is based on a cross section of forty-five of the one hundred largest U.S. industrial corporations and used sales (S), executive compensation (Z), and profits (P) during 1953 to 1959 as the data. For executive compensation, they used the income of the chief executive, as did Roberts, but they improved on Roberts's study by also including in the definition of the income the market value of stocks given to the executive.[15]

The authors compared the effects of S and P on Z by means of partial correlation coefficients, using several equations (with different uses of lag and the absolute values of the variables versus the changes in them). Their findings were quite similar to Roberts's: Most of the partial correlation coefficients between Z and S were statistically significant, whereas none of the coefficients between Z and P were. As

---

[14] We will return to Simon's model in section 2.4.
[15] Roberts claimed that stock options had been rare until 1950.

with Roberts's study, therefore, their results seem to support Baumol's theory of the firm based on the sales-maximization hypothesis.

More recently, however, adverse criticisms were made of the two studies on two grounds: the statistical procedure used and the adequacy of the definition of executive compensation.

That the executive of a larger company will earn more appears plausible; however, it also seems probable that profits of a larger company, at the absolute level, are greater. Thus it must follow that executive compensation, sales, and profits are all larger for a larger firm. Inevitably, then, a regression on these variables is not free from multicolinearity. Moreover, because the residual variance about the regression function very likely increases with compensation, the regression may not be free from the problem of heteroscedasticity either. Consequently, the estimated results of Roberts and McGuire et al. may well be biased.[16]

Lewellen and Huntsman (1970) criticized the study by McGuire et al. for this reason and proposed to have the equation deflated by the size of the firm. That is, in place of estimating an equation of the form,

$$Z = a_0 + a_1 S + a_2 P \tag{1.1}$$

as used by McGuire et al., they estimated an equation of the form,

$$\frac{Z}{K} = a_0 \frac{1}{K} + a_1 \frac{S}{K} + a_2 \frac{P}{K} \tag{1.2}$$

where K denotes total book-valued assets, a measure they used for the size of the firm. Since S/K and P/K are unlikely to be correlated and the residuals are unlikely to display any clear trend, an application of the ordinary least-squares method to this equation must be legitimate. Lewellen and Huntsman applied a cross-section analysis to the fifty largest industrial corporations in the United States for each year – 1942, 1945, 1948, and so forth, up to 1963. They found that, whether

---

[16] Using the rate of profit instead of the level of profit as an explanatory variable, as in Roberts (1956, p. 277) and Marris (1964, p. 83), may be a way to avoid multicollinearity (but not heteroscedasticity). However, the hypothesis that a manager who has succeeded in achieving a higher rate of profit should receive more compensation appears less convincing to me than the hypothesis that a manager who has succeeded in achieving larger profits should be entitled to a share of the larger profits, that is, larger compensation.

executive compensation Z is defined to include only salary plus bonus or other incomes such as stock options as well, it is the estimate for a_2 and not a_1 in equation (1.2) that is statistically significant in most cases. This led them to conclude that "reported company profits appear to have a strong and persistent influence on executive rewards, whereas sales seem to have little, if any, such impact" (Lewellen and Huntsman, 1970, p. 718). Their result of course implies that the conclusion reached by previous authors that executive compensation is mainly affected by sales is a product of a statistical procedure, incorrectly applied, and cannot be a justification for the sales-maximization hypothesis.

A counterattack to Lewellen and Huntsman's conclusion was recently made, however, by Smyth, Boyes, and Peseau (1975). They argued that the deflation procedure adopted by Lewellen and Huntsman "overcompensated so that heteroscedasticity was still present but, now, with error variances inversely related to the dependent variable" (Smyth, Boyes, and Peseau, 1975, p. 73). This they found by the following procedure. Generally, the equation to be estimated may be written as:

$$\frac{Z}{K^\theta} = a_0 \frac{1}{K^\theta} + a_1 \frac{S}{K^\theta} + a_2 \frac{P}{K^\theta} \tag{1.3}$$

where θ is a weight. If $\theta = 0$, then the equation reduces to equation (1.1), the one used by McGuire et al. (1962); if $\theta = 1$, then it reduces to equation (1.2), the one used by Lewellen and Huntsman (1970). Smyth et al. then tried to determine the value of θ that minimizes the probability of multicollinearity and heteroscedasticity, which turned out to be 0.8;[17] thus followed their conclusion that if $\theta = 1$ is to be used the deflation overcompensates. Based on this fact, the ordinary least-squares method was applied to equation (1.3) with $\theta = 0.8$, using 557 U.S. companies (not limited to industrial), with Z defined by salary plus bonus plus directors' fees; with the result,

$$\frac{Z}{K^{0.8}} = \frac{100,108}{K^{0.8}} + 0.0251 \frac{S}{K^{0.8}} + 1.0731 \frac{P}{K^{0.8}}$$
$$\quad (28.81) \quad (4.48) \quad\quad (9.42)$$
$$R^2 = 0.651$$

where the numbers in parentheses indicate t-values. Obviously, all the coefficients are significant at the conventional significance level,

[17] For the details, see Smyth, Boyes, and Peseau (1975, pp. 75–8).

suggesting that both sales and profits are important in determining the level of executive compensation, a conclusion that appears reasonable to me.

This study by Smyth et al. (1975), as well as those by Roberts (1956) and McGuire et al. (1962), is susceptible to another criticism, however, concerning the definition and measurement of executive compensation. All these studies primarily used salary plus bonus as executive compensation, ignoring the significance of other incomes such as stock option.[18] In the United States, however, these other incomes have become more important forms of payment to executives as documented in the study by Lewellen (1969). Based on the sample consisting of the executives of the fifty largest U.S. manufacturing firms, he found that "in the early 1940's, salaries and bonuses accounted for some 75 to 80 percent of total executive earnings. Since 1955, the figure has been in the range of 35 to 50 percent" (Lewellen, 1969, p. 311). Furthermore, by separating the compensation between stock-based rewards, namely, the income provided by those pay arrangements that make use of the corporation's stock as the means of exchange and fixed-dollar rewards such as salaries, cash bonuses, pensions, and cash deferred compensation contracts, he found that "stock-based rewards were virtually nonexistent a quarter century ago, but lately have supplied anywhere from 20 to 50 percent of total after-tax senior executive earnings" (Lewellen, 1969, p. 312).

Insofar as we can assume rational executives, then, it must be the comprehensive compensation including stock-based rewards as well as fixed-dollar rewards that affects their behavior. Lewellen and Huntsman (1970) and Masson (1971) criticized earlier studies on this ground, conducted statistical analyses, each based on some measure of the comprehensive compensation, and concluded that profits or, more appropriately, the market value of the firm or the rate of return to the stock is what affects executive compensation most.

For instance, Lewellen and Huntsman utilized total after-tax compensation of an executive including the equivalent value[19] of all major deferred and contingent compensation arrangements as the measure of executive compensation and estimated equation (1.2). They found a strong influence of profits but little influence of sales on the compensation thus defined.

[18] McGuire et al. (1962) included the market value of stocks given to the executive but not stock options in general.

[19] Defined as the amount of additional direct cash income the executive would have required to be as well rewarded.

Masson, on the other hand, calculated the present value to each executive of all his financial returns accruing each year, including the present value (after tax) of not only salary plus bonuses but also stock options (net of opportunity cost of exercise of option), as well as deferred compensation and retirement benefits. He then regressed its percentage change over years to the percentage changes in sales, earnings per share, and the rate of return on a share of stock, using time series data over the years 1941 to 1966 for each of thirty-nine electronics, aerospace, and chemical companies. Several statistical tests were carried out, with the results that a significant number of firms do have stock market return as an important determinant of executive compensation and that the hypothesis can be rejected that firms pay their executives primarily for sales maximization.

That the gains from stock options must be included in executive compensation is beyond doubt. Still, however, the results of these two works should be taken with caution, for, as Marris (1972a, p. 492) puts it, "stock-option schemes were invented by managers for the benefit of managers," and, consequently, its importance relative to other forms of compensation may well be the result of managers' choices themselves. In Marris's view, the popularity of stock options from the mid-fifties to 1963, as witnessed by Lewellen, was caused by the bullish stock market of the time and of the 1950 revision of tax law to favor stock-option schemes. Thus once the stock market ceases to be bullish, stock options would be expected to lose popularity. This has in fact occurred. After 1963 average stock prices stopped rising at a rate far exceeding that of nominal gross national product or corporate earnings (see Marris, 1972a, p. 492) and stock options are apparently less popular now than in the early sixties. This suggests that the findings of Lewellen and Huntsman and Masson that executive compensation primarily depends on the rate of return on stock may simply be the result of rising stock prices and big capital gains at the time, which itself is the result of the voluntary choice of executives. Whether their arguments should be valid at other times is, therefore, by no means obvious.

In summing up, we note that several studies have been made to sort out the factors determining the level of executive compensation in U.S. large corporations. From the intense controversy over this matter the following conclusion emerges. If one measures executive compensation mainly by salary plus bonuses, then both sales and profits are important as such factors. If one measures executive compensation in a more comprehensive manner, then profits or the performance of the stock appears to be the major factor, although the generality of this finding is not confirmed.

Unfortunately, as far as I know, no one has ever made a similar statistical study of executive compensation for Japanese corporations. It seems that stock options are a much less important part of executive compensation in Japan than in the United States, which suggests that it is perhaps reasonable to assume that executive compensation is more dependent on the size of the firm in Japan. This conjecture agrees with the observations by Noda (1966, pp. 235-7) and Caves and Uekusa (1976, p. 12), even though neither presents any statistical evidence to support its argument.

1.6   The goal of the management: nonpecuniary motives[20]

It is simplistic to suppose that the level of the utility of management depends only on pecuniary gains. More plausibly, it also depends on nonpecuniary gains, such as economic gains not included in the compensation discussed in the previous section, as well as on psychological satisfaction. Even if executive compensation in fact depends on the performance of the stock of the firm as argued by Masson (1971), therefore, it is still questionable if management intends to maximize the stock price or the market value of the firm and, consequently, the interests of the shareholders, as presumed in the traditional theory of the firm.

Examples of economic gains not included in a pay package are company-paid luxuries such as company-owned airplanes, limousines, with company-employed drivers, and summer houses and company-paid expensive lunches with cocktails. No doubt, these should add to the utility of the management. On what the amount of these benefits depends is difficult to pinpoint; however, it seems natural to expect more of such opportunities in a larger company. If so, there may be an incentive here for management to pursue greater size.

A manager may find satisfaction in commanding many personnel in his corporate hierarchy, possessing the power to influence people inside and outside the company, being a popular figure, receiving admiration from others, or simply being at the top – in short, in having prestige and political power. Apparently, a manager of a larger

---

[20] The influences of Gordon (1945, Chapter 3), Marris (1964, Chapter 2), and Galbraith (1967, Chapters 11-15) on my writing of this section should be evident.

company will have more prestige and more political power, however these are measured.

Most individuals seek pleasure and comfort in their lives, including their work. Recently, Scitovsky (1976) inquired into human satisfaction with the help of psychology and successfully combined the result with the utility analysis of economists. His analysis of human satisfaction centers on the concept of *arousal*, a measure of brain's activity; the level of arousal being measured by the frequency, amplitude, and synchrony of electroencephalographic waves (Scitovsky, 1976, pp. 17–18). He then distinguished between comfort and pleasure; "feelings of comfort and discomfort have to do with the *level* of arousal and depend on whether arousal is or is not at its optimum level, whereas feelings of pleasure are created by *changes* in the arousal level" (Scitovsky, 1976, p. 61). This is a very important finding, yet it agrees very well with our intuition. In fact, it explains "the belief that, in man's striving for his various goals in life, being on the way to those goals and struggling to achieve them are more satisfying than is the actual attainment of the goals" (Scitovsky, 1976, p. 62). One usually enjoys climbing a mountain more than being at the top of the mountain.

A manager is no exception in pursuing comfort and pleasure. He should seek pleasure (perhaps, more than comfort) from the job of managing a company. The pleasure of work may be particularly important to managers because they are well paid and, consequently, need not worry about making a living. What they are after, therefore, is the feeling of achieving goals; that is, the change and not the level is more important to managers. Being at the top of a large company, the manager may be comfortable; however, it is heading toward an even larger corporation that gives him pleasure and more satisfaction. The manager's incentive and ultimately his pleasure, including increased prestige and responsibility, should come from pursuing expansion, or growth, of the company beyond the value-maximizing level. Of course, growth means a larger company in the future and the pursuit of growth and of size are in most instances consistent.

So far it has been shown that, on the one hand, the pecuniary gains of a manager (a top executive) depend probably on both profits or the market value of the firm and the volume of sales. However, on the other hand, the nonpecuniary motives are in favor of growth and size. A natural question to ask next would be: Which is more important? In this regard, we propose to assume that a manager's prime concern is for growth (and hence larger size in the future), subject of course to the constraint that he should retain the position. The immediate reason for this hypothesis is that faster growth satisfies psychological desires of the manager (which must be more important than is commonly thought) and at the same time achieves a larger scale in the future, resulting in larger compensation and greater prestige. However, there is another reason that we believe is more profound. To discuss this we have to turn to the question: What or who is the management?

The management we are concerned with is he or those who make decisions as to the variables under the control of the firm, for example, prices, recruitment, purchase of materials, finance, quality of the product, advertising, research and development, and investment. In its most strict sense, therefore, every member of a company is participating in management in one way or another; a worker in sales may decide how much discount to offer to each customer, a worker in personnel may decide which applicants to hire at what wage, a worker in purchasing may decide from where to buy materials and at what price, and so forth. All these workers, therefore, somehow contribute to management and their choices and actions influence the behavior of the firm. Of course it could solely be the task and responsibility of a top executive to make decisions on key issues; however, this does not deny the facts that all the necessary preparations behind such decisions are made by lower-level employees whose decisions may well affect the executive's decisions by, for instance, deciding not to report to the executive the information they consider to be unimportant or unpleasant and that there are numerous decisions relegated to the lower-level workers to make. The management, therefore, should be thought of as a team of personnel – perhaps from the bottom of the corporate hierarchy to the top – and not a single person.

This becomes more evident when we recall the fact discussed in section 1.3 that modern corporations tend to be larger, more complex, and more diversified. It is well beyond the capacity of a single person, or even a small group of people comprising, say, the chairman, the president, and the vice-presidents, to make all the decisions that influence the behavior of the company. It is only by a team of personnel consisting of numerous workers in the company, with decentralization of authority, that the firm can effectively and swiftly make decisions on all its problems.

Many readers may have already noticed a close resemblance between our argument here and Galbraith's (1967) on what he called the *technostructure*. Galbraith defined the technostructure as the organization formed by all who participate in group decision making and argued that "it extends from the most senior officials of the corporation to where it meets, at the outer perimeter, the white- and blue-collar workers whose function is to conform more or less mechanically to instruction or routine" (Galbraith, 1967, p. 84). This definition of the technostructure quite coincides with our definition of the management, although we have used the more conventional term. (We prefer *management* to a *manager* or an *executive*, however, for the apparent reason.) Now that both Galbraith and we believe that decisions in a firm are made by a team and that this team consists of almost the entire personnel of the corporate hierarchy, the question to be asked is: What is the motivation behind the decisions by this team? Clearly, even if executive compensation depends exclusively on the value of the firm and the top executive is concerned solely for his personal pecuniary gains (a dubious assumption), this does not necessarily mean that the firm makes decisions so as to maximize the value, for the executive is but one of many in the corporate organization. It is important, therefore, to analyze fully the motivation of the management in our sense or of technostructure. As Galbraith (1967, Chapters 11–15) has given a detailed discussion, we will consider this subject only briefly here.

The most important goal of the management is to maintain its operation without interference. Because the management is intended as an autonomous team, it would prefer to be free from any outside interference. If, for example, the firm is taken over by a raider, all the workers (including the executives) are at the mercy of the raider and they cannot make decisions as they would like. Such subordination doubtlessly is unbearable to them. Thus to eliminate any interference from outside and to maintain the operation of the company under their own will must be the prime motive of the management. It should be reasonable to call this motive survival.

Once survival is secured, then the growth of the firm is the principal concern of the management. This assertion basically comes from the observation that as an organization expands, more opportunities are created for promotion and appointment. There are several reasons that this creation of opportunities for promotion is so important.

First, as set forth in Simon's theory of executive compensation explained in the previous section, one's pay usually increases as one goes up the hierarchical ladder. As an organization expands, there is more chance of promotion and, consequently, increased pay – pecuniary reason that growth is attractive to a member of the organization. Second, other gains such as company-paid luxuries and prestige surely increase as one climbs the corporate ladder. Third, as has been argued already, one's level of pleasure depends very much on the change in the level of arousal. With promotions generally bringing greater authority, prestige, and responsibility, members of the corporate organization must be pleased as the firm grows rapidly and opportunities are created for promotion. All these suggest that the management as a team has an ample incentive to seek rapid growth of the firm.

Our argument here is analogous to those by Marris (1964) and Galbraith (1967); see, for example, the following quotation from Galbraith.

> Expansion of output means expansion of the technostructure itself. Such expansion, in turn, means more jobs with more responsibility and hence more promotion and more compensation. "When a man takes decisions leading to successful expansion, he not only creates new openings but also recommends himself and his colleagues as particularly suitable candidates to fill them." The paradox of modern economic motivation is that profit maximization as a goal requires that the individual member of the technostructure subordinate his personal pecuniary interest to that of the remote and unknown stockholder. By contrast, growth, as a goal, is wholly consistent with the personal and pecuniary interest of those who participate in decisions and direct the enterprise. [Galbraith, 1967, pp. 171–2; the double quotation is from Marris, 1964, p. 102.]

At this point a reservation may be in order. Our argument thus far has of course assumed that a vacancy is filled internally with an employee usually in the rank immediately below the vacant position. The relevance of our argument is, therefore, sensitive to the extent of internal promotion as opposed to recruiting officers from outside. Wide variation seems to be observed in this respect among countries and also over time. For instance, it appears that recruiting officers from outside is more common now than before in the United States and more common in the United States than in Japan. Granted this fact, one may expect that Japanese management seeks growth more vigorously than American management. This international comparison will be discussed further in Chapter 7.

In conclusion, a present-day advanced economy, be it the United States, Japan, or elsewhere, is dominated by a limited number of large-scale corporations. These corporations are not only large but also diversified, implying that they are composed of complex organizations, of which the management can be effectively carried out only by decentralizing authority among experienced professional personnel.

Those corporations are also characterized by the separation of ownership from control, giving an ample opportunity to the management for
discretion. In view of these facts, it appears that the traditional concept
that a firm is managed by a single person, namely, the top executive, so
as to maximize shareholders' interest is obsolete and the Galbraithian
view that it is managed through group decision making by a team of
personnel should be adopted.

We then investigated the motives of management. The pecuniary
gains of a top executive are found to depend on the value of the firm
and the volume of sales. The nonpecuniary motives are related more to
the growth rate and the size of the firm. On balance, we hypothesized
that a manager tends to pursue the maximal growth rate (and hence
the maximal size in the future) subject to his survival. This hypothesis
concerning the behavioral rule of the firm is quite consistent with the
fact that the management of a corporation should be regarded not as a
single person but as a team of personnel, for what is important to this
team is, first, to maintain its interference-free operation and, second, to
have as many opportunities for promotion as possible. And only
through expansion of the firm can these opportunities be realized.

CHAPTER 2

Takeovers and managerial choice

2.1   Introduction

In the previous chapter we saw that what the management is really after in most large corporations, presumably, is not the profits and market value of the firm as hypothesized by the traditional theory but the growth of the firm, although survival, of course, must come before everything else. More formally, management is assumed to maximize the growth rate of the firm subject to the constraint that it should survive any outside interference or to maximize a utility function with the probability of survival and the growth rate as its arguments, each with positive marginal utility. The growth rate of the firm in this context is defined as the rate of growth of assets the firm owns; however, in the analysis that follows this is not too important because it is confined to a steady state in which assets, sales, profits, and other variables grow at a common rate. This chapter aims to give a detailed analysis of this objective function of the management.

The idea that management does not maximize profits (or value) is not new and in fact several efforts have been made in the past few decades to develop *new* theories of the firm. Setting aside the satisficing or behavioral models [see, e.g., Simon (1955); Cyert and March (1963); Winter (1971); and Radner (1975)], we find that these works are usually brought together under the name of the *managerial theory of the firm*. The common assumption is that management pursues its own goal rather than the shareholders' welfare. However, not all authors agree on what the management goal should be. As already explained, it is the maximal growth rate of the firm for Marris (1964, 1971a) and Galbraith (1967)[1]: Other examples are the maximal amount of sales as proposed by Baumol (1959) and the maximization of a utility function that comprises administrative expense, managerial

[1] Strictly speaking, it is the growth rate of assets for Marris and the growth rate of sales for Galbraith; however, the difference is not important for the reason given in the previous paragraph.

emoluments, and discretionary profits as proposed by O. Williamson (1963). These authors do agree, however, that survival is more important than anything else and for this reason profits or market value should be regarded as a constraint to management. In fact, the concept of profits as a constraint to the discretionary behavior of management was presented as early as 1945 by Gordon as follows: "The profits criterion can never be disregarded by salaried executives. As a minimum, it is necessary to keep directors and stockholders passive. Beyond this, however, the executive group may or may not seek, with every decision to be made, to enlarge profits still further. There is a considerable opportunity to follow other goals" (the paperback edition, 1961, p. 327).

But how can the minimum or satisfactory profits be determined or estimated by the management? These "managerialists" have not succeeded in providing a persuasive answer to this question. For example, Williamson said, "the existence of satisfactory profits is necessary to assure the interference-free operation of the firm to the management. Precisely what this level will be involves a complicated interaction of the relative performance of the rivals, the historical performance of the firm, and special current conditions that affect the firm's performance" (O. E. Williamson, 1963, p. 1035). Despite this consideration, he assumed its level to be exogenously given.

Marris, on the other hand, argued that "if shareholders in general possess countervailing power, it must be found mainly ... in the transferability of shares and in the existence of an organized stock-market" (Marris, 1964, p. 18). Furthermore, he argued that the existence of takeover discipline is the only effective constraint to management.[2] He then analyzed the working of the stock market, particularly the nature of takeovers, and formulated the constraint to a manager as a minimum valuation ratio (market value of the firm divided by its assets). That is, "we suppose that managers set some value of the (valuation) ratio below which either fear of take-over or the sense of guilt becomes intolerable" (Marris, 1964, p. 45, my parentheses). Nevertheless, in his analysis, Marris assumed this mini-

---

[2] Marris (1964, p. 29). The same point was raised in a normative context by Manne: "Only the take-over scheme provides some assurance of competitive efficiency among corporate managers and thereby affords strong protection to the interests of vast numbers of small, non-controlling shareholders" (Manne, 1965, p. 113).

num ratio to be constant, similarly to Williamson's treatment of satisfactory profits.

The treatment of minimum profit (or minimum valuation ratio) as given, namely, as something that cannot be determined in the system, was a serious weakness of these earlier managerial models because the optimal values for management of its policy variables heavily depend on this minimum requirement.[3] If one intends to perform comparative analysis, this weakness becomes even more serious because the change in the environment of the firm may well change the minimum requirement at the same time. This weakness may explain, at least in part, why the traditional theory continues to be preferred over managerial theories.

The purpose of this chapter is to resolve this unfortunate situation by offering a theory to explain how the minimum requirement is determined. Only by doing this can one formulate a managerial theory of the firm that is useful in comparative analyses. As an analytical apparatus we follow Marris's (1971a) analytical framework of corporate growth, which is explained in the next section. We also follow Marris's argument that the threat of being taken over is the only effective constraint to management which seeks the maximal growth rate of the assets of the firm. Obviously, then, it is necessary to investigate the nature of takeovers first, which we do in section 2.3 by first ignoring uncertainty. The optimal strategies in a takeover for a raider and for an incumbent management are discussed, and it is shown that the minimum valuation ratio depends on the maximum feasible valuation ratio. The determination of the optimal growth rate under uncertainty is then discussed in section 2.4. A brief summary of our analysis and some additional remarks are given in the last section.

2.2 The v-g frontier

The essence of Marris's (1971a) model lies in his derivation of what we will call the *valuation-growth frontier* or, in short, the *v-g frontier* (or, in Marris's term, the *growth-valuation function*), namely, the trade-off between valuation ratio v and growth rate g on which management must make its decision. In order to derive it, we make the following assumptions:

Some later managerial models attempted to make the constraint, namely, the minimum valuation ratio, endogenous. See J. H. Williamson (1966) and Yarrow (1976). These will be criticized subsequently, however.

2.1   Management intends to determine the rate of growth of capital (assets) g, given the initial amount of capital, K_0. It considers only the growth along a steady-state path in which sales, profit net of depreciation but not of capital cost P, capital K, total dividends paid D, and the total value of bonds B grow at a common and constant rate for an indefinitely long time. By definition, in such a steady state, profit rate p ($\equiv P/K$), retention rate r ($\equiv (P - D - iB)/P$) and debt-assets ratio stay constant over time. (Let i denote the interest rate paid to bonds.)

2.2   Shareholders know with certainty the choice by the management of g and the rate of profit, and that a steady state is expected.

2.3   The total market value of the shares of the firm E ($\equiv V - B$, where V is the total market value of the firm) is equated at stock market to the present value of its dividend stream (discounted to infinite future) received by the current shareholders, the discount rate of shareholders being i and a given constant to the management.[4]

2.4   There is no corporate tax.

2.5   There is no cost of adjusting the stock of capital.

Under these assumptions it can be shown that

$$v \equiv V/K = (p - g)/(i - g) \qquad (2.1)$$

for g smaller than i. Now assume furthermore that p is determined as a function of the growth rate g, that is, $p = p(g)$, given prices, in such a manner that $p'(g) < 0$ and $p''(g) < 0$ for any $g > 0$. Basically, this is because, in order to achieve faster growth of sales and profits, the firm must increase advertising and/or R & D expenditures. The more detailed analysis of this function and also the proof of equation (2.1) will be covered in the next chapter. By substituting this function into equation (2.1), one can immediately see that v is a function of g only as long as i is given; that is, $v = v(g)$. It is straightforward to show that $v'(g) \gtreqless 0$ as $g \lesseqgtr g^{**}$ and $v''(g^{**}) < 0$ by defining g^{**} accordingly,

---

[4] Assumptions 2.1 and 2.3 together imply that the rate of return is equated between stock and bond markets. This holds if arbitrage is freely carried out between the two markets, as is usually assumed. Strictly speaking, however, there is difficulty here because later we assume that the transaction cost is not negligible in a takeover. In this regard, we speculate that although in buying the large amount of shares that is necessary in a takeover the transaction cost is significant, such a cost is negligibly small for the transaction at the margin. If so, arbitrage between shares and bonds would be done almost without any transaction cost, and the equivalence of the rate of return between the two types of financial assets should be realized. This point will be discussed in more detail in the next section.

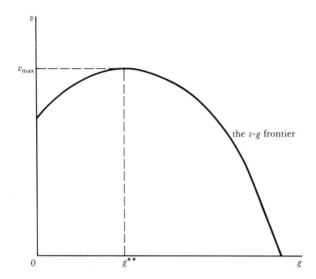

v_{max}

0   g^{**} g

Figure 2.1 The v-g (valuation-growth) frontier.

implying that g^{**} maximizes v at least locally. Since $V = vK_0$ and K_0 is historically given, g^{**} also maximizes V. Also, since $V = E + B$ and B is given today as a result of past financial policy, g^{**} maximizes E, too. The locus of v and g that satisfies the $v(g)$ function is illustrated in Figure 2.1. We will hereafter call it the v-g frontier.

The management choice variable is g. Obviously, the optimal value, g^*, of g would be determined in the region where $g^{**} \leq g^*$ but $v(g^*) > 0$, because if $g^* < g^{**}$ both v and g can be increased. In this region higher g is achieved only by reducing v, and this reduction may increase the probability of being taken over. Taking account of this trade-off between v and g, Marris, as was discussed in the last section, formulated the managerial objective function as follows:

$$\text{Maximize } g \qquad \text{subject to } v \geq \bar{v} \qquad\qquad (2.2)$$

where $\bar{v}$ is the minimum valuation ratio previously discussed. Marris (at least in 1964) assumed that the management can somehow set this value, $\bar{v}$, on the basis of considerations outside of his model and thus he treated it as a constant.[5] In the following sections we will show that this is not correct and $\bar{v}$ is determined as a function of v_{max} among other

[5] Criticizing equation (2.2), J. H. Williamson (1966) formulated the constraint as $v \geq c_1 v_{max}$, whereas Yarrow (1976) formulated it as $v \geq v_{max} - c_2/K(0)$. However, each assumed that c_1 or c_2 is constant, which in the next section we will show to be incorrect.

things, where v_{max} is the maximum value of v along the v-g frontier namely, $v_{max} = v(g^{**})$. To do this, we must first analyze the nature o takeovers.

2.3   A model of takeovers

Suppose that a potential raider is looking for an opportunity to make a profit from some takeover. He might be an individual or a firm. We assume that, even if he is a firm himself, no extra profit accrues from integrating the organization of the firm taken over with the raider's. In other words, following Alberts's (1966) terminology, we assume that no synergistic effect exists in this takeover. For this reason, even though we proceed as if the raider keeps the firm he takes over as an independent organization, the discussion applies equally well to the case where the firm is merged with the raider's.

We also assume that a potential raider is a profit maximizer Suppose that he is to decide whether or not to take over a firm (call it Alpha). Denote by θ the proportion of shares he chooses to purchase of the total shares of Alpha. Then, the raider can acquire Alpha's $100 \times \theta$ percent shares by paying θE plus any transaction cost incurred in this purchase (say C). He knows that if θ is greater than one half, he can manage Alpha himself and maximize its market value by changing its growth rate along the v-g frontier. Suppose that he knows with certainty the shape of the v-g frontier. Then, if he sells his $100 \times \theta$ percent Alpha shares after v_{max} is achieved, his receipt would be θE_{max} where E_{max} denotes the total market value of its shares that corresponds to v_{max}. If this whole operation could be done instantaneously, the expected profit from this takeover, Π, would be the difference between expense and return, that is, $\Pi = \theta E_{max} - \theta E - C$, and the raider will take over if and only if Π is positive for some θ. We assume that the raider sells his Alpha shares to the public as soon as he achieves v_{max}. Therefore the takeover considered here can be interpreted as a sort of arbitrage. In fact, the operation the raider undertakes is almost the same as arbitrage, say, in a commodity market except that in a takeover he has to work as a manager during the transition.

It should be noted that the preceding discussion understates the chance of a takeover because some potential raiders may well be growth-maximizing or size-maximizing managers themselves. Even if the expected profit from the takeover is negative, a growth (or ize)-maximizing raider will take Alpha over as long as the marginal utility of merging Alpha with the raider's own company and thus achieving a greater size of the company outweighs the marginal disutility of the expected loss (see Mueller, 1969). No doubt, however, he should take over if the expected profit is positive, because by acting just as an arbitrager he can increase the wealth of his company without altering the growth rate, which surely helps his growth strategy.

Another assumption in the previous discussion is that the raider can achieve v_{max} instantaneously. In view of the fact that changing the managerial policy usually requires the reorganization of Alpha and adjustment in many aspects of Alpha's activities, it may be more realistic to assume that it takes time T (> 0) to achieve v_{max} where T may be a given number or a choice variable for a raider. If T is positive, the following facts complicate the analysis: (1) Assets, K, grow during the transition. (2) The raider receives dividends for the shares of Alpha he owns during the transition. (3) Since g changes during the transition, v and g do not satisfy the v-g frontier during this period. (4) What matters to a raider is the present value of profit evaluated at the time of the takeover and the raider's discount rate may or may not equal the market interest rate i. We will not investigate this case in detail because the analysis turns out to be mathematically complicated and rather tedious. Interested readers should refer to Odagiri (1977, Appendix to Chapter 1) where it is shown that no essential correction of the result is needed even if T is assumed positive instead of zero.

By using definitional identities, $vK_0 = V = E + B$ and $v_{max}K_0 = E_{max} + B$, we can rewrite the expression for Π, already stated, as follows:

$$\Pi = \theta(v_{max}K_0 - B) - \theta(vK_0 - B) - C$$
$$= \theta(v_{max} - v)K_0 - C \tag{2.3}$$

Let us now consider on what C, the transaction cost, depends. The transaction cost would consist of three categories: The first is the cost that is proportional to the value of the transaction. Examples are the stock price increase due to the revelation of the intention of a takeover or due to the demand increase when the raider purchases the shares at the open market, and the premiums to be paid to shareholders so that they accept the bid if the raider adopts a tender offer or takeover bid (T.O.B.). The rate of the stock price increase or the rate of premium may depend on many factors, for example, the managerial ability of the raider relative to the incumbent management estimated by the shareholders, the shareholders' expectations about the future, whether or not there exist stable shareholders such as firms of which shares Alpha owns, and whether or not the main creditors such as banks trust the incumbent management. The second type of transaction cost is the cost that depends on the number of shares to be acquired, for instance, brokerage fees paid to stock exchange markets and middlemen. The third type is the fixed cost such as the cost of announcing the raider's intention of a T.O.B. and miscellaneous legal expenses.

Hence C depends on θN and θE, where N is the total number of Alpha shares, with a positive value at $\theta N = \theta E = 0$, assuming that the rate of the price increase or of the premium depends on no other variable. It appears, however, that the second type of cost is negligibly small compared to the first, which perhaps is substantial;[6] hence we assume that $C = C(\theta E)$ where $C(0) > 0$ and $0 < C'(\theta E) < 1$. Define x to be the ratio E/V so that debt-equity ratio B/E equals $(1 - x)/x$. Then $C = C(\theta E) = C(\theta x v K_0)$.

By substituting this assumption into equation (2.3), we now have the following expression for Π:

$$\Pi = \theta(v_{max} - v)K_0 - C(\theta x v K_0) \tag{2.4}$$

This equation should make it clear that Π depends on five variables: v, v_{max}, θ, x, and K_0. Among them, K_0 is historically given and v_{max} is given as long as the v-g frontier is given. θ is a choice variable for the raider, whereas x and v are choice variables for the incumbent management. In the rest of this section, we will discuss how the optimal values of these three choice variables are determined.

Obviously, the raider would choose the optimal value, θ^*, of θ so that Π is maximized, subject to the constraint that $\tfrac{1}{2} < \theta \leq 1$. By differentiating equation (2.4) with respect to θ, we have

$$\partial\Pi/\partial\theta = (v_{max} - v)K_0 - C'(\theta x v K_0)x v K_0$$
$$= \Pi/\theta + (1 - \epsilon(C))C/\theta \tag{2.5}$$

where

$$\epsilon(C) = C'(\theta x v K_0)\theta x v K_0/C(\theta x v K_0)$$

that is, $\epsilon(C)$ is the elasticity of the transaction cost C with respect to the

---

[6] However, the existence of such cost may explain the frequent use of share splitting by management as a tactic to defend against raiders. See Cary (1969, p. 322).

market value of the purchase, $\theta x v K_0$, evaluated at the price before its possible increase due to the takeover. Hence if $\epsilon(C) \leq 1$, then $\partial \Pi / \partial \theta > 0$ as long as $\Pi > 0$, implying that if $\epsilon(C) \leq 1$, then the raider would choose $\theta^* = 1$ as long as he expects positive profit from the takeover (otherwise he will not take over). Note that since $C(0) > 0$ and $C'(\theta x v K_0) > 0$, $\epsilon(C) < 1$ if $C''(\theta x v K_0) \leq 0$, that is, if the transaction cost increases as $\theta x v K_0$ increases but only at a constant or a decreasing rate. If, on the other hand, $\epsilon(C) > 1$, which requires that $C''(\theta x v K_0) > 0$, then we may have an interior solution such that $\frac{1}{2} < \theta^* < 1$ and $v_{max} - v = C'(\theta^* x v K_0) x v$, or a corner solution $\theta^* = (N + 1)/2N$ if N is odd and $\theta^* = (N + 2)/2N$ if N is even.[7]

Let us now turn our discussion to the optimal strategy of the incumbent management to prevent being taken over. Its optimal strategy for this purpose is to determine the value of its choice variables x and v so that Π remains nonpositive irrespective of θ. Since x does not affect the management utility, its optimal value x^* is such that Π is minimized. By differentiating equation (2.4) with respect to x, we have

$$\partial \Pi / \partial x = -C'(\theta x v K_0) \theta v K_0 \qquad (2.6)$$

which is negative irrespective of the level of θ and v. Since it must be that $0 < x \leq 1$ because E must be positive and B must be nonnegative, equation (2.6) implies that $x^* = 1$. In other words, the optimal strategy for the incumbent management is to let $B = 0$, that is, to finance only through the retention of profits or the new issue of shares.[8] Why would this be true? Recall that v_{max} does not depend on x [see equation (2.1)]. Then, equation (2.4) indicates that if v is kept constant, Π depends on x only through the transaction cost, which depends not on θV but on θE. Because a larger x implies a larger value

---

[7] Robin Marris in a personal correspondence pointed out another force to make θ unity in a real takeover. Tender offers are commonly used in the United States (and also in the United Kingdom). U.S. law permits the raider to refuse the purchase of shares from those shareholders who turned down the offer at the time of the bid but changed their mind after the success of the bid. Thus many shareholders tend to rush into the acceptance of the offer, provided it is at all attractive, so that they will not be "locked in" after the takeover.

[8] Note that we have been assuming that there is no corporate tax. If there are corporate taxes that discriminate between interest payment to bondholders and dividend payment to shareholders, x^* may well be less than unity.

of the purchase, $\theta x v K_0$, and consequently, a larger transaction cost, it also implies a smaller profit from the takeover. Hence x should be maximized in order to prevent the takeover. This result, for the most part, coincides with Stiglitz's, who concluded that "it would seem that there is some presumption that, in general, actions which increase the value of the equity of the firm will make a take-over bid less easily managed" (Stiglitz, 1972, p. 476).

Stating it differently, there exists an optimal debt-equity ratio if the possibility of takeover is taken into account even though as is shown in equation (2.1) the market value of the firm V does not depend on debt-equity ratio as long as profit rate and growth rate are given, as the Modigliani–Miller theorem (1958) predicts. In this regard, it may be of interest to see from equation (2.6) that an optimal debt-equity ratio does not exist if and only if $C'(\theta x v K_0) = 0$, that is, if and only if there exists no transaction cost in a takeover except a fixed one. Naturally, this condition is quite similar to the assumption of no transaction cost in the Modigliani–Miller theorem but perhaps more restrictive than the latter since a negligible transaction cost at a *marginal* arbitrage between bonds and shares is sufficient for the Modigliani–Miller theorem to hold, whereas our condition requires a negligible transaction cost in the purchase of more than one half of the total shares of a firm.

Another choice variable for the incumbent management is v, the valuation ratio. Since

$$\partial\Pi/\partial v = -\theta K_0 - C'(\theta x v K_0)\theta x K_0 < 0 \qquad (2.7)$$

for any $\theta > 0$, Π is minimized by maximizing v. It has been assumed, however, that the objective of the management is twofold: first to avoid being taken over and second to maximize the growth rate. In view of equation (2.7) and our v-g frontier, this management decision problem can be formulated as minimizing v subject to $\Pi \leq 0$ with the sufficient condition being that $\partial v/\partial g \leq 0$ around the optimal value of v or, equivalently, as setting $v = \bar{v}$ where $\bar{v}$ is defined by the level of v such that Π equals zero, that is,

$$\theta^*(v_{\max} - \bar{v})K_0 - C(\theta^* x^* \bar{v} K_0) = 0 \qquad (2.8)$$

with the same sufficient condition. Note that in equation (2.8) θ and x are evaluated at their optimal values previously analyzed because to avoid a takeover, Π must be nonpositive for any θ and because by setting x at its optimal level so that Π is minimized, v can be minimized without increasing Π. Since K_0 is historically given and θ^* and x^* are optimal values, one can see that $\bar{v}$ depends only on v_{max}. By differentiating equation (2.8) with respect to v_{max} and collecting terms, we have

$$\theta^* K_0 - \theta^* K_0(1 + C'x^*)\frac{d\bar{v}}{dv_{max}} + (v_{max} - \bar{v} - C'x^*\bar{v})K_0\frac{d\theta^*}{dv_{max}}$$

$$- C'\theta^*\bar{v}K_0\frac{dx^*}{dv_{max}} = 0 \quad (2.9)$$

where the argument of the C' function is suppressed. However, by the definition of θ^* and x^*, $dx^*/dv_{max} = 0$ (since $x^* = 1$) and either $d\theta^*/dv_{max} = 0$ (in the case of a corner solution) or $\bar{v}_{max} - \bar{v} = C'x^*\bar{v}$ [in the case of an interior solution as shown in equation (2.5)]. Hence equation (2.9) reduces to

$$\frac{d\bar{v}}{dv_{max}} = \frac{1}{1 + C'x^*} \quad (2.10)$$

which is positive but smaller than unity because C' is positive. It should be worth noting that equation (2.10) implies a smaller $d\bar{v}/dv_{max}$, namely, a smaller response of $\bar{v}$ to the change in v_{max} for a larger C'; whereas equation (2.8) implies a larger discrepancy between v_{max} and $\bar{v}$ for a larger C.

To summarize, the optimal strategy for the incumbent management is to set $x = x^* = 1$ and $v = \bar{v}$ with[9]

$$\bar{v} = \Phi(v_{max}) \quad (2.11)$$

where

$$0 < \Phi' = [1 + x^*C'(\theta^*x^*\bar{v}K_0)]^{-1} < 1$$

2.4 Managerial decision making under uncertainty

So far the shape of the v-g frontier, particularly the value of v_{max}, is assumed to be known with certainty to any potential raider. In the real world this obviously is not true. Each potential raider may well be uncertain as to v_{max}, expecting it with a subjective probability distribution. Different potential raiders may possess different expectations. The incumbent management (simply called the management here-

[9] Odagiri (1977, pp. 55–9) shows that even if a raider cannot achieve v_{max} instantaneously, this result is sustained, except that a possibility, perhaps meager, of Φ' exceeding unity cannot be ruled out.

after) may not know with certainty who the potential raiders are and what expectations each potential raider has as to v_{max}. In such a situation the management cannot be certain as to $\bar{v}$, the minimum value of v such that a takeover is prevented, and may estimate the probability of being taken over in the following manner:

Prob [a takeover takes place given v and v_{max}]

$$= \text{Prob}[\bar{v} > v, \text{ given } v_{max}]$$

$$= \pi(v, v_{max}) \qquad (2.12)$$

where

$$\pi(v, v_{max}) = 1 \qquad \text{for } v \leq 0$$

$$0 \leq \pi(v, v_{max}) \leq 1$$

$$\pi_1(v, v_{max}) \leq 0$$

where v_{max} should be taken as the maximum value of v expected by management itself. The condition that $\pi_1 \leq 0$ follows because, as v increases given v_{max}, fewer and fewer raiders will find the takeover profitable.

As shown in the previous section, $d\bar{v}/dv_{max}$ ($= \Phi'(v_{max})$) is positive but less than unity when v_{max} is known with certainty by any raider. What does this imply in terms of the π function? To answer this question, let us consider the following situation. Suppose each potential raider estimates the probability distribution of v_{max} based on his knowledge of the environment that surrounds the firm. He then calculates for each value of v_{max} the value of $\bar{v}$ that satisfies equation (2.11) and by doing so constructs the probability distribution of $\bar{v}$. The decision of whether or not to take over the firm is made by comparing this distribution of $\bar{v}$ with the actual value of v, namely, the value of v chosen by the management. Now suppose that the value of v_{max} or, more plausibly, the value of v_{max} expected by management is increased. Because this must be the result of a change in the environment such as prices the firm faces, the raider's estimated distribution of v_{max} will also shift upward and, because $\Phi'(v_{max}) > 0$, his estimated distribution of $\bar{v}$ will shift upward as well. Consequently, the probability of earning positive profit from the takeover increases if the actual v is kept constant and the raider is surely more likely to undertake the takeover. Hence it should be appropriate to assume that $\pi_2(v, v_{max}) > 0$. Suppose, on the other hand, that both v_{max} and v are increased by exactly the same amount. Then the raider's estimated distribution of v_{max} and hence of $\bar{v}$ will shift upward as before. Unlike before, however, v is also increased, and therefore the relative location of the distribution of $\bar{v}$ and the actual v is not so simple to determine as previously. Recall that $0 < \Phi'(v_{\max}) < 1$. This implies that the distribution of $\bar{v}$ shifts in the same direction but to a smaller degree in comparison to the shift in the estimated distribution of $v_{\max}$. Because the increase in the true value of $v_{\max}$ is assumed to equal that of v, the shift of the estimated distribution of $\bar{v}$ would be *less* than the change in v as long as the raider's subjective probability distribution of $v_{\max}$ shifts as much as the increase in the true value of $v_{\max}$. Therefore the expected profitability of the takeover would be estimated to be smaller by any raider, and, as a result, the probability of a takeover would decrease. This suggests that we assume the following:

$$\left.\frac{d\pi}{dv_{\max}}\right|_{dv=dv_{\max}} = \pi_1(v, v_{\max}) + \pi_2(v, v_{\max}) < 0 \qquad (2.13)$$

Now with this subjective probability distribution, what is the optimal decision for the management that has the managerial objective function discussed earlier? At least two types of techniques can be applied to solve this problem. The first is the use of a chance-constrained programming method and the second is the use of the concept of a hazard rate.

A chance-constrained programming method that was introduced by Charnes and Cooper (1959) is defined as a problem to "select certain random variables as functions of random variables with known distributions in such a manner as (a) to maximize a functional of both classes of random variables subject to (b) constraints on these variables which must be maintained at prescribed levels of probability" (Charnes and Cooper, 1959, p. 73). In our present context the chance-constrained programming problem for the management is formulated as follows:

$$\text{Maximize } g \qquad \text{subject to Prob[a takeover]} \leq \beta \qquad (2.14)$$

where β is the "prescribed level of probability." Given the v-g frontier and equation (2.12), this constraint is equivalent to $\pi(v(g), v_{\max}) \leq \beta$, where $\partial\pi/\partial g = \pi_1(v, v_{\max})v'(g) > 0$ in the region where $\pi_1(v, v_{\max}) < 0$ and $v'(g) < 0$. Hence the optimal growth rate g^* and the optimal valuation ratio v^* as the solution to equation (2.14) are obtained by solving the equation

$$\pi(v^*, v_{\max}) = \pi(v(g^*), v_{\max}) = \beta \qquad (2.15)$$

Marris's lexicographic managerial utility function, equation (2.2), may be interpreted as being based on this type of approach. A difficulty in this approach, obviously, lies in determining β. Is it plausible to assume that β is a priori given independently of the level of g or v? Can one not, for instance, accept a higher subjective probability of a takeover if he has an opportunity to enjoy a higher growth rate? It might be that the choice of β itself is another decision problem. Marris, in this regard, did not investigate further than to say that β is to be determined at a level "below which either fear of take-over or the sense of guilt becomes intolerable" (Marris, 1964, p. 45).[10]

Since β is assumed to be exogenously given in this approach, we have $\pi_1(v^*, v_{max}) \, dv^* + \pi_2(v^*, v_{max}) \, dv_{max} = 0$ by totally differentiating equation (2.15), or

$$\frac{dv^*}{dv_{max}} = - \frac{\pi_2(v^*, v_{max})}{\pi_1(v^*, v_{max})}$$

which is positive but less than unity in view of equation (2.13). This appears reasonable because it is the same rule as that obtained under the assumption of certain knowledge of v_{max}. However, it should be reemphasized that this result is dependent on the assumption of the constancy of β, for as we will soon show, the relaxation of this assumption may reverse the result.

The second method of solution to our problem uses the concept of a hazard rate, as developed by Kamien and Schwartz (1971, 1972). To apply this method, let us define $F(t)$ to be the probability that a takeover has taken place by time t, with $F(0) = 0$. By the definition of a conditional probability, $F'(t)/(1 - F(t))$ is a measure of the probability of a takeover at time t given that a takeover has not taken place before t. This measure is called a hazard rate and is denoted by $h(t)$. In view of equation (2.12), $h(t)$ is dependent on $v(t)$ and v_{max} (suppressing the indication of time for v_{max} since it is assumed stationary). By analogy to the properties of the π function, the following conditions are assumed to be satisfied:

$$h(t) = h(v(t), v_{max}) \tag{2.16}$$

where

---

[10] Yaari (1965), who applied chance-constrained programming to the problem of consumer allocation over time under uncertain lifetime, recognized this difficulty and considered only the case where $\beta = 0$, which he claimed to be "the case where it is physically or institutionally impossible to violate the constraint under any circumstances" (Yaari, 1965, p. 139).

$h_1(v(t), v_{max}) < 0$

$h_2(v(t), v_{max}) > 0$

$h_1(v(t), v_{max}) + h_2(v(t), v_{max}) < 0$

ignoring, for simplicity, the posssibility that $h_1(v(t), v_{max}) = 0$ for some $v(t)$.

Suppose that management gains positive utility, u, in each period before a takeover takes place but none[11] after a takeover and that u depends on the growth rate of the firm. That is, $u(t) = u(g(t))$, where we assume that $u(g(t)) > 0$, $u'(g(t)) > 0$, and $u''(g(t)) < 0$. Also, suppose that it maximizes the present value of its expected utility stream over the future, U_a, where

$$U_a = \int_0^\infty u(g(t))e^{-\rho t}(1 - F(t))\, dt \qquad (2.17)$$

denoting by ρ the discount rate of the management, which may or may not equal i but is assumed to be constant, subject to

$$F'(t) = h(v(t), v_{max})(1 - F(t))$$
$$F(0) = 0 \qquad (2.18)$$

and the v-g frontier, which we now write as

$$v(t) = v(g(t), v_{max}) \qquad (2.19)$$

summarizing the effects of the factors that determine the position of the v-g frontier by the value of v_{max}. By definition, $\partial v(t)/\partial v_{max} = 1$ at $g(t) = g^{**}$, and we would expect that $v_2(g(t), v_{max}) \equiv \partial v(t)/\partial v_{max} > 0$ for any $g(t)$. As before, $v_1(g(t), v_{max})$ is negative for $g(t) > g^{**}$.

This problem may look like an optimal control problem. It should be recalled, however, that we have assumed that the management considers only a steady-state path where $g(t)$ is constant, in order to obtain the v-g frontier (assumption 2.1 in section 2.2). Hence only a steady state, where $g(t) = g$ is constant for any $t \geq 0$, is considered here.[12] The v-g frontier then implies that v is also constant, which in turn implies that h is constant. We can then solve the differential

[11] It does not change the substance of our argument to assume a positive but constant utility during this period.

[12] It can be shown that the solution to this optimal control problem, without assuming the constancy of $g(t)$ but assuming equation (2.19), yields the same result, namely, the constancy of $g(t)$ with its level determined by equation (2.22). The proof is almost parallel to Kamien and Schwartz (1971). In this formulation, however, one may be unable to justify equation (2.19).

equation in equation (2.18) to obtain (see Kamien and Schwartz, 1971, p. 445)

$$F(t) = 1 - \exp(-h(v, v_{max})t) \tag{2.20}$$

By substituting this equation into equation (2.17), we have

$$U_a = \int_0^\infty u(g) \exp(-\rho t - h(v, v_{max})t)\, dt$$
$$= u(g)/[\rho + h(v, v_{max})] \tag{2.21}$$

The original optimal control problem of maximizing equation (2.17) now reduces to a regular maximization problem. Substituting equation (2.19) and assuming an interior solution, we obtain the first-order condition as follows (the asterisk refers to the optimal value as before):

$$\left. \frac{\partial U_a}{\partial g} \right|_{g=g^*} = \frac{u'(g^*)[\rho + h(v^*, v_{max})] - u(g^*)h_1(v^*, v_{max})v_1(g^*, v_{max})}{[\rho + h(v^*, v_{max})]^2} = 0$$

where

$$v^* = v(g^*, v_{max})$$

or

$$\frac{u'(g^*)}{u(g^*)} = \frac{h_1(v^*, v_{max})v_1(g^*, v_{max})}{\rho + h(v^*, v_{max})} \tag{2.22}$$

Interpretation of this equation is simple. The ratio in the left-hand side expresses the proportional increase in utility due to an infinitesimal increase in g, whereas the ratio in the right-hand side expresses the proportional increase in $\rho + h$, which can be interpreted as a capitalization rate adjusted for uncertainty, due to the increase in g. The necessary condition (2.22) requires that these ratios be equal at the optimal growth rate g^*.

The second-order condition is as follows (the arguments for the u, h, and v functions and their derivatives are suppressed):

$$\frac{\partial^2 U_a}{\partial g^2} = \frac{u''(\rho + h) - u(h_{11}v_1^2 + h_1v_{11})}{(\rho + h)^2} < 0 \tag{2.23}$$

Since $u'' < 0$ and $\rho + h > 0$, a sufficient condition for equation (2.23) to hold is that

$$h_{11}v_1^2 + h_1v_{11} = \frac{\partial^2 h}{\partial g^2} > 0 \tag{2.24}$$

that is, h increases with g at an increasing rate.

Alternatively, one can solve the problem by means of a diagram in

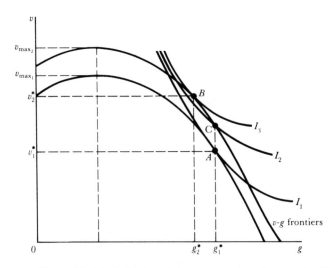

Figure 2.2. Maximization of the present value of expected utility stream U_a, where (1) I_1, I_2, and I_3 are indifference curves, that is, the locus of constant U_a, such that I_1 (I_2 and I_3) is drawn given that the value of v_{max} is v_{max_1} (v_{max_2}), and I_3 corresponds to a higher level of U_a than I_2 and (2) the two v-g frontiers are parallel, for example, the vertical distance between points C and A equals $v_{max_2} - v_{max_1}$.

the (g, v) plane. Regard the right-hand side of equation (2.21) as a function of two variables, v and g. Then by fixing U_a, a collection of indifference curves are obtained with the slope,

$$\left.\frac{dv}{dg}\right|_{U_a=\text{const.}} = \frac{u'(g)[\rho + h(v, v_{max})]}{u(g)h_1(v, v_{max})} \tag{2.25}$$

which is negative because $u'(g) > 0$ and $h_1(v, v_{max}) < 0$. Then the solution to maximizing equation (2.21) subject to equation (2.19) is obtained at the point (g^*, v^*) where one of the indifference curves is tangent to the v-g frontier, with the condition for this tangency being equation (2.22) because the slope of the v-g frontier is $v_1(v, v_{max})$. The point A in Figure 2.2 illustrates this. Since the slope of the indifference curves is negative everywhere by equation (2.25), the slope of the v-g frontier at (g^*, v^*) must also be negative. This implies that $g^* > g^{**}$ and $v^* < v_{max}$; that is, the management that has the managerial objective function as previously defined never maximizes v.

We will now investigate the effect of v_{max} on v^*. Totally differentiate equation (2.22) and (2.19) and rearrange them. Then in matrix notation we have (the arguments for the functions are suppressed)

$$\begin{bmatrix} u''(\rho + h) - u'h_1 v_1 - uh_1 v_{11} & u'h_1 - uh_{11} v_1 \\ -v_1 & 1 \end{bmatrix} \begin{bmatrix} dg^* \\ dv^* \end{bmatrix}$$

$$= \begin{bmatrix} -u'h_2 + uh_{12} v_1 + uh_1 v_{12} \\ v_2 \end{bmatrix} dv_{max} \quad (2.26)$$

By applying Cramer's rule and rearranging, we obtain the desired expression,

$$\frac{dv^*}{dv_{max}} = v_2 + [uh_{11} v_1^2 v_2 - u'v_1(h_1 + h_2) + u'h_1 v_1(1 - v_2)$$

$$+ uh_{12} v_1^2 + uh_2 v_1 v_{12}]/[u''(\rho + h) - uh_1 v_{11} - uh_{11} v_1^2] \quad (2.27)$$

By the second-order condition (2.23), the denominator of the fraction in the right-hand side is negative; however, the sign of the numerator is ambiguous. For instance, assume a parallel shift of the v-g frontier; then, $v_2 = 1$ for any g and $v_{12} = v_{21} = 0$. Also suppose that h_{12} is negligibly small. Then equation (2.27) reduces to

$$\frac{dv^*}{dv_{max}} = 1 + \frac{uh_{11} v_1^2 v_2 - u'v_1(h_1 + h_2)}{u''(\rho + h) - uh_1 v_{11} - uh_{11} v_1^2} \quad (2.28)$$

The second term in the numerator of the fraction in the right-hand side is positive in view of equation (2.16), whereas the sign of the first term in the numerator cannot be determined unless the sign of h_{11} is specified. It appears more plausible to assume h_{11} to be positive, which implies that as v is increased the hazard rate decreases but only at a diminishing rate. This positivity of h_{11} also makes it easier for the second-order condition (2.23) to hold, particularly because v_{11} is negative.[13] If so, the first term in the numerator is positive and it is ambiguous whether dv^*/dv_{max} is less than or greater than unity. Consider the case where h_{11} is relatively small in absolute value. Then dv^*/dv_{max} is greater than unity in contradiction to the prediction made when there is no uncertainty or when the chance-constrained programming method is applied. Since

$$dh/dv_{max} = h_1 \, dv/dv_{max} + h_2 < (dv/dv_{max} - 1)h_1$$

by equation (2.16), the fact that $dv^*/dv_{max} > 1$ implies that $dh^*/dv_{max} < 0$ where $h^* = h(v^*, v_{max})$; that is, the hazard rate is decreased when v_{max} increases, making the assumption of constant β in the chance-constrained programming method unconvincing.

[13] Since $p''(g) < 0$, $v_{11} = (p''(g) + 2v_1)/(i - g) < 0$ in the region where $v_1 < 0$.

Also note that by equation (2.26), $dv/dv_{max} = v_1 dg/dv_{max} + v_2$. Therefore $v_2 = 1$ and $dv^*/dv_{max} > 1$ imply that $dg^*/dv_{max} < 0$; that is, as v_{max} increases, the growth rate is decreased. Figure 2.2 illustrates this. As v_{max} increases from v_{max_1} to v_{max_2}, the tangency of the v-g frontier and an indifference curve moves from point A to B and g^* decreases. Note that at point C in the diagram the level of U_a is greater than at point A since as it moves from A to C, g stays constant but v and v_{max} increase by the same amount and hence reduce h. What our analysis has shown is that the management further decreases the hazard rate and increases the security against a takeover even at the sacrifice of the growth rate in order to increase the level of intertemporal utility U_a, which is why the optimal point B is located northwest of C in the diagram. In this sense one may say with analogy to consumer theory that the growth rate is an inferior good for this management.

The preceding determination of the optimal growth rate thus avoids our criticism of the chance-constrained programming method, because the maximum tolerable probability of being taken over is now endogenously determined. However, another criticism might be raised. We assumed that the instantaneous utility function u depends on g, and this is more restrictive than to assume that the objective function like U_a is an increasing function of g, the latter probably being what Marris intended. Marris, for example, argued that "if the analysis assumes that the 'initial' size of a firm is historically determined and that steady-state growth begins from this point, ... it is clear that we can be indifferent to the question of whether management satisfactions are derived directly from size as such or from the rate of change" (Marris, 1971a, p. 16). In this context our previous analysis has dealt only with the latter (the rate of change). To deal with the former (size), the instantaneous utility function u may have to be such that $u(t) = u(K(t)) = u(K(0) \exp (\int_0^t g(s)\, ds))$. The analysis based on this hypothesis, however, did not yield an interesting result. For this reason, we consider only a special case of it as formulated by Simon (1957).

Simon attempted to explain how executive compensation is determined based on the sociological considerations discussed in section 1.5. According to him, the salary of a top executive Z is determined as follows (Simon, 1957, p. 33):

$$Z(t) = kS(t)^a \tag{2.29}$$

where

S = the number of executives in the firm
a = log b/log n
n = the number of immediate subordinates of each executive
b = the ratio of the salary of an executive to the salary of his immediate subordinates
k = a number determined as a function of n, b, and A
A = the salary of the executives at the lowest level

and he argued that n, b, and A are sociologically or economically determined and are given for a firm. Let us suppose, as Simon did, that $S(t)$ is proportional to the size of the firm $K(t)$ and hence grows at rate $g(t)$. Then we have

$$Z(t) = k\left(S(0)\exp\int_0^t g(s)\,ds\right)^a = Z(0)\exp\left(a\int_0^t g(s)\,ds\right)$$

where $Z(0)$ depends on n, b, A and $K(0)$, and hence is given. Suppose now that the management makes decisions so as to maximize the present value of the top executive's expected salary stream over the future, U_b, namely,

$$U_b = \int_0^\infty Z(t)e^{-\rho t}(1 - F(t))\,dt$$
$$= \int_0^\infty Z(0)\left[\exp\left(a\int_0^t g(s)\,ds - \rho t\right)\right](1 - F(t))\,dt$$

subject to equation (2.18) and the v-g frontier, equation (2.19). In a steady state where $g(t) = g$ for any t, equation (2.20) again holds, and we have

$$U_b = Z(0)/[\rho - ag + h(v, v_{max})] \tag{2.30}$$

Since $Z(0)$ is a constant, the maximization of U_b is equivalent to the minimization of $\rho - ag + h(v, v_{max})$ ($\equiv U_c$). The first-order condition for an interior solution to this maximization problem is

$$\left.\frac{\partial U_c}{\partial g}\right|_{g=g^*} = -a + h_1(v^*, v_{max})v_1(g^*, v_{max}) = 0 \tag{2.31}$$

and the second-order condition is

$$\frac{\partial^2 U_c}{\partial g^2} = h_{11}v_1^2 + h_1 v_{11} = \frac{\partial^2 h}{\partial g^2} > 0 \tag{2.32}$$

Equation (2.31) shows that, at the optimal growth rate, the increase of the hazard rate due to an infinitesimal increase in g must equal a, the elasticity of the top executive's salary to the size of the firm. Since

$$\left.\frac{dv}{dg}\right|_{U_c=\text{const.}} = \frac{a}{h_1(v, v_{max})} < 0$$

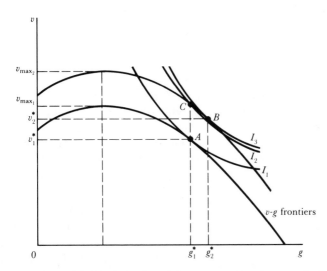

Figure 2.3. Maximization of the present value of expected salary stream U_b, where (1) I_1, I_2 and I_3 are indifference curves, that is, the locus of constant U_b, such that I_1 (I_2 and I_3) is drawn, given that the value of $v_{\max}$ is $v_{\max_1}$ ($v_{\max_2}$) and I_3 corresponds to a higher level of U_b than I_2, and (2) the two v-g frontiers are parallel, for example, the vertical distance between points C and A equals $v_{\max_2} - v_{\max_1}$.

one can again employ a diagrammatic analysis as illustrated in Figure 2.3. It should be obvious that $g^* > g^{**}$ and $v^* < v_{\max}$, as in the previous model.

The effect of $v_{\max}$ on the optimal solution in this model can be analyzed analogously to the previous model. The equation analogous to equation (2.27) (the derivation of which is not difficult and is not given here) is as follows:

$$\frac{dv^*}{dv_{\max}} = v_2 - \frac{h_{11}v_1^2v_2 + h_{12}v_1^2 + h_1v_1v_{12}}{h_1v_{11} + h_{11}v_1^2} \qquad (2.33)$$

The denominator of the fraction in the right-hand side is positive by equation (2.32) and the numerator is also positive if $h_{11} > 0$, $h_{12} = 0$, and the shift of the v-g frontier is parallel, that is, $v_2 = 1$ and $v_{12} = 0$. Hence in this case $dv^*/dv_{\max}$ is less than unity and, consequently, $dg^*/dv_{\max}$ is positive as illustrated in Figure 2.3. This result conforms to the one obtained when there is no uncertainty or when the chance-constrained programming method is applied but may contradict the one obtained when the expected present value of utility stream U_a is maximized. Since by equations (2.16) and (2.33),

$$\frac{dh^*}{dv_{max}} = h_1 \frac{dv^*}{dv_{max}} + h_2$$

$$= (h_1 + h_2) - h_1 h_{11} v_1^2 / (h_1 v_{11} + h_{11} v_1^2)$$

under the same assumption as to the value of v_2, and so on, and since both the terms in the first parentheses and the fraction in the right-hand side are negative, it is ambiguous whether dh^*/dv_{max} is positive or negative.

In summing up, we have demonstrated how the management decision problem under uncertainty can be formulated by means of a hazard rate. Two models have been presented, each assuming a particular objective function. The results of the analysis of these two models might be summarized as follows. First, in either formulation, it was shown that the management never maximizes the market value of the firm, indicating that the managerial theory of the firm always predicts the behavior of a firm differently from the traditional theory in which the shareholders' welfare is assumed to be maximized. Second, it was shown that whether or not dv^*/dv_{max} is less than unity and whether or not dg^*/dv_{max} is positive cannot be determined a priori even if the v-g frontier shifts in a parallel fashion, unlike the conclusion reached under the assumption of certain knowledge of v_{max} or by means of the chance-constrained programming method.

2.5   Summary and concluding remarks

Let us briefly summarize this chapter.

First, we argued that the serious weakness common to any managerial theory of the firm lies in the absence of a theory to explain how the minimum profit or the minimum market value is determined, in spite of its crucial role as a constraint to the discretionary behavior of management in such a theory. Following Marris's argument that such a constraint arises mostly from the threat of being taken over, we emphasized that the nature of takeovers needs to be analyzed first; thus a model of takeovers was formulated based on the concept of a v-g frontier. The optimization behavior of raiders and of incumbent management was then investigated to show that if the value of the maximum feasible valuation ratio v_{max} of a firm is known to any raider with certainty, the growth-maximizing management should set the valuation ratio at the level $\bar{v}$ such that the profit from taking over the firm is zero and that $\bar{v}$ depends on v_{max} in such a manner that $d\bar{v}/dv_{max}$ is positive but less than unity. In a more realistic situation where v_{max} is not known with certainty, $\bar{v}$ may be a random variable. In such a case the optimal valuation ratio and the optimal growth rate can be determined by means of either a chance-constrained programming method or the maximization of the present value of expected utility (or salary) stream, making use of the concept of a hazard rate.[14]

Our argument has made extensive use of the concept of the transaction cost of a takeover. It was shown that the larger this cost is the smaller $\bar{v}$ is relatively to v_{max} and that the more responsive this cost is to the value of transaction, the less responsive $\bar{v}$ is to v_{max}. Therefore how sensitive the transaction cost is to the value of transaction may give a good clue to the question of whether or not the managerial theory of the firm is significantly differentiated from the traditional theory in regard to predictions. Fortunately, two pieces of evidence concerning the transaction cost are available. Hayes and Taussig (1967), on the one hand, investigated fifty takeover bids that were resisted by the incumbent management, to find out that the total premium paid to the shareholders (which is a part of the transaction cost as defined in this chapter) amounted to 16 percent of the total market value of shares purchased at the median and 44 percent at the maximum. Smiley (1976), on the other hand, using data from forty-nine takeovers, estimated the ratio of the total transaction cost to the total market value of shares (assuming $\theta = 1$) to be 16 percent at the median.[15] Whether or not the number, 16 percent, on which the two studies interestingly agree, is large enough to claim that the management owns significant discretionary power, is not an easy question to answer. However, in view of the fact that the median total value of the transaction cost, $0.16 \times E$, could be huge for many corporations, it seems reasonable to me to expect a substantial discrepancy between the predictions of the managerial theory and those of the traditional theory.

Now, turning our attention to a comparison among managerial

[14] The management in our model may be regarded as trading the difference in the valuation ratio, $v_{max} - v^*$, for the difference in the growth rate, $g^* - g^{**}$.

[15] Smiley based his analysis on the Marris model and estimated the transaction cost as the difference between E_{max} and actual E. Two methods (TCPRE and TCPOST) were used to estimate E_{max}. The figure quoted in our text is the one calculated from TCPOST. According to the other (namely, the one calculated from TCPRE), the ratio amounted to 102 percent, which does not seem reasonable.

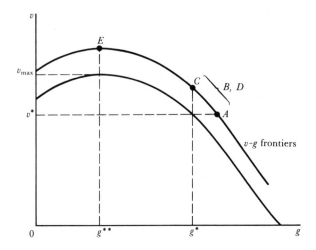

Figure 2.4. Comparison of five models, where (1) two v-g frontiers are parallel, (2) g^*, g^{**}, v^*, and v_{max} refer to the values before the upward shift of the v-g frontier occurs, and (3) A refers to the new equilibrium under Marris's model, B under J. H. Williamson's, C under Yarrow's, D under ours, and E under the traditional.

theories, our discovery that $d\bar{v}/dv_{max}$ is positive but less than unity and is a function of $\bar{v}$, in the case of certain knowledge of v_{max}, shows that neither Marris (1964), Yarrow (1976), nor J. H. Williamson (1966) dealt with the general case. Marris's formulation that $\bar{v}$ is constant holds only if $C'(\theta E)$ is infinite. Yarrow's formulation that $\bar{v} = v_{max} - c_2/K(0)$, where c_2 is constant, holds only if $C'(\theta E)$ is zero. And Williamson's formulation that $\bar{v} = c_1 v_{max}$, where c_1 is a constant, holds only if $C'(\theta E)$ is a constant; that is, only if the transaction cost is a linear function of the value of the transaction. These differences among the formulations could lead to differences in their predictions once a comparative analysis is undertaken. Suppose, for example, that the v-g frontier shifts upward for some reason and that the shift is parallel. Figure 2.4 illustrates how these models predict differently not only in the quantitative sense but also in the qualitative sense. A precise formulation of the managerial objective function, particularly of the managerial constraint, if any, is thus vital to our understanding of the behavior of firms.

Finally, a preliminary remark is made concerning the effect of takeovers on industrial concentration. Consider a situation where there are two types of firms: growth-maximizing firms, namely, those firms

hat maximize the rates of growth subject to the threat of takeovers as
discussed in this chapter, and neoclassical value-maximizing firms.
Then, from what has been discussed so far it is obvious that growth-
maximizing firms are more vulnerable to takeovers (i.e., their hazard
rates are larger) than neoclassical firms; hence the number of growth-
maximizing firms should tend to decrease relatively to that of neoclassical firms. It should be recalled, however, that most likely raiders
(acquirers) are growth-maximizing firms themselves as discussed in
section 2.3. Most probably, therefore, growth-maximizing firms take
over other growth-maximizing firms, which suggests a neutral effect of
takeovers to the relative share (in terms of size) between the two types
of firms but a relative decrease in the number of growth-maximizing
firms. At the same time, we know that by the definition of growth
maximization, the size of a growth-maximizing firm must increase
faster than the size of a neoclassical firm. Adding these two effects,
then, we should expect an increase in the share in size of growth-
maximizing firms in the economy and further concentration to fewer
and bigger growth-maximizing firms of assets, employment, and sales
in the long run. This argument admittedly is simplistic in considering
only the effect of takeovers: without doubt, to make a better prediction
on the change in industrial concentration, a detailed inquiry is
required into the effects of other factors as well, such as new entry of
firms and the shift of demand across industries. Nevertheless, it
provides an interesting and useful explanation for the observed
upward trend in aggregate business concentration in the United States
and other countries, witnessed by, for instance, Scherer (1970, pp.
41–4).

CHAPTER 3

The value and growth of the firm

3.1   Introduction: Optimization in two stages

In Chapter 2 we analyzed decision making under the threat of a takeover for management whose utility depends on the growth rate of the firm. To do so, we assumed a priori that a trade-off exists between the valuation ratio v and the growth rate g of the firm, which we have called the v-g frontier. We now analyze in more detail why such a frontier exists and how it is derived.

A firm has a set of policy variables: the amount of labor to employ, the amount to produce, the amount and the means of advertising, the amount of R & D expenditure, which industry to diversify, and so on, and of course the growth rate of capital or investment. The management of the firm determines the values of these variables so as to optimize according to some criteria. Suppose that this problem is solved in two stages: (1) Given the growth rate g, determine the optimal values of other policy variables and (2) determine the optimal growth rate. Then, by the first stage of the optimization, the optimal values of all the policy variables except g are determined as functions of g and relevant prices. Hence with these optimal values substituted, the market value of the firm or the valuation ratio is a function of a single variable, the growth rate, given prices.

Now suppose, as before, that the management utility depends on v and g but not on anything else and that the marginal utility of v is positive. Then, in the first stage of the optimization, it should determine the values of other variables so as to maximize v for any fixed value of g. If v is evaluated at these optimal values, it changes accordingly as g changes, and as a result, a functional relation is obtained between g and this v. This is the basic notion of what we have called the v-g frontier. It is a frontier because points on it can be attained if and only if the firm operates efficiently for any g.

Once the frontier is thus obtained as a consequence of the first stage

68

of the optimization, its second stage is performed in the manner analyzed in the previous chapter.

In this chapter optimization in two stages is analyzed in detail. The next section proves that $v = (p - \psi)/(i - g)$, where $\psi \equiv I/K$, under the assumption of, among others, a steady state. Equation (2.1) is, of course, a special case of this equation. As discussed in section 2.2, Marris argued that p is a decreasing function of g. His rationale for his function is examined in section 3.3. We will first look at Marris's own explanation and then reformulate it using more conventional concepts such as production and demand functions. We will argue, however, that his assumption is not quite convincing. Another method for obtaining the frontier is to introduce the concept of the cost of adjusting the stock of capital, as was done by Uzawa (1969), whose model is examined in section 3.4. In section 3.5 we incorporate research activity by the firm into Uzawa's model. In these sections production functions and the marginal product of labor are used as the analytical tools. In this sense one may view the present analysis as a derivation of the v-g frontier from a neoclassical framework (with adjustment cost). We often find that neoclassical theorists disregard managerial theories on the grounds that the latter are based on ad hoc assumptions and not on solid foundations as in the neoclassical theory, whereas managerial theorists criticize neoclassical theories on the basis of its being fanciful and unrealistic. The derivation developed in this chapter should help bridge this gap.

Later, in Chapter 5, the models of the firm analyzed in the present chapter will prove to be useful as bases for macroeconomic growth models.

3.2   The value of the firm

Let us maintain assumptions 2.1 to 2.4 of section 2.2. In addition to the notation defined there, denote the rate of growth of dividend per share by g_d, the price of a share (namely, stock price) by q, and the cost of net investment by I. Also, following the usual convention, $\dot{K}$, and so on, will denote the time derivative of K, and so on. Then it should be self-evident that the following six equations hold as identities:

Definition of E

$$E = qN \tag{3.1}$$

Definition of V

$$V = E + B = vK \tag{3.2}$$

Distribution of profits

$$D + iB + rP = P = pK \tag{3.3}$$

Financing net investment

$$I = rP + q\dot{N} + \dot{B} \tag{3.4}$$

Definition of g_d

$$g_d = [d(D/N)/dt]/(D/N) = \dot{D}/D - \dot{N}/N \tag{3.5}$$

Definition of g

$$\dot{K} = gK \tag{3.6}$$

Assumption 2.1 – the assumption of steady state – requires that

$$\dot{K}/K = \dot{B}/B = \dot{D}/D = g \tag{3.7}$$

Substituting equations (3.1) and (3.2) into equation (3.4), we get

$$I = rP + (\dot{N}/N)(vK - B) + \dot{B}$$

or by dividing both sides by K and using equation (3.7), we have

$$I/K = rp + (\dot{N}/N)(v - B/K) + gB/K$$

Solve this equation for $(\dot{N}/N)$ and substitute it into equation (3.5). Also substitute equation (3.7) into equation (3.5). Then, we obtain the following equation after some rearrangement:

$$g_d = (rp + vg - I/K)/(v - B/K) \tag{3.8}$$

So far we have not explicitly indicated time in any variable since all the preceding equations must hold at any time. Let us now use the notation $E(0)$, and so on, to denote today's value of E, and so on. Assumption 2.3 states that today's market value of total shares $E(0)$ is determined as follows:

$$E(0) = \int_0^\infty D(0)e^{g_d} e^{-it} dt$$
$$= D(0)/(i - g_d) \tag{3.9}$$

provided that $i > g_d$, which is satisfied as long as $i > g$ and $\dot{N} \geq 0$ in view of equation (3.5). Substitute equations (3.2) and (3.3) into equation (3.9) and divide both sides by $K(0)$. Then, since $v \equiv V(0)/K(0) \equiv (E(0) + B(0))/K(0)$,

$$v - B(0)/K(0) = [p - rp - iB(0)/K(0)]/(i - g_d)$$

We now substitute equation (3.8) into this equation and rearrange. Then, several terms are canceled out and

$$v = (p - \psi)/(i - g) \tag{3.10}$$

where ψ denotes I/K.

Obviously, if we further assume that $I = \dot{K}$ (assumption 2.5), then $\psi = g$ and equation (3.10) reduces to $v = (p - g)/(i - g)$, which is exactly equation (2.1).

It can be shown that v also equals the present value per initial capital of the net cash flow, $P(t) - I(t)$, discounted at rate i, for

$$\int_0^\infty [P(t) - I(t)](1/K(0))e^{-it}\, dt = \int_0^\infty (p - \psi)(K(t)/K(0))e^{-it}\, dt$$

$$= \int_0^\infty (p - \psi)e^{gt}e^{-it}\, dt$$

$$= (p - \psi)/(i - g)$$

if p, ψ, i, and g are constant over time and $i > g$. This equivalence of the two methods of calculating v coincides with the theorem proved by Miller and Modigliani (1961).

To repeat, assumptions required to establish equation (3.10) are those of steady state (assumption 2.1), certain knowledge (assumption 2.2), the perfect and rational stock market (assumption 2.3), and the absence of corporate tax (assumption 2.4). Needless to say, therefore, equation (3.10) is applicable not only in Marris's model but in any instance where these conditions are satisfied.

3.3   Marris's model

Marris presented his model of corporate growth in a book (1964) and then in an article (1971a). We will base our examination of his model on the latter because it appears more succinct.

He begins his analysis with what he calls a

> demand curve for the corporation [which is] a relation between total capacity, measured in replacement value of total corporate assets, and total profits, defined for the time being as the gross profit net only of depreciation as reported in a firm making no attempt to grow. [Marris, 1971a, p. 8]

This profit, after being divided by book-valued assets or capital, he calls the operating profit rate.

> The 'creative' corporation, however, has the capacity to shift the demand curve, either by means of advertising or by research and development expenditure designed to expand its potential catalog. [Marris, 1971a, p. 10]

He assumes that the initial amount of capital $K_0 (\equiv K(0))$ is fixed and considers only a steady-state growth path starting from this K_0.

> That is to say, given our starting point on the curve, we want to find the optimum rate of progress along the ray through the origin which passed through the starting-point, so that profits and assets may grow through time at a common, constant, exponential rate. [Marris, 1971a, p. 10]

In order to shift the demand curve continuously, however, the firm must make demand-shifting expenditures or development expenditures as already argued. He further assumes

> that a constant value of these expenditures, relative to a measure of the current scale of output (a convenient normalizing variable is book-value of assets, a commonly used alternative is sales) will be just sufficient to produce a constant growth rate; the higher however, the constant normalized value of growth creating expenditure, the higher the associated constant growth rate – an effect which is likely to be subject to diminishing effectiveness or dynamic diminishing returns. [Marris, 1971a, p. 10; his parentheses]
>
> If development expenditure is normalized by assets, the reported profit rate is precisely defined as the operating profit rate less normalized development expenditure. Then because higher growth rate requires higher normalized development expenditure, we can say that the steady reported profit rate is a function of steady growth rate. [Marris, 1971a, p. 11.]

Now let us translate Marris's argument into a mathematical and more familiar form. For simplicity, assume that the firm produces a single product and sells it in a monopolistic market. It is not difficult to extend the analysis to the case of multiproducts as long as the number of products is fixed. Denote by Q the amount of output produced, by K the amount of capital, and by L the amount of labor employed, and assume a constant-returns-to-scale production function, $Q = F(K, L)$, with the usual assumption on the sign of the derivatives; that is, $F_1 (K, L) > 0$, $F_2(K, L) > 0$, $F_{11}(K, L) < 0$, and $F_{22}(K, L) < 0$. For simplicity, inventory is neglected. Denote what Marris called development expenditures by M, and assume that the required amount of M to produce the demand growth of rate g at a constant price is determined by the following function: $M = M(gK, K) \equiv M(K, K)$, where $M_1(gK, K) > 0$ and $M_{11}(gK, K) > 0$ for any g, and the M function is homogeneous of degree one. In other words, when development expenditure is made by exactly the amount determined by the M function, the inverse demand function for this monopolistic firm is written as $\pi(t) = \pi(Q(t)e^{-gt})$, where π is the price of the output and $\pi'(Q(t)e^{-gt}) < 0$ as usual.

The reported profit rate at time t is calculated as an accounting residual to be

$$[\pi(t)Q(t) - wL(t) - M(g(t)K(t), K(t))]/K(t)$$

where w is the wage rate and is assumed to be constant over time. Denote the labor-capital ratio, $L(t)/K(t)$, by $l(t)$. Then at a steady state where $g(t)$ is constant and equal to g and hence $K(t) = K_0 e^{gt}$, this reported profit rate is rewritten as

$$\pi(F(K_0, l(t)K_0))F(1, l(t)) - wl(t) - M(g,1)$$

since both F and M functions are assumed to be homogeneous of degree one. Now suppose that the optimal value $l(t)^*$ of $l(t)$ is determined so that this reported profit rate is maximized given g (the first stage of the optimization). Then, without going into the mathematical detail, it should be obvious that $l(t)^*$ is determined, given K_0, as a function of w only so that the value of the marginal product of labor is equated to w with $\partial l(t)^*/\partial w < 0$. This implies that $l(t)^*$ is constant over time as long as w is constant as assumed. Denote this constant by l^*, evaluate the reported profit rate at l^*, and denote it by p. Then p is also constant over time and

$$p = \pi(F(K_0, l^*K_0))F(1, l^*) - wl^* - M(g, 1) \equiv p(g, w) \quad (3.11)$$

Obviously, $\partial p/\partial g = -M_1(g, 1) < 0$ and $\partial^2 p/\partial g^2 = -M_{11}(g, 1) < 0$, as argued by Marris. Also, $\partial p/\partial w = -l^* < 0$ since $\partial p/\partial l^*)(\partial l^*/\partial w) = 0$ by the envelope theorem.

This is the function assumed in section 2.2. Since there is no cost in adjusting the stock of capital in Marris's model, $\psi = g$. Therefore $v = p(g, w) - g)/(i - g)$ at the frontier,[1] which is a function of g as well as of i and w, as has been extensively used in the previous chapter.

Two questions may be immediately raised regarding this model: (1) What is the development expenditure? (2) What is the rationale behind the M function? These are perhaps closely related. As the

---

Hereafter, the notation v is used only for the value of the valuation ratio at the frontier, that is, evaluated with the optimal values obtained by the first stage of the optimization.

development expenditure, Marris seems to consider expenditures for two activities: advertising and R & D to create new products. However, if his reference to advertising is for existing products, why does he not use more conventional formulation such as the one by Nerlove and Arrow (1962)? The reason perhaps is that he regards the latter, the development of new products, more important as his emphasis on diversification of the firm indicates in his book. However, continuous diversification of the firm, namely, continuous expansion of the catalog of products the firm produces and sells, would create a serious problem in attempting to formulate it in terms of production functions and demand functions. This perhaps explains why Marris formulated his model without recourse to those concepts more familiar to economists. The question remains, however, as to why an M function as previously defined is used. It appears that Marris restricted the choice of the management a priori to a steady-state growth path and then proceeded to argue that at such a steady-state growth path the required development expenditure increases as the target rate of growth increases in a rather mechanical fashion. It is mechanical because the amount of M is not something to be determined optimally for a given g.[2] For many readers, not to mention neoclassical theorists, this may not appear to be a persuasive argument.

Let us return to our preceding mathematical formulation of Marris's model and ask whether any interpretation other than Marris's is possible. In view of equation (3.11), the net cash flow per unit of capital at time t, $p(t) - g(t)$, equals

$$\pi(F(K_0, l^*K_0))F(1, l^*) - wl^* - M(g(t), 1) - g(t)$$

when l is evaluated at its optimal value l^*. Now redefine the rate of profit p by $\pi(F(K_0, l^*K_0))F(1, l^*) - wl^*$ (Marris's operating profit rate). Also, redefine *the cost of investment* $I(t)$ by $[M(g(t), 1) + g(t)]K(t) \equiv M(\dot{K}(t), K(t)) + \dot{K}(t)$ or, equivalently, $\psi(t) \equiv I(t)/K(t)$ by $M(g(t), 1) + g(t)$, so that $I(t) > \dot{K}(t)$ and $\psi(t) > g(t)$ as long

---

[2] Otherwise, M would be determined so that $\partial p/\partial M = 0$; hence $(\partial p/\partial M) \cdot (\partial M/\partial g) = 0$, implying that p is not dependent on g and

$$\frac{\partial v}{\partial g} = \frac{p(w) - i}{i - g} \gtreqless 0 \quad \text{as } p(w) \gtreqless i$$

In this case, therefore, there is no positive, finite, and unique value of g that maximizes v.

s $M(\dot{K}(t), K(t)) > 0$. The net cash flow per capital at time t is then
rewritten as $p - \psi(t)$, where p is now a decreasing function of w only,
and $\psi(t)$ is an increasing function of $g(t)$. Consequently, if $g(t)$ is
constant over time,

$$v = (p(w) - \psi(g))/(i - g^*)$$

and we again obtain the v-g frontier that, by definition, has exactly the
same properties as before. Because this is nothing more than Uzawa's
model, let us now discuss his model in detail.

3.4 Uzawa's model

Uzawa (1969) assumed that due to the cost of adjusting "the index of
real capital" K,[3] the cost of investment I, namely, the cost of increasing K by $\dot{K}$ exceeds $\dot{K}$ for any $\dot{K} > 0$ and is determined by the
following function

$$\psi = \psi(g) \tag{3.12}$$

where $\psi \equiv I/K$ and $g \equiv \dot{K}/K$ as before and that $\psi(g) \geq 0, \psi'(g) > 0$,
and $\psi''(g) > 0$ for all $g \geq 0, \psi(0) = 0$, and $\psi'(0) = 1$.[4] This relation
between ψ and g he named the "Penrose curve" after Penrose, who
regarded "the firm as a collection of physical and human capital"
(Penrose, 1959, p. 24). To explain the rationale for this Penrose curve,
let us reproduce Uzawa's explanation.

> The index of real capital $K(t)$ reflects the managerial and adminis-
> trative abilities of the firm as well as the quantities of physical factors
> of production such as machinery and equipment. The actual increase
> in the index of real capital $K(t)$ due to a certain amount of
> investment is also constrained by the magnitude and quantities of
> managerial resources possessed by the firm at that moment ... If we
> suppose that the administrative, managerial and other abilities
> which are required by the firm in the process of growth and
> expansion are present in proportion to the index of real capital $K(t)$,
> the schedule relating the rate of interest, $g = \dot{K}/K$, in real capital
> with the investment-capital ratio, $\psi = I/K$, may be assumed to
> remain invariant over time, independently of the level of real capital

For the adjustment cost in general, see Brechling (1975).
In terms of the M function in the previous section, these conditions,
respectively, correspond to: $M(g, 1) \geq -g, M_1(g, 1) > -1$, and $M_{11}(g, 1)$
> 0 for all $g \geq 0, M(0, 1) = 0$, and $M_1(0, 1) = 0$.

possessed by the firm at each moment of time. [Uzawa, 1969, p. 64⬛ our notation][5]

In the following, let us assume for simplicity that the output marke⬛ is competitive and normalize the output price to be unity. It is no⬛ difficult to extend the analysis to a firm facing a downward-slopin⬛ demand curve along the line in the previous section, although admit⬛ tedly an introduction of oligopolistic interdependence to the model i⬛ difficult. The present value of the net cash flow per initial capital K_0 i⬛ then defined as

$$\int_0^\infty [F(K(t), L(t)) - w(t)L(t) - \psi(g(t))K(t)] (1/K_0)e^{-it} \, dt$$

$$= \int_0^\infty [F(1, l(t)) - w(t)l(t) - \psi(g(t))] \exp\left[\int_0^t g(s)ds - it\right]d⬛$$

where $l(t) = L(t)/K(t)$ as before. The latter expression follows b⬛ using $K(t) = K_0 \exp \int_0^t g(s)ds$ and the assumed linear homogeneity o⬛ F.

The first stage of the optimization is to maximize this expressio⬛ with respect to $l(t)$, the first-order condition being, obviously,

$$F_2(1, l(t)^*) = w(t)$$

Therefore $l(t)^*$ is constant as long as $w(t)$ is constant. Denoting bot⬛ these constants simply by l^* and w, we have $l^* = l(w)$ with $l'(w) < 0$⬛ The present value of the net cash flow per K_0 evaluated at l^*, which w⬛ again denote by v, is then as follows:

$$v = \int_0^\infty [F(1, l(w)) - wl(w) - \psi(g)] \exp(-(i-g)t)dt$$

assuming that g is constant over time. Therefore if $i > g$,

$$v = \frac{p(w) - \psi(g)}{i - g} \equiv v(g, i, w) \tag{3.13⬛}$$

where

$$p(w) = F(1, l(w)) - wl(w)$$

---

[5] Marris (1964) also emphasized the importance of this Penrose effect. Se⬛ the section entitled "the internal restraint on the growth rate" (pp. 114–18⬛ For example, he says that "the internal restraint arose mainly from th⬛ inability of a management team to expand at an indefinitely rapid rat⬛ without endangering efficiency" (Marris, 1964, p. 230).

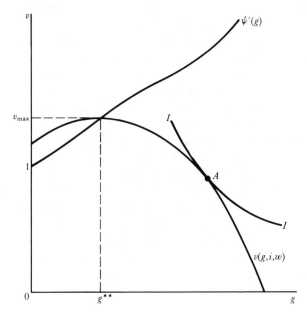

Figure 3.1 Uzawa's model: the decision making of the firm.

ith

$$p'(w) = -l(w) < 0$$

This is the v-g frontier and coincides with our argument at the end of the previous section. Since

$$\frac{\partial v}{\partial g} = \frac{1}{i - g}\left(\psi'(g) - \frac{p(w) - \psi(g)}{i - g}\right)$$

$$= \frac{1}{i - g}(\psi'(g) - v(g, i, w))$$

$v/\partial g \gtreqqless 0$ as $g \lesseqqgtr g^{**}$, where g^{**} satisfies $\psi'(g^{**}) = v(g^{**}, i, w)$. The determination of g^{**} is illustrated in Figure 3.1 using the fact that $\psi''(g) > 0$ and $\psi'(0) = 1.$[6] Since an increase in either w or i decreases v for any g, it should be obvious from the diagram that

For the existence of g^{**}, see Uzawa (1969, p. 643). Note that

$$\frac{\partial^2 v}{\partial g^2} = \frac{1}{i - g}\left[2\frac{\partial v}{\partial g} - \psi''(g)\right] < 0 \qquad \text{for } g \geq g^{**}$$

the intersection of $\psi'(g)$ and $v(g, i, w)$ curves moves southwest as i or w increases. Hence g^{**} depends adversely on both i and w.

The second stage of the optimization is to choose the set of value (g^*, v^*) along the v-g frontier. If the management wants to maximiz the market value of the firm, then it should choose g^{**} as the optima growth rate.[7] It can be shown that if it is a value maximizer, then th policy of a constant growth rate at the level g^{**} is in fact optima (Uzawa, 1969, pp. 642–3). If, on the other hand, the managemer preference is such as that discussed in the previous chapter, then should choose a point such as A in Figure 3.1, where curve II is th managerial indifference curve derived in section 2.4. Note here that th analysis in sections 2.3 and 2.4 depends only on the fact that v is function of g, and hence the result obtained there can be applie irrespective of whether $v = (p(g) - g)/(i - g)$ as assumed in sectio 2.2 or $v = (p - \psi(g))/(i - g)$ as in the present model.

We may now summarize the choice of the growth rate by th management as follows:

$$g^* = g(i, w, z) \tag{3.1}$$

where z is a new parameter, which we would like to call the index management preference toward growth. Specifically, define z so tha the management maximizes the value if and only if $z = 0$ and that larger value of z implies the preference inclined more toward growth that is, $g(i, w, 0) = g^{**}(i, w)$ and $g_3(i, w, z) > 0$.

The value of z depends on many factors. Given the v-g frontier, th point of tangency A in Figure 3.1 usually moves as the indifferenc curves shift. The location and shape of these indifference curves, w have already shown, depend on the instantaneous utility function the management, the rate to be used by the management to discour the future utility stream, and the hazard rate [see equations (2.21) an (2.30)]. This last variable, the hazard rate, is related inversely to th transaction cost to take over the firm, which consists not only of th transaction cost in its narrow sense, such as the premiums to be paid the shareholders and brokerage fees, but also the cost of changing th managerial policy of the acquired firm, which in turn depends on th flexibility of the corporate organization among other things. In addi tion, the hazard rate depends on the amount of information possesse

---

[7] Remember that maximizing v is equivalent to maximizing $V = vK_0$, sin K_0 is historically given.

y potential raiders on the shape of the v-g frontier of the firm, their ttitudes toward risk, and the expectation of the management on the ehavior of potential raiders. All these factors, therefore, affect the osition of the tangency between the v-g frontier and an indifference urve and, by definition, the value of z.

A special simple case occurs when the value of v_{max} is known to veryone with certainty and the adjustment of managerial policy after takeover is instantaneous. In this case, as we have shown in section .3, g^* is determined so that $v = \bar{v}$ where $\bar{v}$ is determined by an ncreasing function of v_{max} and the transaction cost to be incurred to ake over the firm. Since given the v-g frontier a smaller $\bar{v}$ results in a arger g^*, the amount of the transaction cost solely determines z in this pecial case. Of course, in a more general case where v_{max} is not know vith certainty, the value of z also depends on many other factors iscussed in the previous paragraph: Some of them are economic but thers may be legal, institutional, sociological, historical, or even sychological.[8] The considerations as to the value of z are particularly mportant in a comparison among countries, because each country nust differ from others considerably as to these factors. We will return o this subject later in Chapter 7 and argue that an analysis of these actors suggests a larger value of z for Japanese firms than for those in he United States.

Let us now turn to the other two variables that affect g^*: the rate of nterest i and the wage rate w. We have already shown that $\partial g^{**}/\partial i <$ and $\partial g^{**}/\partial w < 0$. For the case of the management with $z > 0$, it is ot easy to determine the signs of $\partial g^*/\partial i$ and $\partial g^*/\partial w$ as the analysis in ection 2.4 has revealed. In the following we assume, with analogy to he case of a value maximizer, that $\partial g^*/\partial i < 0$ and $\partial g^*/\partial w < 0$ for ny z. Hence the g function is assumed to satisfy the following onditions

$$g_1(i, w, z) < 0 \quad g_2(i, w, z) < 0 \quad g_3(i, w, z) > 0$$

ince the desired level of investment is immediately obtained by ubstituting equation (3.14) into $I = \psi(g)K$, (3.14) may be interpreted s a variation of the investment function.

Readers should be warned that z, despite its being called the index of management preference, represents not only management preference in its strict sense but also various other factors previously discussed that determine the *effectiveness* of the preference.

3.5   Research activity and the growth of the firm

We will now incorporate research activity for the purpose of cost reducing technical progress into the previous model. Assume Harrod neutral and disembodied technical progress. Then, as Uzawa (1961 has shown, we need to separate the amount of labor measured in physical units (say, man-hours) from the amount of labor measured in efficiency units. Let L denote the latter and N the former. Also define A by L/N, which can be interpreted as the index of labor productivity The production function is written as $Q = F(K, L) = F(K, AN)$ where the function F is assumed to satisfy the same properties as in the previous section.

Let us assume that $\dot{A}$, the increment in the productivity of each labor, is *produced* according to the following equation:

$$\dot{A} = Fr(R/L)A \tag{3.15}$$

with $Fr'(R/L) > 0$ and $Fr''(R/L) < 0$ for $R \geq 0$, where R is the amount of goods spent for research activity. An immediate interpretation of this formulation is that the firm allocates the fraction R/Q of its output to research activity. Or one may interpret it as the firm allocating the fraction R/Q of their sales revenue to the purchase of inputs to research activity. Whatever the interpretation, it says that a larger input to research activity per labor in efficiency units results in a higher *proportional* increase in labor productivity, subject to diminishing returns. Or remembering that $L \equiv AN$, equation (3.15) can be rewritten as

$$\dot{A}N = \widetilde{Fr}(R, AN) = \widetilde{Fr}(R, L)$$

if $\widetilde{Fr}$ function is homogeneous of degree one and $\widetilde{Fr}(R/L, 1) \equiv Fr(R/L)$, which says that the increase in the productivity of all the labor employed, $\dot{A}N$, is produced with R and L as the inputs and that doubling both R and L doubles $\dot{A}N$.[9]

---

[9] Similar formulation of "the production function for technology" has been used by several researchers. Shell (1973), for example, assumed that $\dot{A} = R - \rho A$ where ρ is a constant, whereas Kamien and Schwartz (1969) and Ruff (1969) assumed that $\dot{A}/A$ is a function of R, although the formulation by Kamien and Schwartz is more general in that they took into consideration the substitution between labor-augmenting technical progress and capital-augmenting technical progress. These formulations, however, are not free from scale effect because a larger firm can achieve the same *rate* of increase of labor productivity by spending a smaller fraction of their total cost. Our formulation does not have this property.

Since Fr has been assumed to be a unique function of R/L, we can ↸vert it to obtain

$$R = \phi(a)L$$

↸here a denotes $\dot{A}/A$, and it can be readily proved that $\phi'(a) > 0$ and ↸"(a) > 0$ for $R \geq 0$. The value of a when R is zero depends on ↸hether there is any exogenous technical progress and whether A ↸eteriorates over time. Let us assume for simplicity that there is ↸either exogenous technical progress nor deterioration of labor ↸roductivity so that $\phi(a) \geq 0$ as $a \geq 0$, though one can easily introduce ↸em by assuming that $\phi(a) \geq 0$ as $a \geq a_0$, where a_0 is the rate of ↸xogenous technical progress net of the rate of deterioration. Further-↸ore, let us assume that the result of research activity can neither be ↸ought (or stolen) from other firms nor sold to other firms.[10]

Under these assumptions, the present value of the net cash flow per ↸$_0$ is

$$\int_0^\infty [F(K(t), L(t)) - w(t)N(t)$$
$$- \psi(g(t))K(t) - \phi(a(t))L(t)](1/K_0)e^{-it}\, dt$$

The first stage of the optimization is to determine the optimal values ↸ $L(t)$, $N(t)$, and $a(t)$, given $g(t)$ subject to $L(t) = A(t)N(t)$ and $\dot{A}(t)$ ↸ $a(t)A(t)$. Let us assume that management considers only a steady-↸ate growth path such that $g(t)$, $a(t)$, and $L(t)/K(t)$ are constant over ↸me and respectively equal g, a, and l. Also, assume that it expects ↸(t) to be increasing at a given constant exponential rate ξ^e. (ξ denotes ↸e rate of wage increase and the superscript e refers to the expectation ↸y management). We will show later in section 5.4 that this policy of ↸llowing a steady-state path is in fact optimal in a general equilibri-↸m.

This assumption may not be acceptable to some readers in that it neglects the peculiar characteristic of technology and knowledge as discussed by Arrow (1962b). At least for the purpose of the macroeconomic analysis to be made in Chapter 5, however, this assumption, in our opinion, is not so crucial as it may appear, provided the transmission of technical knowledge is not perfect among firms (perhaps a reasonable assumption), and provided any firm behaves in a Cournot-like fashion – each firm takes the level of research activity of other firms as given. Ruff's (1969) interesting article analyzes the effect of the degree of the transmission of technical knowledge on the equilibrium level of research activity in such a Cournot economy.

The present value of the net cash flow per K_0 is rewritten unde
these assumptions as follows:

$$\int_0^\infty [F(1, l) - wl \exp((\xi^e - a)t) - \psi(g) - \phi(a)l]$$

$$\times \exp(-(i - g)t)\, dt \quad (3.16$$

by setting the historically given initial value of A to unity without los
of generality and by denoting the initial wage rate simply by w. W
now maximize this expression with respect to l and a. The first-orde
condition is satisfied if the optimal values, l^* and a^*, satisfy

$$\frac{F_2(1, l^*)}{i - g} = \frac{w}{(i - g - \xi^e + a^*)} + \frac{\phi(a^*)}{i - g} \quad (3.17$$

$$\frac{w}{(i - g - \xi^e + a^*)^2} = \frac{\phi'(a^*)}{i - g} \quad (3.18$$

assuming that $i > g$ and $i > g + \xi^e - a^*$.[11] It is not difficult to give a
economic interpretation to these equations. Equation (3.17) says tha
at the optimal values, the present value (adjusted for the growth) of th
marginal product of labor in efficiency units must be equated to th
sum of the present values of wage cost and research cost, both per labo
in efficiency units. Equation (3.18), on the other hand, says that th
present value of wage cost per labor in efficiency units, namely, th
marginal benefit of increasing labor productivity, $w/(i - g - \xi^e + a$
must be equated to the marginal cost of the proportional increase o
labor productivity, $\phi'(a)$, adjusted by $(i - g - \xi^e + a)/(i - g)$, th
ratio of discounting factors between wage cost and research cost.

Let us solve these equations to obtain l^* and a^* as functions of w,
$- g$, and ξ^e; that is,

$$l^* = l(w, i - g, \xi^e)$$

$$a^* = a(w, i - g, \xi^e) \quad (3.19$$

It is straightforward to prove that $\partial l^*/\partial w < 0$, $\partial l^*/\partial \xi^e < 0$, ∂a^*
$\partial w > 0$, and $\partial a^*/\partial \xi^e > 0$. These appear reasonable because the highe
the wage rate is today or the expected rate of wage increase, the highe
will be the present value of wage cost and, consequently, the smalle
will be the optimal labor-capital ratio and the greater will be th
incentive for research activity to reduce future labor costs. On the othe

[11] It can be shown that the second-order condition is locally (in the neighbo
hood of l^* and a^*) satisfied. Unfortunately, whether or not it is global
satisfied is ambiguous.

and, the sign of the effect of $i - g$ on l^* or a^* depends on the magnitude of $\xi^e - a^*$, because the ratio of discounting factors between wage cost and all other terms, $(i - g - \xi^e + a)/(i - g)$, appears in both equations.

Now substitute l^* and a^* thus obtained into (3.16), the expression for the present value of the net cash flow per K_0, and denote it by v as before; that is,

$$
\begin{aligned}
v &= \int_0^\infty [F(1, l^*) - wl^* \exp((\xi^e - a^*)t) \\
&\quad - \psi(g) - \phi(a^*)l^*] \exp(-(i - g)t)\, dt \\
&= \frac{F(1, l^*) - \psi(g) - \phi(a^*)l^*}{i - g} - \frac{wl^*}{i - g - \xi^e + a^*} \\
&\equiv v(g, w, i, \xi^e)
\end{aligned}
\tag{3.20}
$$

This, of course, is the v-g frontier under the present model. Since $\partial v/\partial g$ when l^* and a^* are optimally adjusted is not different from $\partial v/\partial g$ when l^* and a^* are fixed (the envelope theorem),

$$
\frac{\partial v}{\partial g} = \frac{F(1, l^*) - \psi(g) - \phi(a^*)l^*}{(i - g)^2}
$$

$$
- \frac{wl^*}{(i - g - \xi^e + a^*)^2} - \frac{\psi'(g)}{i - g}
\tag{3.21}
$$

Because $\psi''(g) > 0$, it may be expected that as g gets very large, the last term in the right-hand side becomes dominant and hence $\partial v/\partial g$ becomes negative. We will later analyze the property of this v-g frontier in detail and show that this conjecture is in fact true (section 3.4). For the time being, let us assume that $\partial v/\partial g \gtreqless 0$ as $g \lesseqgtr g^{**}$ where g^{**} depends on i, w, and ξ^e. Then the management would determine the optimal growth rate g^* so as to maximize its managerial utility function $U(g, v)$, subject to equation (3.20). If $U(g, v)$ is such that $U_1(g, v) = 0$, that is, if the management maximizes the value, then g^* equals g^{**}. If $U_1(g, v) > 0$, then g^* would be greater than g^{**}. At any rate, g^* would be dependent on i, w, and ξ^e. Therefore, again taking into account the difference in management preference,

$$
g^* = g(i, w, \xi^e, z)
\tag{3.22}
$$

where by definition $\partial g^*/\partial z > 0$. The signs of other partial derivatives will be discussed later.

In sum, this section investigated the behavior of the firm that undertakes research activity as well as production activity subject to the Penrose dynamic effect. This research activity was confined to the aimed at Harrod-neutral technical progress, that is, to that of process innovation to raise labor productivity. A specific production function for the research activity was assumed in the manner that a larger input to research per labor in efficiency units results in a higher rate of increase of labor productivity subject to diminishing returns. The optimal behavior of the firm was then investigated concerning labor research, and growth. For instance, the optimal rate of technical progress or, more accurately, the optimal rate of increase of labor productivity was shown to be determined so that the marginal benefit of increasing labor productivity, that is, the present value of wage cost saved by the technical progress, equals the marginal research cost. The optimal rate of growth depends on wage rate, its expected rate of increase, interest rate, and the index of management preference toward growth.

3.6   Summary and concluding remarks

In this chapter we have examined three models of the firm: Marris model, Uzawa's model, and the model of the firm with research activity. The last model was established as an extension of Uzawa model.

Marris's and Uzawa's models may appear distinct at first sight, for the former assumes that $p = p(g)$ and $\psi = g$, whereas the latter assumes that p is independent of g and $\psi = \psi(g)$. With a closer look, however, they are quite similar. In fact, it was shown that an superficial difference disappears if the variables are appropriately redefined. Therefore the analysis of the behavior of a firm or of its management can be carried out in either of the two models and should yield the same result. For example, our analysis in Chapter 2 of the behavior of management that prefers a higher growth rate but subject to the threat of a takeover can be equally applied to Uzawa model as well as to Marris's model because our analysis there depended only on the fact that there is a trade-off between v and g.

The difference between them probably exists in interpretation rather than in implication. Marris argues that the cost of increasing capital by $\dot{K}$ exceeds $\dot{K}$ because the firm has to pay demand-shifting expenditures or development expenditures, whereas Uzawa argues that it is because of the Penrose effect. However, this difference again may be trivial especially if one recalls Marris's emphasis of the importance of the Penrose effect in his earlier work (see footnote 5).

In Chapter 5, we will present models of economic growth, first, based on Uzawa's model and, then, on the model with research activity, for the assumption in Uzawa's model appears more acceptable than Marris's as our discussion at the end of section 3.3 suggests and the concept of adjustment cost now seems broadly accepted. Uzawa's model is particularly more convenient to use in analyzing macroeconomic growth than Marris's model because one can easily compare the model of economic growth based on Uzawa's model to other models, due to their common analytical tools such as production functions for a fixed number of products and exogenously given consumer preference under the absence of advertising.

PART II

Macroeconomics

CHAPTER 4

The role of corporate shares in general equilibrium

4.1 Introduction

There has been a long tradition in the literature on the theory of economic growth, whether written in Cambridge, United Kingdom, or in Cambridge, Massachusetts,[1] to neglect the role of corporate shares in the process of capital accumulation. This neglect constrained researchers to formulate the equilibrium condition in such a manner that whenever net saving takes place, additional real capital is purchased by the same amount (less the increment in the holdings of money and government bonds, if any). That is, in such an economy net saving must always be balanced by net investment in real capital unless money or government bonds are introduced into the model to fill in the gap between them. Such a treatment may be justified if one's intention is to analyze an economy where most firms are single proprietorships or partnerships; however, in order to analyze a modern economy where most firms are corporations, the neglect of the role of corporate shares could result in a serious misunderstanding.

In a corporation the decision of management to invest in real capital and the decision of investors to purchase shares do not have a direct relationship, unlike a single proprietorship in which these two decisions are actually equivalent. Management and ownership are funcionally separated even though an executive could be a shareholder himself.[2] As a consequence, in an economy where most firms are corporations, which we call a corporate economy, the decision by the

---

See Foley and Sidrauski (1971) or Burmeister and Dobell (1970) and the literature cited therein for the studies along the Cambridge, Massachusetts, tradition. For the work done in Cambridge, United Kingdom, see Robinson (1962) and Pasinetti (1962). Uzawa (1969), in the Cambridge, Massachusetts, tradition, should be referred to here as an exception to our criticism. Shareholdings by the executives constitute only minor portions of the total shares in most corporations; recall the evidence cited in section 1.4.

89

corporate sector on investment in real capital and the decision by th
noncorporate sector on saving are functionally separated and ma
diverge. An equilibrium of the economy may be achieved even if such
divergence between saving and investment exists because stock pric
will be adjusted accordingly; that is, saving without any offsettin
investment will be absorbed by an increase in stock price, just as for
corporation an increase in demand for its shares without new issue o
the shares results in an increase in its price. This increase will yiel
capital gains to current shareholders as additional income, which ma
increase their saving further. An equilibrium stock price will b
attained at the level where saving and the increment of the total marke
value of shares, possibly both depending on stock price, are equated.

The rate of profit to corporations and the rate of return t
shareholders are no longer equivalent in such an equilibrium. If th
demand for shares increases, then as a consequence of the increase i
the price, the rate of return to shareholders will decline even if the rat
of profit stays constant. One may argue that such divergence betwee
the rate of profit and the rate of return should disappear in the lon
run because, if the former is higher, shareholders would rather set u
corporations themselves than purchase the shares of existing corpora
tions in order to enjoy the higher rate.[3] However, as discussed in detai
in Chapter 1, in a modern corporate economy where many corpora
tions are characterized by large-scale operation and diversification
management requires special skills most shareholders lack. In view o
this fact, arbitrage by shareholders between the profit from running
corporation and the return from purchasing shares does not seem
practical possibility. Hence in a corporate economy, saving can diverg
from real investment, the rate of profit can diverge from the rate o
return to shareholders, and the total assets owned by corporations ca

---

[3] Strictly speaking, the rate of profit in the previous sentence should b
understood as Marris's reported profit rate (see section 3.3), $p - (\psi - g)$
namely, the rate of profit after deducting the cost of capital in excess of th
value of the increment of capital, because $v = 1$ if and only if $p - (\psi - g) =$
i [see equation (3.10)]. If $v > 1$, then the present value of net cash flow from
starting a corporation by employing a certain amount of capital is greate
than the cost of the capital, and hence every investor will attempt to star
one if there were no barriers to entry; whereas if $v < 1$ then everyone wil
attempt to exit from the corporate sector. The long-run equilibrium in th
absence of barriers to entry, therefore, requires that $v = 1$ or, equivalently
$p - (\psi - g) = i$.

liverge from the total wealth – the number of shares multiplied by the
price – owned by shareholders.

The purpose of this chapter is to investigate the steady-state
equilibrium condition of a corporate economy where shares are the
only type of financial assets, that is, where there is neither money nor
government bonds. Such an analysis has been made recently by Moore
(1973, 1975) based on two assumptions: (1) households apply a
constant average propensity to save irrespective of the form in which
income is received and (2) average propensities to save differ according
to the form in which income is received. He seems to favor the latter
assumption on the ground that "due to the high concentration of
wealth ownership, the very much more uncertain nature of capital
gain, and the moral stigma associated with the consumption of capital,
saving propensities are higher out of capital gain income" (Moore,
1973, p. 537). It seems to me, however, that he failed to formulate
these observations properly with the exception of the third, which is
probably not very important, for the following two reasons. First, a
redistribution of wealth ownership does not affect aggregate saving
unless propensities to save differ between the rich and the poor. Hence,
for his assertion to be valid, it must be that there exist several classes in
the economy and that different classes have different structures of
income sources and different propensities to save, whereas each class
may have a single propensity to save irrespective of income source. If
so, to analyze an economy where only one class exists is improper. The
simplest assumption one can make to analyze the effect of the
distribution of wealth on the equilibrium condition is the one used by
Pasinetti (1962), namely, the assumption that there are two classes –
workers and capitalists – the former receiving wages and possibly
returns from their share ownership and the latter receiving only
returns from their share ownership. Pasinetti has proved that at a
steady-state equilibrium the rate of profit must be equated to the
growth rate of capital divided by capitalists' propensity to save
irrespective of workers' propensity to save. However, because he did
not take into account the role of corporate shares, his theorem may or
may not hold in a corporate economy.

Secondly, if capital gains are regarded as more uncertain than other
sources of income, namely, dividends and wages, then it should mean
that shareholders regard the certainty equivalent of capital gains as
less than their actual value. Because they are likely to consume only
this certainty equivalent multiplied by their propensity to consume and

save the rest including actual capital gains less the certainty equiva
lent, the ratio of actual saving to actual capital gains must be greater
than the propensity to save applied to wages and dividends. This is not
the same, however, as Moore's treatment, where shareholders recognize all their capital gains as income but multiply them with a greater
propensity to save than that applied to wages and dividends, and may
well yield different results.

These considerations suggest that four cases should be distinguished
according to (1) whether there is one class or two classes and (2)
whether shareholders recognize their capital gains fully or only partly
as income. In this chapter we analyze the steady-state equilibrium
conditions for these four cases, to show that the equilibrium conditions
are diverse among the cases. We also show that a proposition quite
analogous to Pasinetti's holds in a two-class economy where both
classes recognize their capital gains fully. These results are to be
discussed in section 4.4 (for a one-class economy) and in section 4.5
(for a two-class economy). In sections 4.2 and 4.3 notation, definitions
and assumptions and the determination of the rate of return are
explained, respectively. The final section summarizes the results.

4.2   Notation, definitions, and assumptions

We maintain the notation in previous chapters; however, because our
concern is now macroeconomic, each variable should be reinterpreted
in a macroeconomic context. The following summarizes the notation in
this chapter, including several new variables:

D total dividends
G total capital gains
I total cost of net investment
K total amount of capital
N total number of shares issued
P total profit net of depreciation and gross of capital cost
Q net national product
S total saving by the noncorporate sector (i.e., outside corporations)
V total market value of shares
W total wages
Y total income of the noncorporate sector (including capital gains)[4]

---

[4] Y includes capital gains and usually is not equal to net national product Q.
Moore called it "household comprehensive income." Obviously, it is not the
national income defined in most national income accounts.

g the growth rate of K ($\equiv \dot{K}/K$)

g_d the growth rate of dividend per share

i the rate of return from shares (also to be called the rate of interest because shares are the only type of financial assets)

p the rate of profit ($\equiv P/K$)

q stock price, namely, the price of a share in terms of goods

r retention rate

s the propensity to save

v valuation ratio ($\equiv V/K$)

γ the relative portion of capital gains recognized by a shareholder as income

ψ the cost of investment per unit of capital ($\equiv I/K$)

Subscripts to be used are

c   capitalists
h   households
w   workers

The following are definitional identities:

$$Q = W + P \tag{4.1}$$
$$Y = W + D + G \tag{4.2}$$
$$V = vK = qN \tag{4.3}$$
$$D_w + D_c = D = D_h \tag{4.4}$$
$$G_w + G_c = G = G_h \tag{4.5}$$
$$D + rP = P \tag{4.6}$$
$$G = \dot{q}N \tag{4.7}$$

The following constraints must always be satisfied:

$$0 \le r \le 1$$
$$0 \le s_i \le 1, \quad i = c, h, w$$
$$0 \le \gamma_i \le 1, \quad i = c, h, w$$

We define five terms as follows:

1. *A steady state* is defined as a state in which g, ψ, p, and v are constant and in which the relative share of wealth owned by each class is also constant.
2. *A one-class economy* is defined as an ecomomy in which only one class exists. This class is called households and receives both wages and returns from their share ownership.
3. *A two-class economy* is defined as an economy in which two classes exist: workers, who receive both wages and returns from their share ownership, and capitalists, who receive only returns from their share ownership; that is, capitalists do not receive wages.

4. A shareholder is called *rational* if and only if he is indifferent to whether the income is in the form of dividends or in the form of capital gains, in the sense that he recognizes both of them fully as income.

5. A shareholder is called *myopic* if and only if he recognizes all dividends paid to him as income but only a portion, γG, of his capital gains as income. In other words, a shareholder is myopic if and only if $0 \leq \gamma < 1$ and is rational if and only if $\gamma = 1$.

Two remarks are in order here regarding these definitions. First, when we call an economy a one(two)-class economy, it means that one(two) class(es) exist(s) in the noncorporate sector, namely, outside corporations. Hence if one counts the corporate sector, namely, corporations, as another class as Uzawa (1969) did, it in fact is a two(three)-class economy. Secondly, as was argued in the previous section, the major reason for a shareholder recognizing his capital gains only partly may be that capital gains are regarded as more uncertain than other sources of income and are discounted by the amount to be regarded as a premium to risk, assuming that the shareholder is risk averse. If so, according to the conventional usage of the word, he probably should be called rational and not myopic. However, as far as our analysis here is concerned, whether he in fact is rational but discounts capital gains because of uncertainty or he in fact is myopic in the sense of shortsightedness does not make any difference. For this reason, we will maintain the definition of term 5.

The assumptions to be maintained throughout this chapter are as follows:

4.1 Shares of common stock are the only type of financial assets. There exists neither money nor bonds. The economy consists of three markets: labor, goods, and stock. For a moment we assume that the labor market is dichotomized from the other two markets and consider only the equilibrium of goods and stock markets (the general equilibrium of all three markets is discussed in Chapter 5).

4.2 The propensities to save and the retention rate are constant and given.

4.3 Wages received are always fully recognized as income.

4.4 If one is myopic, one consumes only the portion of income equal to his recognized income multiplied by his propensity to consume. Hence the actual saving (actual income less consumption) is greater than the amount he intends to save. For households, for example, the actual saving equals

$$Y - (1 - s_h)(W + D + \gamma_h G) = s_h(W + D) + (1 - (1 - s_h)\gamma_h)G$$

4.5 Q, K, and W are positive; N and g are nonnegative; $p > \psi$; and $i > g$.

By assuming that $N \geq 0$, we exclude the situation in which corporations are creditors. $i > g$ and $p > \psi$ are assumed because these are the sufficient conditions for v to be nonnegative. Also, these conditions, together with the others given in assumption 4.5, imply that $Y > 0$ at a steady state. These properties will be proved in footnote 5 in the next section. Because corporations will not operate unless v is nonnegative, these assumptions should be reasonable.

The necessary and sufficient condition for both goods and stock markets to be in equilibrium is that either of the two markets is in equilibrium. This, of course, is due to the Walras law, the proof of which follows. Consider first the stock market. On the one hand, because shares are the only means of holding wealth available to the noncorporate sector, the desired increase in the total value of shares, namely, the demand for shares in terms of flow, is the total saving S. On the other hand, the total value of available shares is V and hence the amount of its increase, namely, the supply of shares in terms of flow, is $\dot{V}$. Therefore the stock market is in equilibrium if and only if

$$S = \dot{V} \tag{4.8}$$

Now consider the budget constraint for the corporate sector. The corporate sector finances investment by either issuing new shares (and selling them at the market price) or retaining profits; hence

$$I = q\dot{N} + rP \tag{4.9}$$

Combining equations (4.8) and (4.9), substituting $G = \dot{q}N = \dot{V} - q\dot{N}$ (equations (4.3) and (4.7)), we have $S = G + I - rP$ or

$$(S + rP) - I = G \tag{4.10}$$

This equation demonstrates that the excess of total saving by both corporate and noncorporate sectors, $S + rP$, over the demand for funds, I, must be absorbed by exactly the same amount of capital gains. Now the noncorporate sector budget constraint is $Y = C + S$, where C is the consumption; hence, using equations (4.1), (4.2), and (4.6) – respectively the definition of Q, Y, and r – we can rewrite equation (4.10) as

$$Q = C + I$$

This of course is the equilibrium condition for the goods market, for Q is the aggregate supply of goods and $I + C$ is the aggregate demand for goods. (Implicitly assumed here is that no input of goods is made to R&D, or Q, in this chapter only, is net of such input.) Therefore the goods market is in equilibrium if and only if equation (4.8) is satisfied that is, if and only if the stock market is in equilibrium. This completes the proof of the Walras law.

4.3   The rate of return and valuation ratio

Let us investigate how the amount of capital gains G is determined. By definition, $G = \dot{q}N = \dot{V} - q\dot{N}$. Combining this equation with equation (4.9) to eliminate $q\dot{N}$, we have

$$G = \dot{V} + rP - I \tag{4.11}$$

At a steady state where v is constant and hence $\dot{V} = v\dot{K} = vgK$, we have after dividing both sides by K and substituting $p = P/K$ and $\psi = I/K$,

$$G/K = vg + rp - \psi \tag{4.12}$$

implying that capital gains are greater than or less than retained profits accordingly as v is greater than or less than ψ/g. If there is no Penrose effect, that is, no cost of adjusting the stock of capital, then $\psi = g$, and equation (4.12) implies that $G \gtreqless rP$ accordingly as $v \gtreqless 1$. If, on the contrary, there is the Penrose effect as discussed in section 3.4, then $G = rP$ requires $v > 1$, and if perfect arbitrage forces v to be unity, then G must be less than rP. That is, in this situation, shareholders receive as capital gains less than what the firm has retained for reinvestment. This is an important and rather unexpected result which so far as I know no one has ever mentioned. However, this by no means implies that shareholders should prefer not to retain the earnings to finance the target rate of growth, because as we proved in the previous chapter and will prove again presently in the macroeconomic context, the valuation ratio v does not depend on the retention rate r at all.

We now investigate how the rate of return is determined. First, assume that shareholders are rational. Then, by definition, the rate of return equals the sum of dividends and capital gains per dollar invested; that is,

$$i = (D + G)/V$$
$$= [(1 - r)p + G/K]/v$$

because, by equation (4.6), $D = (1 - r)P = (1 - r)pK$. Assuming a steady state and substituting equation (4.12), we have

$$i = [(1 - r)p + vg + rp - \psi]/v$$
$$= [vg + p - \psi]/v$$

or

$$v = \frac{p - \psi}{i - g} \qquad (4.13)$$

This of course is the same equation as that derived in section 3.2, proving that the market value of the firm and the total market value, $V = vK$, is determined by either: (1) the sum of dividends and capital gains divided by i, (2) the present value of dividends stream received by the current shareholders, or (3) the present value of the net cash flow. That is, mathematically,

$$V = vK = (D + G)/i$$
$$= \int_0^\infty D e^{g_d t} e^{-it} \, dt$$
$$= \int_0^\infty (P(t) - I(t)) e^{-it} \, dt \qquad (4.14)$$

This result, which is less obvious than might be supposed, is a powerful one.

Now let us turn to the case where shareholders are myopic. In the case of a two-class economy we will confine our analysis to the case $\gamma_c = \gamma_w = \gamma.$[5] In the case of a one-class economy, γ in the following should be interpreted as γ_h. The (perceived) rate of return for such myopic shareholders is then defined as

If $\gamma_c \neq \gamma_w$, the rate of return would be perceived to be different between the classes because stock price and v must be uniquely determined in the market. For example, if $\gamma_c > \gamma_w$, the perceived rate of return is larger for capitalists than for workers, provided that capital gains are positive. If so, it may be reasonable to suppose that arbitrage takes place; that is, capitalists would borrow from (sell bonds to) workers to finance the purchase of shares, for if the rate of interest paid to these bonds is less than the rate of return perceived by capitalists but larger than that perceived by workers, and if workers recognize the interest receipt fully as income, then obviously both parties would be willing to participate in this transaction. We will not discuss this case further, but the equilibrium for such an economy may differ from what we obtain later in section 4.5.

$$i = (D + \gamma G)/V$$
$$= [(1 - r)p + \gamma G/K]/v$$

Assuming a steady state and substituting equation (4.12), we get

$$i = [(1 - r)p + \gamma(vg + rp - \psi)]/v$$

which by rearranging yields

$$v = \frac{(1 - r + \gamma r)p - \gamma\psi}{i - \gamma g} \qquad (4.15)$$

Similarly to equation (4.14), one can prove that

$$V = (D + \gamma G)/V$$
$$= \int_0^\infty De^{\gamma g_d t} e^{-it} \, dt$$

This indicates that shareholders underestimate the growth of the dividend per share.[6]

The important difference between the two cases is that v does not depend on r when shareholders are rational but does depend on r when they are not. Obviously, this corresponds to the Modigliani–Miller theorem, which says that "the market value of any firm is independent of its capital structure" (Modigliani and Miller, 1958, p. 268) if shareholders do not differentiate between dividends and capital gains. In the case of myopic shareholders $\partial v/\partial r = -(1 - \gamma)p/(i - \gamma g) < 0$. Hence the management can attain a higher market value of its corporation by financing investment by means of the new issue of shares instead of the retention of profits. Since r is restricted to be nonnegative, this indicates that, *ceteris paribus*, the optimal retention

---

[6] Now we are in a position to prove the remarks made in the previous section in relation to assumption 4.5. If shareholders are rational, $v = (p - \psi)/(i - g)$. Hence $p > \psi$ and $i > g$ imply $v > 0$ unless i is infinite, in which case $v = 0$. If shareholders are myopic, $v = [(1 - r + \gamma r)p - \gamma\psi]/(i - \gamma g)$. Hence if $p > \psi$ and $i > g$, $v \geq [(1 - r + \gamma r)\psi - \gamma\psi]/(i - g) = (1 - r)(1 - \gamma)\psi/(i - g) \geq 0$, where equality holds if $\gamma = 0$ and $r = 1$ and/or if i is infinite. Hence $p > \psi$ and $i > g$ are sufficient for v to be nonnegative. Also by using equation (4.12), we can show that if assumption 4.5 holds, then $Y > 0$ at a steady state, for $Y = W + D + G = W + (1 - r)P + (vg - \psi)K + rP = W + (p - \psi)K + vgK > 0$. The result just obtained, $v \geq 0$, was used to prove the last inequality.

ate is zero if $\gamma < 1$, whether the management maximizes the market value or the utility function comprising g and v.

This conclusion may appear dubious to some readers because in practice new issues are not frequent. It is simply a logical consequence of the definition of myopic shareholders, however. That is, if shareholders are myopic, they prefer dividends to capital gains and current dividends to future dividends. Hence decreasing retention and consequently capital gains but increasing dividends by decreasing r increases the utility of shareholders and thus v. Of course, in reality, there may well be factors neglected here that affect corporate dividend policy. For instance, in most countries personal taxes are levied fully to dividends but only partly to capital gains, making retention more favorable than otherwise. Another reason for the infrequent new issue may be substantial costs associated with it, such as brokerage fees. Admittedly, therefore, the optimal dividend policy may not be this simple, even if shareholders are myopic. In the following analysis we do not bind r to any specific value.

4.4   The steady-state equilibrium in a one-class economy

The steady-state equilibrium condition for a one-class economy can be stated in terms of the following two propositions.

Proposition 4.1. If households are rational and if $0 < s_h < 1$,[7] then a one-class economy is in a steady-state equilibrium if and only if

$$v = \frac{s_h}{1 - s_h} \frac{Q/K - \psi}{g}$$

Proof: Since $S = s_h Y$, the economy is in equilibrium if and only if

The case where either $s_h = 0$ or $s_h = 1$ is omitted because neither appears realistic. If $s_h = 1$, then there is no consumption by households, and this surely is unrealistic. If $s_h = 0$, all investment must be financed through retained profits; hence $\psi = rp$. In this case the equilibrium requires that $G = 0$ because $I = rP$ and $S = 0$ in equation (4.10), which implies that $vg = 0$ by equation (4.12). Therefore if $s_h = 0$, then at equilibrium it must be either that $v = 0$, namely, there is no corporate share of any value, or that the economy is in a stationary state such that $r = \psi = g = G = \dot{N} = 0$.

$$\dot{V} = s_h Y = s_h(W + D + G) = s_h(Q - rP + G) \tag{4.16}$$

using $Y = W + D + G = Q - rP + G$. Substituting equation (4.11) and rearranging, we have

$$(1 - s_h)\dot{V} = s_h(Q - I)$$

At steady state v is constant and $\dot{V} = vgK$; hence we have

$$(1 - s_h)vg = s_h(Q/K - \psi) \tag{4.17}$$

To obtain the desired result, we need to show that if $0 < s_h < 1$, then $g \neq 0$. Suppose on the contrary that $0 < s_h < 1$ and $g = 0$. Then equation (4.17) reduces to $Q/K = \psi$. But since $Q = W + P$, this implies that $W + (p - \psi)K = 0$, which contradicts assumption 4.5. Hence if $0 < s_h < 1$, then $g \neq 0$. By dividing both sides of equation (4.17) by $g (1 - s_h)$, we complete the proof.   Q.E.D.

Proposition 4.2. If households are myopic and $0 < s_h < 1$, then a one-class economy is in a steady-state equilibrium if and only if

(i) $v = \dfrac{s_h(Q/K - \psi) - (1 - s_h)(1 - \gamma_h)(\psi - rp)}{(1 - s_h)\gamma_h g}$ if[8] $\gamma_h > 0$

(ii) $\psi = s_h Q/K + (1 - s_h)rp$ if $\gamma_h = 0$

Proof: Since

$$S = Y - (1 - s_h)(W + D + \gamma G)$$
$$= s_h(W + D) + [1 - (1 - s_h)\gamma_h]G$$

the economy is in equilibrium if and only if

$$\dot{V} = s_h(W + D) + [1 - (1 - s_h)\gamma_h]G \tag{4.18}$$

By substituting equations (4.1), (4.6), and (4.11), we get

$$\dot{V} = s_h(Q - rP) + [1 - (1 - s_h)\gamma_h](\dot{V} + rP - I)$$

Rearranging yields

$$(1 - s_h)\gamma_h \dot{V} = s_h(Q - I) - (1 - s_h)(1 - \gamma_h)(I - rP)$$

At steady state, $\dot{V} = vgK$; hence

---

[8] This equation holds even if $s_h = 0$ as long as $r > 0$.

$$v(1 - s_h)\gamma_h g = s_h(Q/K - \psi) - (1 - s_h)(1 - \gamma_h)(\psi - rp) \quad (4.19)$$

It is straightforward to prove (ii) from this equation. To prove (i), we need to show that $g \neq 0$. Suppose on the contrary that $g = 0$. Then equation (4.19) reduces to

$$s_h Q/K + (1 - s_h)(1 - \gamma_h)rp = -[(1 - s_h)(1 - \gamma_h) + s_h]\psi$$

By assumption, at least either the first term or the second term of the left-hand side is positive and both are nonnegative. On the other hand, $\psi = 0$ when $g = 0$ by our assumption of the Penrose curve (see section 3.4), and hence the right-hand side is zero. This contradiction implies that $g \neq 0$. By dividing both sides of equation (4.19) by $(1 - s_h)\gamma_h g$, (i) is immediate.   Q.E.D.

When $\gamma_h = 0$, all capital gains are automatically saved and the equilibrium condition reduces to $I = s_h(W + D) + rP = s_h(Q - P) + rP$. Therefore as long as Q, I, and P do not depend on v or i, the equilibrium condition does not depend on v or i, as shown in proposition 4.2(ii). In other words, in this case ψ, p, and Q/K cannot be all exogenously given.

In the presumably more usual case where $0 < \gamma_h \le 1$, however, the equilibrium can be obtained even if g, ψ, p, and Q/K are all exogenously given if v is adjusted so that the equation in proposition 4.1 or 4.2(i) is satisfied. This is the point stressed by Moore, who expressed this fact as follows: "the introduction of equities and capital gains thus provides an additional escape from the Harrod–Domar knife-edge problem" (Moore, 1975, p. 876). In the case of rational shareholders, proposition 4.1 shows that if $\psi = g$, $v \gtreqless 1$ as $g \lesseqgtr s_h Q/K$. Therefore $v = 1$ if Harrod–Domar's equation, $g = s_h Q/K$, holds. But even if saving in Harrod–Domar's sense, $s_h Q$, exceeds (is less than) investment, gK, an equilibrium is attained with a v greater (less) than unity, because the excess (shortage) of saving over investment is absorbed by the increase (decrease) in the total market value of shares. This argument holds even if shareholders are myopic, although the equilibrium level of v is different from the one in the case of rational shareholders.

It might be of interest to investigate the effect of γ_h to v (when $0 < s_h < 1$) and compare the value of v between propositions 4.1 (when

shareholders are rational) and 4.2(i) (when shareholders are myopic)
Let $v(j)$ denote the equilibrium value of v obtained in proposition
(proposition 4.2(i) if $j = 2$). Also, let $\dot{V}(j)$ denote $v(j)gK$, namely, the
increment in the total market value of shares or in the total wealth
owned by the noncorporate sector, corresponding to proposition j
Then, the Appendix shows that insofar as capital gains are positive,

    (i) $\partial v/\partial\gamma_h < 0$ for $0 < \gamma_h \leq 1$
    (ii) $v(2) = v(1) + (1 - \gamma_h)G/gK > v(1)$
    (iii) $\dot{V}(2) = \dot{V}(1) + (1 - \gamma_h)G > \dot{V}(1)$

Here (iii) indicates that the total market value increase is greater, by
the amount of the neglected capital gains, if shareholders are myopic
than if they are rational. Consequently, as (ii) indicates, the equilibrium valuation ratio is greater if they are myopic than if they are
rational, provided capital gains are positive. More generally, it is
shown in (i) that the smaller γ_h is, the larger v is, provided capital
gains are positive. The reason for these results is as follows. Provided
$G > 0$, a smaller γ_h means that smaller capital gains are recognized at
the time households make their consumption-saving decision and
consequently, households spend less for consumption. Because actual
saving equals actual income (including the portion of capital gains that
is neglected by households) less actual consumption (which we
assumed equals intended consumption), less consumption results in
greater actual saving. Hence the demand for shares is larger and the
total market value has to be greater to be in equilibrium. Given K, this
means that v has to be larger.

Once the equilibrium valuation ratio is thus determined, the equilibrium rate of return is obtained using either equation (4.13) or
(4.15). It is shown in the Appendix that $di/d\gamma_h > 0$ if $G > 0$. That is, if
capital gains are positive, the larger γ_h is, namely, the less myopic
households are, the larger must be the rate of return perceived by
shareholders. This is so because of two effects: (1) since v and i are
inversely related, given γ_h, a smaller v as a result of a larger γ_h results
in a larger i and (2) for any given v, a larger γ_h results in a larger i [see
equation (4.15)]. These two effects thus reinforce each other.

Another important difference between the two propositions is that
the retention rate does not affect either the equilibrium valuation ratio
or the equilibrium rate of return if households are rational but does
affect both of them if households are myopic. In other words, the
equilibrium valuation ratio and the equilibrium rate of return are

ndependent of the choice of the means of financing investment by orporations if and only if households are rational. This result shows hat the Modigliani–Miller (1958) theorem, which was proved origi-ally in a partial equilibrium analysis, holds even in a general quilibrium analysis based on aggregate variables.[9] It is not difficult to xplain why. An equilibrium requires that $\dot{V} = S$. Since $\dot{V} = vgK$ at teady state, the solution of V does not depend on r if and only S is ndependent of r. Using equations (4.1) and (4.6), and the equation in ssumption 4.4 for the household saving, however, one can easily see hat S is independent of r if and only if $(1 - s_h)(1 - \gamma_h) = 0$. Therefore if $s_h < 1$, r does not affect v if and only if $\gamma_h = 1$, that is, if nd only if households are rational.

4.5   The steady-state equilibrium in a two-class economy

This section investigates the steady-state equilibrium conditions for an conomy with two classes.

Proposition 4.3. If both workers and capitalists are rational and $0 \le$ $_w < s_c < 1$, then a two-class economy is in a steady-state equilibrium if nd only if

$$v = \frac{s_c}{1 - s_c} \frac{p - \psi}{g}$$

r, equivalently,

$$g = s_c i$$

Proof: The economy is in equilibrium if and only if

$$\dot{V} = s_w(W + D_w + G_w) + s_c(D_c + G_c) \tag{4.20}$$

Since dividends received and capital gains are proportional to the number of shares owned,

---

We should note, however, that to examine the validity of the Modigliani–Miller theorem, our framework may not be general enough, in that corporate shares are assumed to be the only means of external finance for corporations. For an examination of the theorem under a general equilib-rium analysis taking into account both corporate shares and corporate bonds, see Stiglitz (1969). His analysis, however, assumed a priori that household wealth and household saving are given and that corporations do not retain their profits.

$$\frac{D_w}{D_c} = \frac{G_w}{G_c} = \frac{D_w + G_w}{D_c + G_c} = \frac{N_w}{N_c} = \frac{qN_w}{qN_c} = \frac{V_w}{V_c}$$

where $V_w \equiv qN_w$, and $V_c \equiv qN_c$ are the wealths owned by workers and capitalists, respectively. Since saving equals the increment of shares multiplied by their price plus capital gains.

$$\frac{s_w(W + D_w + G_w)}{s_c(D_c + G_c)} = \frac{q\dot{N}_w + G_w}{q\dot{N}_c + G_c} = \frac{q\dot{N}_w + \dot{q}N_w}{q\dot{N}_c + \dot{q}N_c} = \frac{\dot{V}_w}{\dot{V}_c}$$

At a steady state the wealth owned by each class must grow at a common rate because otherwise the relative share of wealth changes between the two classes; hence

$$\frac{s_w(W + D_w + G_w)}{s_c(D_c + G_c)} = \frac{\dot{V}_w}{\dot{V}_c} = \frac{V_w}{V_c} = \frac{D_w + G_w}{D_c + G_c}$$

by using the previous equations. Multiplying both sides by $s_c(D_c + G_c)$ yields

$$s_w(W + D_w + G_w) = s_c(D_w + G_w) \tag{4.21}$$

Since $W > 0$, this equality can hold only if $s_w < s_c$. Now by substituting this equation into equation (4.20), we obtain

$$\dot{V} = s_c(D_w + G_w) + s_c(D_c + G_c)$$
$$= s_c(D + G) \tag{4.22}$$

since $D_w + D_c = D$, and so on. We now substitute the definition of the rate of return, $i = (D + G)/V$, to this equation to get

$$\dot{V} = s_c i V \tag{4.23}$$

At a steady state, where v is constant, $\dot{V} = vgK = gV$; hence we obtain

$$g = s_c i$$

The first equation of the proposition follows by combining this equation with (4.13). Finally, if $s_c = 1$, then $g = i$ and this contradicts assumption 4.4; hence it must be that $s_c < 1$. Q.E.D.

Proposition 4.4. If both workers and capitalists are myopic, $\gamma_w = \gamma_c = \gamma$ and $0 \le s_w < s_c < 1$, then a two-class economy is in a steady-state quilibrium if and only if

$$\text{(i)} \quad v = \frac{s_c(p - \psi) - (1 - s_c)(1 - \gamma)(\psi - rp)}{(1 - s_c)\gamma g} \qquad \text{if } \gamma > 0$$

r, equivalently,

$$i = \frac{(p - \psi)\gamma g}{s_c(p - \psi) - (1 - s_c)(1 - \gamma)(\psi - rp)} \qquad \text{if } \gamma > 0$$

nd

$$\text{(ii)} \quad \psi = [s_c(1 - r) + r]p \qquad \text{if } \gamma = 0$$

Proof: The economy is in equilibrium if and only if

$$V = s_w(W + D_w) + [1 - (1 - s_w)\gamma]G_w + s_c D_c + [1 - (1 - s_c)\gamma]G_c$$

By the same reasoning as in the proof of proposition 4.3, the following equation must be satisfied at a steady state.

$$\frac{D_w}{D_c} = \frac{G_w}{G_c} = \frac{V_w}{V_c} = \frac{\dot{V}_w}{\dot{V}_c} = \frac{s_w(W + D_w) + [1 - (1 - s_w)\gamma]G_w}{s_c D_c + [1 - (1 - s_c)\gamma]G_c}$$

Hence

$$\dot{V} = [s_c D_c + (1 - (1 - s_c)\gamma)G_c](1 + D_w/D_c)$$
$$= s_c D + (1 - (1 - s_c)\gamma)(G_c/D_c)D$$
$$= s_c D + (1 - (1 - s_c)\gamma)G \qquad\qquad (4.24)$$

because $G_c/D_c = G/D$. Substituting equations (4.6) and (4.11), we get

$$\dot{V} = s_c(1 - r)P + (1 - (1 - s_c)\gamma)(\dot{V} + rP - I)$$

At steady state, $\dot{V} = vgK$; hence after rearranging and dividing by K, we have

$$(1 - s_c)\gamma v g = s_c(p - \psi) - (1 - s_c)(1 - \gamma)(\psi - rp)$$

By setting $\gamma = 0$, proposition 4.4(ii) follows. If $\gamma > 0$, then by dividing both sides by $(1 - s_c)\gamma g$, the first equation in proposition 4.4(i) follows.

Because under the assumption of myopic shareholders i is determined by equation (4.15), substitute equation (4.15) into the equation just obtained. Then, after necessary rearrange-

ment and division the second equation in proposition 4.4(i
follows.   Q.E.D.

The similarity between proposition 4.3 and Pasinetti's theorem i
striking. Pasinetti proved that in a two-class economy where shares d
not exist and consequently the rate of profit to firms and the rate c
return to investors cannot diverge, the rate of profit and hence the rat
of return equal the growth rate of capital divided by the propensity t
save of capitalists at a steady-state equilibrium. Proposition 4.3 show
that if shares are explicitly introduced into the model, the equilibriun
rate of return to shareholders equals the growth rate divided by th
propensity to save of capitalists, as is the case with Pasinetti's, but th
rate of profit can take any value in the sense that it need not have an
relation to the equilibrium rate of return. In other words, Pasinetti'
theorem may be regarded as a special case of ours where it is somehov
enforced that the rate of profit always equals the rate of return
Moreover, there is another generalization of Pasinetti's theorem in ou
proposition: The propensity to save of workers does not affect th
equilibrium rate of return not only when shareholders are rational bu
also when they are myopic.

But why is the equilibrium rate of return independent of s_w? Th
answer to this question is found in equations (4.22) and (4.24) in th
proofs of the two propositions. These equations indicate that, at
steady state, the total saving made by both workers and capitalist
exactly equals the saving capitalists would have made if they ha
owned all the shares in the economy. That is, at a steady state, share
and the return from shares are distributed among classes so that th
total saving by workers exactly equals the amount capitalists would
have saved if they had received the workers' return from shares. As
result, the equilibrium rate of return depends on s_c but not on s_w.[10]

An implication of these arguments is that because capitalists sav
only out of their return from shares, whereas households in a one-clas
economy save not only out of their return from shares but also out o
wages, the total saving in a two-class economy must be smaller tha
the total saving in a one-class economy even if s_c equals s_h. That thi
statement is correct can be easily verified by comparing equation

[10] The argument here is perfectly parallel to Pasinetti's. See Pasinetti (1962
p. 273).

4.16) with equation (4.22) and equation (4.18) with equation (4.24). Consequently, the only difference between $v(1)$ and $v(2)$ and between $v(3)$ and $v(4)$, following the notation used in the previous section, is that Q/K in the propositions for a one-class economy is replaced by p in the propositions for a two-class economy if $s_c = s_h$. Since $Q/K - p = (Q - P)/K = W/K > 0$ by our assumption, total saving is larger in a one-class economy if $s_c = s_h$ and $v(1) > v(3)$ and $v(2) > v(4)$. In other words, for the total saving in a two-class economy to be greater than that in a one-class economy, the propensity of capitalists to save must be sufficiently larger than that of households so that the extra saving out of the return from shares [i.e., $(s_c - s_h)(D + G)$] more than offsets households' saving out of wages (i.e., $s_h W$).

So far we have compared the total savings of two different economies, one with only one class and the other with two classes, when $s_h = s_c$. Conversely, one can ask what the saving propensity of households should be if a one-class economy is to save exactly as much as a two-class economy. It appears reasonable to call this rate an *average* saving rate of a two-class economy. If we denote it by $\bar{s}$, therefore

$$\bar{s} = \frac{s_w(W + D_w + G_w) + s_c(D_c + G_c)}{W + D + G} = \frac{s_c(D + G)}{W + D + G}$$

where the latter equality holds because of equation (4.22). Obviously, $\bar{s} < s_c$ consistently with our argument in the previous paragraph. It is also easy to verify that $s_w < \bar{s}$ if $s_w < s_c$, which is no wonder since $\bar{s}$ is a weighted average of s_w and s_c.

Now turn to the comparison between $v(3)$ and $v(4)$. This is also easy because we know that they respectively differ from $v(1)$ and $v(2)$ only in that p and s_c in the former, respectively, replaces Q/K and s_h in the latter and that $v(1) < v(2)$ if $G > 0$. Therefore we again have the following results, assuming that $G > 0$ and $0 \leq s_w < s_c < 1$.

(i) $\partial v / \partial \gamma < 0$ if $0 < \gamma \leq 1$
(ii) $v(4) = v(3) + (1 - \gamma)G/gK$
(iii) $\dot{V}(4) = \dot{V}(3) + (1 - \gamma)G$
(iv) $di/d\gamma > 0$ if $0 < \gamma \leq 1$

The reasons for these results are perfectly parallel to those in the previous section.

Similarly, our argument in relation to the Modigliani–Miller theorem in the previous section again holds here. That is, at a steady-state equilibrium in a two-class economy, the valuation ratio

and the rate of return are independent of the financial policy of th
corporate sector if and only if shareholders (workers and capitalist
are rational.[11]

Proposition 4.4(ii) is analogous to proposition 4.2(ii), again replac
ing Q/K and s_h in the latter by p and s_c, respectively, In this case ψ an
p cannot be both exogenously given, and any value of the valuatio
ratio or the rate of return can sustain the equilibrium as long as ψ an
p satisfy the condition.

4.6   Summary and concluding remarks

In this chapter we have investigated the steady-state equilibriur
condition for an economy where shares are the only type of financia
assets.[12] Four cases were separated for this purpose, each characterize
by (1) whether there is one class or two classes in the noncorporat
sector and (2) whether shareholders are rational or myopic. Th
results of these analyses are summarized as follows, assuming that r, s
and γ (for any subscript) are given:

1. If $0 < s_h < 1$ and $0 < \gamma_h \le 1$ in a one-class economy, then v i
   determined as a function of Q/K, g, ψ, and p; or if $0 \le s_w < s_c <$
   and $0 < \gamma_w = \gamma_c \le 1$ in a two-class economy, then v is determined a
   a function of g, ψ, and p.
2. If $\gamma_h = 0$ in a one-class economy, then ψ, Q/K, and p must satisfy
   functional relationship; hence all these variables cannot be exoge

---

[11] Note that we have confined our analysis to the case where $\gamma_c = \gamma_w$. Th
Modigliani–Miller theorem may hold in the case where capitalists ar
rational but workers are not, because v does not depend on the savin
behavior of workers. However, the possible complication in such a situa
tion, as discussed in footnote 5, may prevent this statement from bein
true.

[12] The equilibrium of an economy where shares are the only type of financia
assets was analyzed also by Kaldor (1966) and Marris (1972b), both in th
appendixes, as well as Moore (1973, 1975), mentioned earlier. These thre
authors derived the results equivalent to our proposition 4.1, although al
are confined to the case where $\psi = g$. In addition, Kaldor attempted to dea
with a two-class economy; however, his argument is misleading in the sens
that he derived his equation (6), $p = \psi(1 - j)/r$, where $j = q\dot{N}/I$ (th
notation is mine), and argued that "it is similar to the Pasinetti theorem i
that the rate of profit will be independent of s_w." (Kaldor, 1966, p. 318)
This equation, however, can be rewritten as $I = rP + q\dot{N}$, which i
nothing more than the budget constraint for the corporate sector. Hence i
is an identity that has nothing to do with an equilibrium of an economy.

nously determined. If $\gamma_w = \gamma_c = 0$ in a two-class economy, then a functional relationship must be satisfied with respect to ψ and p.

3.   A two-class economy can be sustained only if $s_w < s_c$.

The equilibrium condition, therefore, depends on what economy one analyzes. In case (1), which presumably is the most natural assumption to make, an equilibrium can be attained even if the Harrod–Domar condition, $\psi = s_h Q/K$, is not satisfied, because the discrepancy between ψ and $s_h Q/K$ is absorbed by the rise in stock price. In this sense, as Moore argued, the Harrod–Domar knife-edge dilemma can e avoided when one takes into account the role of corporate shares in n economy.

The most interesting result in this chapter, perhaps, is that a roposition quite similar to Pasinetti's holds even if his neglect of orporate shares is remedied. Unlike Pasinetti's, however, the rate of eturn to shareholders can diverge from the rate of profit to corporations in our model, and it was shown that Pasinetti's theorem holds ith respect to the former but not necessarily to the latter.

We are now ready to discuss comprehensive models of economic rowth. This will be considered in the next chapter, based on the nodels of the firm presented in the previous chapter and the steady-tate equilibrium condition of goods and stock markets proved in this hapter. Specifically, we will use the condition for a two-class economy ith rational shareholders, namely, proposition 4.3, primarily because f its simplicity and powerfulness. It should be appropriate here to emind readers that proposition 4.3 does not depend on the magnitude f the share of either class in a national economy. To take an extreme ase, proposition 4.3 holds even if there is only a handful of capitalists, ay, Rockefellers and Mellons, but millions of workers. Probably, herefore, it is not whether there is a class of capitalists as defined here ut whether the economy is in a steady state as defined here, if the dequacy of proposition 4.3 is to be questioned.[13] That is, whether or ot the share of each class in national wealth stays constant over time nay have to be asked. This we can only leave as an empirical uestion.

Of course, these two questions are not independent; for example, if the share of capitalists steadily declines over time, then capitalists would eventually (probably in thousands of years!) vanish. Samuelson and Modigliani (1966) argued that this is more likely than the constancy of the relative share.

Appendix: Propositions 4.1 and 4.2 compared

The effect of γ_h on v

By proposition 4.2 (i),

$$v(2) = s_h(Q/K - \psi)/(1 - s_h)g\gamma_h - (1 - \gamma_h)(\psi - rp)/\gamma_h g$$
$$= v(1)/\gamma_h + (1 - \gamma_h)(G/K - v(2)g)/\gamma_h g$$

Proposition 4.1 and equation (4.12) were used to derive the last equality. Multiplying both sides by γ_h and rearranging, we get

$$v(2) = v(1) + (1 - \gamma_h)G/gK \tag{A4.1}$$

Since $v(1)$ does not contain γ_h in its argument, $\partial v(1)/\partial \gamma_h = 0$. Hence by partially differentiating both sides of (A4.1) with respect to γ_h, we have

$$\partial v(2)/\partial \gamma_h = -G/gK + [(1 - \gamma_h)/gK][\partial G/\partial v][\partial v(2)/\partial \gamma_h]$$

By substituting $\partial G/\partial v = gK$, which is obtained by differentiating equation (4.12), and rearranging, we obtain

$$\partial v(2)/\partial \gamma_h = -G/\gamma_h gK \tag{A4.2}$$

Multiply both sides of (A4.1) by gK and use the definitional identity $\dot{V} = vgK$. Then, we have

$$\dot{V}(2) = \dot{V}(1) + (1 - \gamma_h)G$$

The effect of γ_h on i

By partially differentiating equation (4.15), we get

$$\partial i/\partial v = -(i - \gamma_h g)/v \tag{A4.3}$$

and

$$\partial i/\partial \gamma_h = (vg + rp - \psi)/v = G/vK \tag{A4.4}$$

The use of equation (4.12) was made in deriving the last equality. If g, r, and s_h are constant, then

$$di/d\gamma_h = \partial i/\partial \gamma_h + (\partial i/\partial v)(\partial v/\partial \gamma_h)$$

Substituting (A4.2), (A4.3), and (A4.4), we obtain

$$di/d\gamma_h = G/vK + [(i - \gamma_h g)/v](G/\gamma_h gK)$$
$$= iG/\gamma_h vgK \gtreqless 0 \qquad \text{as } G \gtreqless 0$$

CHAPTER 5

The model of economic growth

.1 Introduction

A look at the facts will now show why present-day economists think
hat scientific and engineering progress has been quantitatively the
ingle most important factor for growth in the advanced countries"
Samuelson, 1976, p. 738). As Samuelson asserted in his popular
conomics textbook, few economists would deny the important role
echnical progress plays in modern economic growth.

The question to be asked, then, is how this technical progress is
enerated. It may be due to experience or learning by doing, as Arrow
1962a) argued. Or it may be due to governmental expenditures on
esearch and development.[1] The largest input toward technical
rogress, however, is made by business firms that undertake it to
mprove production efficiency and reduce costs and/or to develop new
roducts and expand sales. For example, Nelson, Peck, and Kalachek
ound that "industrial research and development probably accounts for
ignificantly more than half of the total national effort to advance
echnological knowledge" (Nelson et al., 1967, p. 45). Furthermore,
hey found that "industrial R & D is concentrated in about 400 largest
irms" (Nelson et al., 1967, p. 65). These facts suggest that it is
usiness firms, especially a limited number of large firms, that play a
najor role in advancing and applying our technological knowledge.

The purpose of this chapter is to present a model of economic
rowth that takes this observation into account. We have already
nalyzed in section 3.5 the behavior of the firm that engages in
esearch activity for the purpose of increasing labor productivity

---

It is true that the role of government is more important in R & D than in
other activities, such as the accumulation of real capital. However, the
governmental expenditure in R & D is extremely concentrated in a few
fields, most notably defense, nuclear, and space. See Matthews (1973,
p. 17).

besides the production and marketing of goods. It was shown that the firm determines, according to some criteria, both the optimal growth rate of capital g and the optimal rate of increase of labor productivity as functions of prices, i and w, and the expected rate of increase ξ^e of w. We will now show that a model of macroeconomic growth can be constructed based on this analysis of the optimization behavior of the firm. In this model, those functions that determine the desired level of g and a, together with the macroeconomic equilibrium condition obtained in the previous chapter and the equilibrium condition for labor market, determine the equilibrium values of prices, the rate of economic growth, and the rate of technical progress, namely, the rate of increase of labor productivity. In this model, therefore, the microeconomic aspect of the economy is explicitly taken into account and forms the basis for analyzing the macroeconomic equilibrium under growth. Only by doing this should one be able to analyze the dynamics of an economy where research activity undertaken by firms is the major force of technical progress and economic growth, and also to analyze effectively the influences of management preference in a growing economy.

In spite of these facts, there are surprisingly few who have presented analyses along these lines. As for the latter problem – the effect of management preference on economic growth – the only analysis I know of is that of Marris (1972b, Appendix). The basic idea behind Marris's is similar to that of the present analysis; unfortunately however, his model is far from complete and depends on several rather ad hoc assumptions.[2]

As for the first problem – the macroeconomic effect of industrial research activity – the lack of analysis is still more impressive if one remembers that Schumpeter stressed as early as 1911 the importance of innovation by firms in the process of economic development.[3] There have been several studies on the socially optimal rate of technical progress (Phelps, 1966; Shell, 1966, 1967; Uzawa, 1965) and on the optimal direction of technical progress (Kennedy, 1964; Samuelson 1965). Also, a model to combine microeconomic research activity

---

[2] Marris (1964) also made a verbal analysis of macro implications of his model of the firm in the last chapter of his book. No formal model is presented there.

[3] See Schumpeter (1934), the first edition of which was published in 1911 in German.

and macroeconomic technical progress was presented by Shell (1973) for the case where research activity is undertaken by a single firm that is a monopolist in the investment goods market and rents the machines to other firms that produce and sell consumption goods in a competitive market. Nordhaus (1969a) made another attempt to introduce inventive activity to economic growth; however, he assumed that invention is undertaken not by production firms but by individual inventors who earn profits by selling their patents. In view of the observations by Nelson et al. cited earlier, therefore, none of these models appear satisfactory; that is, all of them failed to depict the economy as an aggregation of firms engaged in research activity as well as in production activity.

Our analysis of economic growth begins with a model of economic growth without research activity so that the importance of incorporating research activity into growth models should become clearer in later sections. Firms in this model behave in the manner examined in section 3.4. Basically, the model of economic growth is identical to Uzawa's (1968); however, two alterations have been made: (1) Uzawa confined his analysis to the firms maximizing their values, whereas ours does not. (2) Uzawa's dubious saving-investment balancing condition is replaced by ours, proved in the last chapter.[4]

A model of economic growth with firms engaged in research activity as well as in production activity is presented in section 5.3, based on the model of the firm in section 3.5. Section 5.4 examines in more detail the determination of the optimal growth rate by firms, and section 5.5 shows that the policy of steady state is in fact optimal for firms at any steady-state general equilibrium. Section 5.6 gives the summary and concluding remarks.

We should hasten to add that the model presented here is by no means a comprehensive and complete model of economic growth, for it is dependent on several assumptions that simplify analysis but are not necessarily easy to justify; for instance, Harrod-neutral disembodied technical progress, no dissemination of new technological knowledge among firms, no sales promotion activity, and identical firms. We

---

Uzawa assumed that $G = rP$ to derive his balancing condition. This, however, implies that $vg = \psi$ by our equation (4.12) and that g, p, i, and ψ are mutually dependent by the v-g frontier, equation (4.13). Nevertheless, in Uzawa's model, four independent equations other than $G = rP$ are supposed to determine the equilibrium values of these four values. Therefore, it is overdetermined.

believe, however, that this model is helpful at least as a starting point toward a more comprehensive analysis (Parts IV and V of this book present some attempts) and that it makes the mechanism of growth and technical progress in our modern economy much clearer than previous models.

5.2   The model without research activity

We have already presented a model of the firm in the absence of research activity in section 3.4; hence, those assumptions and results are used without explanation in this section. As a macroeconomy we follow the assumptions in proposition 4.3; that is (1) corporate shares are the only type of financial assets in the economy, (2) there are two classes in the noncorporate sector, workers and capitalists, and (3) both workers and capitalists are rational.[5] In addition, we assume that all firms are identical to avoid any complication that may arise from aggregation and confine our analysis to a steady state as defined in section 4.2. Then , by proposition 4.3, the goods and stock markets are in equilibrium if and only if

$$g = s_c i \tag{5.1}$$

where s_c is the saving propensity of capitalists.

As proved in section 3.4 as equation (3.14), the desired rate of growth is determined as a function of the rate of interest i, the wage rate w, and the index of management preference toward growth z as [6]

$$g = g(i, w, z) \tag{5.2}$$

where

$$g_1(i, w, z) < 0, \quad g_2(i, w, z) < 0 \quad \text{and} \quad g_3(i, w, z) > 0$$

An equilibrium in the labor market requires that

$$g = n \tag{5.3}$$

where n is the rate of increase of labor supply which is assumed to be

---

[5] Analyses based on other assumptions, namely, the assumptions behind propositions 4.1, 4.2, and 4.4, can be made similarly to the analysis in the text; however, readers should note that shareholders were assumed rational in Chapters 2 and 3 and the results there have to be modified if shareholders are myopic.

[6] Asterisks used in Chapter 3 to indicate the optimal values of firms are omitted hereafter.

Table 5.1. *The sign of the effect of parameters on equilibrium values*

Equilibrium values	Parameters		
	s_c	n	z
g^0	0	+	0
i^0	—	+	0
w^0	+	—	+
p^0	—	+	—

given, because at a steady state in which the labor-capital ratio stays constant the demand for labor grows at rate g.

We now have three equations and three unknowns, g, i, and w. Hence the equilibrium values, g^0, i^0, and w^0, of these unknowns are determined given three parameters, s_c, z, and n. The equilibrium profit rate p^0 is then determined as a decreasing function of w^0 by equation (3.13).

The determination of the equilibrium is quite simple. Since n is given, g^0 is immediately determined equal to n by equation (5.3). Then equation (5.1) determines i^0 at the level n/s_c. w^0 is then determined by equation (5.2) so that $g^0 = g(i^0, w^0, z)$, namely, $n = g(n/s_c, w^0, z)$. Accordingly, the comparative analysis is also easy. Since g^0 is dependent only on n, neither s_c nor z affects g^0; i^0 is affected positively by n and negatively by s_c but not by z; w^0 is affected by all three parameters; and by equation (5.2) it can be easily proved that s_c and z affect w^0 positively, whereas n affects w^0 negatively. Since $dp/dw < 0$, the effect of any parameter on p^0 is of the opposite sign to that on w^0. These results are summarized in Table 5.1.

The results are interesting but hardly surprising. For instance, because there is no technical progress, g^0 is constrained to n. The effort of management to achieve a higher growth rate is, therefore, fruitless in the economy as a whole and ends up with a higher wage rate so that every management is content with the growth at exactly the rate n. A similar statement can be made as to the effect of s_c. This suggests that in order to explain differences in the rate of economic growth, say, among countries, by factors other than the difference in the rate of increase in population, one should incorporate some kind of technical progress into the model. The easiest way to do this may be to incorporate Harrod-neutral exogenous technical progress into the model. Then, the full employment condition (5.3) is replaced by $g =$

$n + \bar{a}$, where $\bar{a}$ is the rate of exogenous technical progress.[7] In such a model the difference in g^0 can be explained by the difference in $\bar{a}$ as well as in n. Still, however, neither z nor s_c affects the equilibrium growth rate in this model as long as $\bar{a}$ is assumed to be an exogenously given number. This suggests clearly that if one believes that these parameters are the important factors determining the equilibrium growth rate, as I do, then, he has to incorporate an analysis of how technical progress is generated into model.

5.3   The model with research activity

We now proceed to the model of economic growth based on our model of the firm in section 3.5. The assumptions as to the macroeconomy are as in the previous section. Therefore the saving-investment balancing condition is

$$g = s_c i \tag{5.1}$$

By equation (3.22), the desired growth rate is determined as

$$g = g(i, w, \xi^e, z) \tag{5.4}$$

An equilibrium in the labor market requires that the rate of growth of labor demand in efficiency units, g, equals that of labor supply, $n + a$, where n is the rate of increase of labor force measured in physical units; hence

$$g = n + a \tag{5.5}$$

where, by equation (3.19),

$$a = a(w, i - g, \xi^e) \tag{5.6}$$

A steady-state equilibrium of course requires that the management expectation on the rate of wage increase ξ^e equals the actual rate ξ, for otherwise the management will revise its expectation; hence

$$\xi^e = \xi \tag{5.7}$$

We now inquire how ξ is determined in the market. Recall that the profit gross of capital cost is defined for any t as an accounting residual, $F(K(t), L(t)) - w(t)N(t) - \phi(a(t))L(t)$, where $L(t) = A(t)N(t)$ and $\dot{a}(t) = \dot{A}(t)/A(t)$ (section 3.5). The marginal product of labor (MPL) in physical units at time t is hence $F_2(K(t), L(t))A(t)$ whereas its marginal cost (MCL) is $w(t) + \phi(a(t))A(t)$. At a steady

---

[7] See, for instance, Allen (1967, Chapter 13).

state where $L(t)/K(t)$ and $a(t)$ are constant and $\dot{A}(t)/A(t) = a(t) = a$ for any t, MPL increases at rate a because $F_2(K(t), L(t))$ is homogeneous of degree zero, whereas MCL increases at rate $(w\xi + \phi(a)aA)/(w + \phi(a)A)$. Therefore MPL increases faster than MCL if and only if $\xi < a$. But since, by assumption, the amount of labor is freely adjustable and the firm maximizes v for any growth rate, MPL is equated to MCL today, implying that if $\xi < a$, MPL exceeds MCL tomorrow and the firm will be able to enjoy additional profit by employing an additional unit of labor tomorrow. This would raise the demand for labor tomorrow and push w and ξ upward. This process would continue as long as $\xi < a$. A similar movement would take place in the opposite direction if $\xi > a$. Consequently, in a steady-state growth path it must be that[8]

$$\xi = a \qquad (5.8)$$

Now we have six equations and six unknowns; g, i, w, a, ξ, and ξ^e. To inquire about the existence and the properties of the equilibrium, substitute this equation and equation (5.7) into equation (5.6). Then, in view of equation (3.18), the desired level of a is obtained by the following equation:

$$\phi'(a) = w/(i - g)$$

Since $\phi''(a) > 0$, we can invert this equation to obtain

$$a = A(w/(i - g)) \qquad (5.9)$$

where $A'(w/(i - g)) > 0$. Similarly, presuming that $\xi^e = \xi = a = A(w/(i - g))$, equation (5.4) can be rewritten as

$$g = G(i, w, z) \qquad (5.10)$$

A detailed discussion of the properties of this function will be given in the next section, but for now assume that $G_1(i, w, z) < 0$, $G_2(i, w, z) < 0$, and $G_3(i, w, z) > 0$.

Equations (5.1), (5.5), (5.9), and (5.10) constitute a system of four equations with four unknowns: g, i, w, and a. An analysis of this model can be made diagrammatically in the following manner. First, substitute equation (5.1) into equation (5.10) to obtain

$$g = G(g/s_c, w, z) \qquad (5.11)$$

---

[8] Notice that the model discussed in the previous section satisfies this condition, where $\xi^e = \xi = a = 0$.

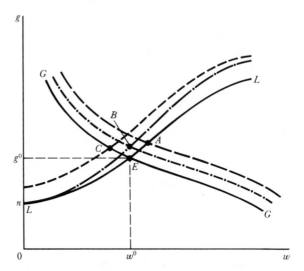

Figure 5.1. Economic growth with research activity: comparative analysis.

In view of the signs of the partial derivatives of the G function, $dg/dw < 0$, given s_c and z. Therefore, given s_c and z, the relation between g and w that satisfies equation (5.11) is depicted as a downward-sloping curve in the (w, g) plane, as illustrated by the solid line marked GG in Figure 5.1. Second, substitute equation (5.1) into equation (5.9) and then into equation (5.5) to obtain

$$g = n + A(s_c w/(1 - s_c)g) \tag{5.12}$$

Since $A'(w/(i - g)) > 0$ and $0 < s_c < 1$, it is easy to show that $dg/dw > 0$ in this equation, given s_c and n. Given s_c and n, therefore the relation between g and w that satisfies equation (5.12) is depicted as an upward-sloping curve, as illustrated by the solid line marked LL in Figure 5.1. These GG and LL curves depict how g and w must be related for the stock (and goods) market and the labor market respectively, to be in steady-state equilibria as i and ξ are accordingly adjusted. The equilibrium growth rate g^0 and the equilibrium wage rate w^0 are then determined at the intersection of these GG and LL curves, as illustrated by the point E in Figure 5.1.

The figure clearly shows that a general equilibrium exists if the LL curve intercepts the g axis below the GG curve. This condition seems generally satisfied for the following reason. When w is zero, the wage rate is always zero no matter how large its growth rate is. Obviously no firm would then have an incentive to spend for research activity that s aimed to reduce future labor costs. Hence it must be that $\phi(a) = 0$ if $w = 0$.[9] But since $\phi(a) = 0$ if and only if $a = 0$ by our assumption section 3.5), $a = 0$ if $w = 0$. Thus the intercept of the LL curve with he g axis, namely, the value of g that satisfies equation (5.12) when $w = 0$, is n. On the other hand, if w equals zero, firms will employ nfinite amount of labor, assuming that MPL is positive for all L [see equation (3.17)]. But if L is infinite, the output and the value of the irm will also be infinite. In this situation the optimal growth rate for he management will be very large and surely will exceed n, implying hat the GG curve intercepts the g axis above the LL curve.

We now proceed to the analysis of the effect of the three parameters, z, n, and s_c, on the equilibrium values. A warning is in order here, however. Note that equations (5.11) and (5.12) presume that $\xi = \xi^e = a$ and $g = s_c i$, both holding only at steady state. Therefore, equations (5.11) and (5.12) hold only at steady state and may not be used either to discuss the transition from one steady-state equilibrium to another or to discuss the stability of an equilibrium.[10] Thus even though we follow convention and use words, such as increase, decrease, and shift, they should be understood as referring to the comparison of two steady states and not to the movement between them.

First, suppose that z increases. Then the GG curve shifts up but the LL curve stays the same. Consequently, both w^0 and g^0 increase (point A in Figure 5.1). Since $a^0 = g^0 - n$, a^0 also increases, and since $g^0 = s_c i^0$, i^0 increases, too. The effect on the equilibrium profit rate p^0 is also easy to see because

$$p = F(1, l(w, a)) - wl(w, a) - \phi(a)l(w, a)$$

provided $\xi^e = a$ and, consequently, p is a decreasing function of w and z. Therefore p^0 decreases if both w^0 and a^0 increase as in the case in which z increases. Suppose next that s_c increases. Then both the LL and GG curves shift up and, as a result, g^0 increases, but it is

If $w = 0$, then the value of the firm is a decreasing function of a [see equation (3.16)]. Hence the optimal rate of productivity increase (subject to the constraint that it is nonnegative) is zero.

[10] We should add that our analysis here does not preclude the possibility that there exists a nonsteady-state general equilibrium. The analysis only says that if there exists a steady-state equilibrium, then it must always satisfy equations (5.1), (5.5), (5.9), and (5.10), and that if there exists a solution to this set of equations, then it is an equilibrium because every agent in the economy is content with it.

Table 5.2. *The sign of the effect of parameters on equilibrium values*

Equilibrium values	Parameters		
	s_c	n	z
g^0	+	+	+
i^0	?	+	+
w^0	?	−	+
a^0	+	−	+
p^0	?	+	−

ambiguous whether w^0 increases or decreases (point B in Figure 5.1). The effect on i^0 is also ambiguous. What if n increases? Then LL shifts up but GG stays the same, implying an increase in g^0 and a decrease in w^0 (point C in Figure 5.1). i^0 increases because $i^0 = g^0/s_c$. Since $s_c w^0/(1 - s_c)g^0$ now decreases, a^0 decreases. These results are summarized in Table 5.2, and the algebraic proof is provided in the Appendix.

The results appear reasonable. If the saving rate of capitalists is larger, then funds are available for more rapid growth. An increase in the rate of increase of the labor force, n, will push the wage rate downward. This shifts the v-g frontier upward and makes rapid growth more attractive to firms. However, faster growth requires larger funds and increases the interest rate. Obviously, a lower wage rate makes labor-saving R & D less attractive. The most interesting result may be that of an increase in z. If the management prefers growth to security, or if the devices such as takeovers to control the discretionary behavior of management are costlier, then the equilibrium growth rate is in fact larger. To sustain a high growth rate, however, labor supply in efficiency units must also increase at a high rate, which in turn means that firms have to spend more on R & D. In this fast growing economy, demands for labor and for funds are large and so their prices, w and i, are pushed up.

The striking contrast of these results to the ones in the previous section cannot be overemphasized. A larger s_c does not necessarily imply a lower i^0 and a higher w^0 any more, and both s_c and z now affect g^0 positively. Of particular interest will be the fact that although z affected neither the equilibrium growth rate nor the equilibrium rate of interest in the model without research activity, it now affects both of them positively. That is, in an economy with research activity undertaken by firms, management, if it intends to achieve faster growth, can increase the level of research activity to achieve a faster increase of labor supply in efficiency units. As a consequence, not only the desired growth rate, given i and w, but also the equilibrium growth rate becomes larger in such an economy. This finding should have important practical implications; for instance, the difference in the actual growth rate between economies can now be explained by the differences in saving behavior and management preference as well as in the rate of population increase, and new considerations may become necessary in policy recommendations.

5.4 The v-g frontier revisited

We now investigate in more detail the nature of the v-g frontier in the model with research activity to verify that the growth rate determined by the G function in the last section is in fact optimal for the management.

For this purpose, three functional relations are defined between v and g as follows:

i. The v-g frontier in the absence of research activity, namely, the v-g frontier in Uzawa's model, which is expressed by a function $\hat{v}$:

$$v = \frac{F(1, l(w)) - wl(w) - \psi(g)}{i - g}$$

$$\equiv \hat{v}(g, i, w) \tag{5.13}$$

and

$$\frac{\partial \hat{v}}{\partial g} = \frac{F(1, l(w)) - wl(w) - \psi(g)}{(i - g)^2} - \frac{\psi'(g)}{i - g} \tag{5.14}$$

ii. The locus of (v, g) such that the optimal value of a equals ξ^e: To construct this locus, let us first define $\tilde{g}$ as the value of g such that the corresponding optimal value of a equals ξ^e. Then, by equation (3.18), $\tilde{g}$ satisfies $w/(i - \tilde{g}) = \phi'(a) = \phi'(\xi^e)$, and depends on ξ^e as well as on i and w. Since $\phi''(a) > 0$, $\tilde{g}$ is unique for any $\xi^e \geq 0$ and $\partial \tilde{g}/\partial \xi^e > 0$. Now change ξ^e continuously to obtain the locus of $\tilde{g}$ and the corresponding value of v. This locus is what we want and is expressed by a function $\tilde{v}$, which can be obtained by substituting $\xi^e = a$ into equation (3.20).

$$v = \frac{F(1, l) - wl - \psi(g) - \phi(a)l}{i - g}$$

$$\equiv \tilde{v}(g, i, w) \tag{5.15}$$

because $l = l(w, a)$ and $a = \xi^e = A(w/(i - g))$. Since $A'(w/(i - g)) = 1/\phi''(a) > 0$,

$$\frac{\partial \tilde{v}}{\partial g} = \frac{F(1, l) - wl - \psi(g) - \phi(a)l}{(i - g)^2} - \frac{\psi'(g)}{i - g} - \frac{\phi'(a)l}{i - g} \frac{\partial a}{\partial g}$$

$$= \frac{F(1, l) - wl - \psi(g) - \phi(a)l}{(i - g)^2} - \frac{\psi'(g)}{i - g} - \frac{\phi'(a)}{\phi''(a)} \frac{wl}{(i - g)^3} \qquad (5.16)$$

iii. The v-g frontier for the model with research activity as obtained in section 3.5:

$$v = \frac{F(1, l) - \psi(g) - \phi(a)l}{i - g} - \frac{wl}{i - g - \xi^e + a}$$

$$\equiv v(g, i, w, \xi^e) \qquad (5.17)$$

because $l = l(w, i - g, \xi^e)$ and $a = a(w, i - g, \xi^e)$. As was shown by equation (3.21),

$$\frac{\partial v}{\partial g} = \frac{F(1, l) - \psi(g) - \phi(a)l}{(i - g)^2} - \frac{wl}{(i - g - \xi^e + a)^2} - \frac{\psi'(g)}{i - g} \qquad (5.18)$$

Several results can be established concerning the relationship among these three.

Lemma 5.1. $\hat{v}(g, i, w) > \tilde{v}(g, i, w)$ and $\partial\hat{v}/\partial g > \partial\tilde{v}/\partial g$ for any i and w and for any $g \geq 0$.

> *Proof:* Denote by $\hat{l}$ and $\tilde{l}$ the optimal values of l, given g, i, and w, corresponding to $\hat{v}$ and $\tilde{v}$, respectively. Then,
>
> $$(\hat{v} - \tilde{v})(i - g) = F(1, \hat{l}) - w\hat{l} - [F(1, \tilde{l}) - w\tilde{l} - \phi(a)\tilde{l}]$$
> $$\geq F(1, \tilde{l}) - w\tilde{l} - [F(1, \tilde{l}) - w\tilde{l} - \phi(a)\tilde{l}]$$
> $$= \phi(a)\tilde{l} > 0$$
>
> The first inequality follows by the definition of $\hat{l}$ and the second inequality holds because $\phi(a) > 0$ for $g \geq 0$. Also,
>
> $$\left(\frac{\partial\hat{v}}{\partial g} - \frac{\partial\tilde{v}}{\partial g}\right)(i - g)^2 = F(1, \hat{l}) - w\hat{l}$$
>
> $$- \left[F(1, \tilde{l}) - w\tilde{l} - \phi(a)\tilde{l} - \frac{\phi'(a)}{\phi''(a)} \frac{w\tilde{l}}{(i - g)}\right] > \frac{\phi'(a)}{\phi''(a)} \frac{w\tilde{l}}{(i - g)} > 0$$
>
> The first inequality follows from the preceding result and the

second inequality holds because $\phi'(a) > 0$ and $\phi''(a) > 0$ for $g \geq 0$. Q.E.D.

f we denote by $\hat{g}^{**}$, $\tilde{g}^{**}$, and g^{**} the values of g that maximize, espectively, $\hat{v}$, $\tilde{v}$, and v, $\hat{g}^{**}$ and $\tilde{g}^{**}$ depend on i and w, whereas g^{**} lepends on i, w, and ξ^e. The following lemma follows immediately rom lemma 5.1:

Lemma 5.2. $\hat{g}^{**} > \tilde{g}^{**}$ for any i and w such that $\hat{g}^{**} > 0$.

Proof: Since by definition $\partial\hat{v}/\partial g = 0$ at $g = \hat{g}^{**}$, $\partial\tilde{v}/\partial g < 0$ at $g = \hat{g}^{**}$ by lemma 5.1. By the definition of $\tilde{g}^{**}$, it must be that $\tilde{g}^{**} < \hat{g}^{**}$. Q.E.D.

We now proceed to the comparison between $\tilde{v}$ and v.

Lemma 5.3. $\partial v/\partial g > \partial\tilde{v}/\partial g$ at any $\tilde{g} > 0$.

Proof: Comparing equations (5.16) and (5.18), if $g = \tilde{g}$, namely, if $\xi^e = a$,

$$\frac{\partial v}{\partial g} - \frac{\partial\tilde{v}}{\partial g} = \frac{\phi'(a)}{\phi''(a)}\frac{wl}{(i-g)^3} > 0 \quad \text{Q.E.D.}$$

Lemma 5.4. $\partial v/\partial g \gtreqless 0$ at any $\tilde{g}$ as $v \gtreqless \psi'(g)$.

Proof: By letting $\xi^e = a$ in equation (5.18), we have at any $\tilde{g}$

$$\frac{\partial v}{\partial g} = \frac{F(1, l) - wl - \psi(g) - \phi(a)l}{(i - g)^2} - \frac{\psi'(g)}{i - g}$$

$$= \frac{\tilde{v}(g, i, w) - \psi'(g)}{i - g} \gtreqless 0 \qquad \text{as } v \gtreqless \psi'(g) \quad \text{Q.E.D.}$$

Let us define $g^{\#}$ by an equation, $\tilde{v}(g^{\#}, i, w) = \psi'(g^{\#})$. Then, by lemma 5.4, $g^{\#}$ is the value of g such that $\partial v/\partial g = 0$ and $a(w, i - g^{\#}, \xi^e) = \xi^e \cdot g^{\#}$ of course depends on i and w.

Lemma 5.5. There exists a unique $g^{\#}$ that is strictly positive if and only f $\tilde{v}(0, i, w) > 1$ or, equivalently, if and only if $F(1, l_0) - wl_0 - \phi(a_0)l_0 > i$, where $l_0 = l(w, a_0)$ and $a_0 = A(w/i)$.

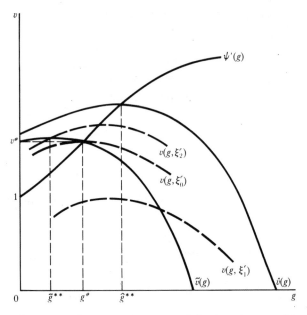

Figure 5.2. The three alternatively defined v-g frontiers ($\xi_2^c < \xi_0^c < \xi_1^c$).

Proof: Suppose that $\tilde{v}(0, i, w) > 1$. Then, since $\psi'(0) = 1$ by our assumption, $\tilde{v}(0, i, w) > \psi'(0)$. $\partial \tilde{v}/\partial g$ may be positive for small g but eventually turns to negative as g increases because of lemma 5.1 together with the property of Uzawa's v-g frontier $\hat{v}$, discussed in section 3.4. Since $\psi''(g) > 0$, therefore there must exist a positive $g^{\#}$ that satisfies $\tilde{v}(g^{\#}, i, w) = \psi'(g^{\#})$. Now suppose that $g^{\#}$ is not unique; that is, in the (g, v) plane the $\tilde{v}(g, i, w)$ curve crosses (or becomes tangent to) $\psi'(g)$ curve at least twice. Then, since $\psi''(g) > 0$ for any $g > 0$ and $\tilde{v}(g, i, w)$ is continuous in g, it must be that $\partial \tilde{v}/\partial g > 0$ at at least one of such $g^{\#}$s. On the other hand, lemmas 5.3 and 5.4 imply that $\partial \tilde{v}/\partial g < 0$ at $g^{\#}$. This contradiction implies that $g^{\#}$ must be unique. Suppose on the contrary that $\tilde{v}(0, i, w) \le 1$. Then, $\tilde{v}(0, i, w) \le \psi'(0)$. Also lemmas 5.3 and 5.4 imply that $\partial \tilde{v}/\partial g < 0$ for any $g > 0$ and hence $\tilde{v}(g, i, w) < 1$ for any $g > 0$. Since $\psi'(g) > 1$ for any $g > 0$, this implies that $\tilde{v}(g, i, w) < \psi'(g)$ for any $g > 0$ and, consequently, there exists no $g^{\#} > 0$. Therefore $g^{\#} > 0$ exists if and only if $\tilde{v}(0, i, w) > 1$.   Q.E.D.

We can now illustrate in the (g, v) plane three functions, $\hat{v}$, $\tilde{v}$, and v, so that they satisfy lemmas 5.1 to 5.5 (Figure 5.2). The values of i and w

are fixed in drawing Figure 5.2 and are suppressed in the denomination of each curve. Note that $\tilde{g}^{**} < g^{\#} < \hat{g}^{**}$ in Figure 5.2. This follows from lemmas 5.1, 5.3, and 5.4.

Now what is the optimal decision for the management in this circumstance? It should be reasonable to assume as in section 3.5 that each management perceives ξ^e as given, namely, as something that its behavior does not affect, as is the case if there are many firms in the economy and no firm possesses any monopsonistic power. Then, each firm will optimize according to some criterion subject to the v-g frontier, $v(g, i, w, \xi^e)$. On the other hand, the economy as a whole cannot be in a steady-state equilibrium unless ξ^e is equated to the value v that firms choose (equations (5.7) and (5.8)). Since all firms are assumed to be identical, this must also be true for each firm, implying that any steady-state equilibrium must satisfy $v = \tilde{v}(g, i, w)$. In sum, v and g must satisfy the following two conditions at any steady-state general equilibrium: (1) it must be optimal along the $v = v(g, i, w, \xi^e)$ curve and (2) it must be on the $v = \tilde{v}(g, i, w)$ curve. These of course imply that (3) it must be at an intersection of the two curves.

Suppose at first that the management is a value maximizer – the management utility function is such that $U_1(g, v) = 0$. It should be obvious, then, that only the pair of values $(g^{\#}, v^{\#})$ where $v^{\#} = \tilde{v}(g^{\#}, i, w)$ can satisfy these two conditions simultaneously. That is, only with $(g^{\#}, v^{\#})$, every value-maximizing management is content and at the same time the economy as a whole can achieve a steady-state equilibrium. Put differently, if there exists a steady-state equilibrium in an economy where every management maximizes the value of the firm, then its growth rate must be $g^{\#}$. This, with the result we have already proved, is summarized as the following proposition.[11]

---

[1] We need to prove that $g^{\#}$ in fact maximizes. Since $\partial^2 v/\partial g^2 = -\psi''(g)/(i - g) < 0$ at $g^{\#}$, the sufficient condition is locally satisfied. Whether or not it is globally satisfied is unfortunately ambiguous. Note that if $\psi(g)$ is linear in g, as in the case $\psi = g$, $\psi''(g) = 0$ and $\partial^2 v/\partial g^2 = 0$ at $g^{\#}$, implying that $g^{\#}$ may not be optimal even locally. This indicates the importance of incorporating the Penrose curve into the model. This is because, even though a and l depend on g, v does not depend on g as long as a and l are optimally adjusted because of the envelope theorem. Incidentally, this is exactly why we have asserted in section 3.3 that Marris's model assumed no optimization behavior concerning the level of development expenditure but instead assumed a *mechanical* relation between the growth rate and the required development expenditure.

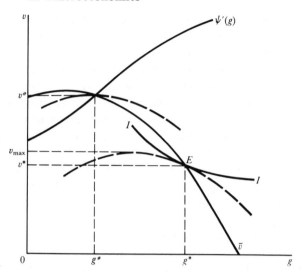

Figure 5.3. Maximization of $U(g, v)$.

Proposition 5.1. If every management is a value maximizer, that is,
$U_1(g, v) = 0$, then $g^{\#}$ is the only optimal steady-state growth rate tha
is consistent with the general equilibrium. $g^{\#}$ is positive and unique
$\tilde{v}(0, i, w) > 1$. Furthermore, $\tilde{g}^{**} < g^{\#} < \hat{g}^{**}$ and $v^{\#} < \tilde{v}_{max} < \hat{v}_{ma}$
where $\tilde{v}_{max} = \tilde{v}(\tilde{g}^{**}, i, w)$ and $\hat{v}_{max} = \hat{v}(\hat{g}^{**}, i, w)$.

For the case that the management does not maximize v but pursues
higher growth rate, the following two propositions should be evident:

Proposition 5.2. If $U(g, v)$ is such that the marginal rate of substitutio
is positive but finite, the optimal steady-state growth rate that i
consistent with the general equilibrium is greater than $g^{\#}$.

Proposition 5.3. If the management maximizes g subject to $v \geq \Phi(v_{max})$
where $0 < \Phi'(v_{max}) < 1$, the optimal steady-state growth rate that i
consistent with the general equilibrium is greater than $g^{\#}$. The optima
valuation ratio, v^{*}, is strictly smaller than $\Phi(v^{\#})$ or, in other words, th
deviation of v^{*} from $v^{\#}$ is greater than what can be attributed to th
transaction cost of a takeover.

The points E in Figures 5.3 and 5.4 illustrate the equilibria describe
in propositions 5.2 and 5.3, respectively, where II denotes a manage

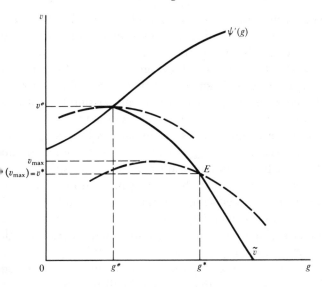

Figure 5.4. Maximization of g subject to $v \geq \Phi(v_{max})$.

ial indifference curve, namely, the locus of constant U. The latter half of proposition 5.3 follows because $v^\# > v_{max}$ and $\Phi' > 0$ so that $\Phi(v^\#) > \Phi(v_{max}) = v^*$. As already shown, the difference, $v_{max} - v^*$, can be accounted for by the transaction cost of a takeover (see section 2.3). The following corollary immediately follows from propositions 5.2 and 5.3 since $\partial a / \partial g > 0$ along the $\tilde{v}$ curve.

Corollary 5.1. The desired level of research activity and the desired rate of increase of labor productivity are greater when management pursues faster growth at the sacrifice of the value of the firm (the case of proposition 5.2 or 5.3) than when it maximizes the value (the case of proposition 5.1) for any fixed i and w.

Among these results, the latter half of proposition 5.3 may be of particular interest. It says that when research activity is undertaken, the value of v chosen by the management is less than $v^\#$ – the value that would have been chosen if it were a value maximizer – and the difference is greater than what can be attributed to the transaction cost of a takeover, because ξ also changes as g is changed but none of the potential raiders will foresee it. If all the firms are taken over and the raiders reduce the growth rate to $g^{\#}$, then ξ is also reduced because a is reduced and, as a result, the profits that the raiders can enjoy are θ $(v^{\#} - v^*)K_0 - C$, which is strictly greater than $\theta(v_{\max} - v^*)K_0 - C$ [see equation (2.4)]. Each raider, however, will not foresee this reduction in ξ because he will not believe that other raiders behave identically as he does and hence will ignore the possibility that ξ is affected by his choice of a. Therefore the raider will not take over even if he can earn positive profits if $v^{\#}$ is attainable, as long as positive profits cannot be expected when $v_{\max}$ is supposed to be the maximum value attainable. Note that a similar result holds for proposition 5.3 in the following sense. Suppose that the management utility function $U(g, v)$ is derived from considering hazard rate h and h is a function of $v_{\max}$ as well as of v, as in section 2.4. Then, since this $v_{\max}$ will be the maximum value of v along the same v-g frontier that passes through (v^*, g^*) by the same reason as previously stated and this $v_{\max}$ is strictly smaller than $v^{\#}$, v^* to be chosen by the management when research activity is undertaken is smaller than $v^{\#}$, and the difference should be greater than what can be attributed to the transaction cost of a takeover.

The optimal steady-state growth rate consistent with the general equilibrium thus obtained, needless to say, depends on prices, i and w (but not on ξ). Let us now inquire how i and w affect the optimal growth rate. For this purpose, we confine our analysis to the case where $g^{\#} > 0$, that is, to the case where $\tilde{v}$ $(0, i, w) > 1$ (lemma 5.5), otherwise, the equilibrium valuation ratio is less than unity for any positive growth rate (see the proof of lemma 5.5), which contradicts most findings.[12] Let us first investigate $g^{\#}$, the optimal steady-state growth rate for the value-maximizing management consistent with the general equilibrium.

[12] Marris (1971b) reported that the average valuation ratio of 335 U.S corporations surviving through 1950–63 was 1.85. [Marris's definition of the valuation ratio only includes total stock market value, E, in the numerator; hence I added the debt-assets ratio, B/K, to get the valuation ratio, $(E + B)/K$, as defined in this book.] Thus Marris's result roughly agrees with my unpublished preliminary result, in which the average valuation ratio of 184 Japanese corporations was 1.59 in 1971. We should note, however, that these figures may be biased upward because assets, K are evaluated at the acquisition cost basis in most instances and, especially during inflation, underevaluate the true current value of assets, thus giving an upward bias in the valuation ratio, $(E + B)/K$.

Proposition 5.4. $\partial g^{\#}/\partial w < 0$.

Proof: In view of equation (5.15),

$$\frac{\partial \tilde{v}}{\partial w} = \frac{-l - \phi'(a)l(\partial a/\partial w)}{i - g}$$

$$= \left[-l - \frac{\phi'(a)}{\phi''(a)} \frac{l}{i - g} \right] \bigg/ (i - g) < 0$$

since $\phi'(a) > 0$, $\phi''(a) > 0$ and, by the envelope theorem, $(\partial \tilde{v}/\partial l)(\partial l/\partial w) = 0$. Therefore, the $\tilde{v}$ curve shifts downward as w increases. On the other hand, the $\psi'(g)$ curve is not affected by the change in w. Thus $g^{\#}$ decreases as w increases. Q.E.D.

Proposition 5.5.

$$\frac{\partial g^{\#}}{\partial i} \gtreqless 0 \quad \text{as} \quad v^{\#} = \psi'(g^{\#}) \lesseqgtr \frac{\phi'(a^{\#})}{\phi''(a^{\#})} \frac{wl(w, a^{\#})}{(i - g^{\#})^2}$$

where

$$a^{\#} = A(w/(i - g^{\#}))$$

Proof

$$\frac{\partial \tilde{v}}{\partial i} = \frac{-v - \phi'(a)l(\partial a/\partial i)}{i - g}$$

$$= -\left[v - \frac{\phi'(a)}{\phi''(a)} \frac{wl}{(i - g)^2} \right] \bigg/ (i - g) \tag{5.19}$$

Hence

$$\frac{\partial \tilde{v}}{\partial i} \gtreqless 0 \quad \text{as } v \lesseqgtr \frac{\phi'(a)}{\phi''(a)} \frac{wl}{(i - g)^2}$$

where $l = l(w, a)$ and $a = A(w/(i - g))$. Because the $\psi'(g)$ curve is not affected by the change in i,

$$\frac{\partial g^{\#}}{\partial i} \gtreqless 0 \quad \text{as } \frac{\partial \tilde{v}}{\partial i} \gtreqless 0 \text{ at } g = g^{\#} \quad \text{Q.E.D.}$$

As a corollary to proposition 5.5, we have

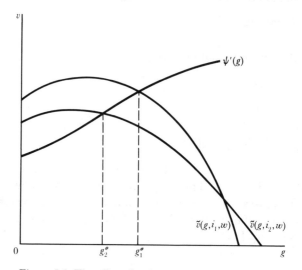

Figure 5.5. The effect of an increase in interest rate ($i_1 < i_2$).

Corollary 5.2.

(i) $\partial \tilde{v}/\partial i < 0$ at $\tilde{g}^{**}$
(ii) $\partial \tilde{v}/\partial i > 0$ at $v = 0$

Proof: (i) By the definition of $\tilde{g}^{**}$, $\partial \tilde{v}/\partial g = 0$ at $\tilde{g}^{**}$; that is, a $\tilde{g}^{**}$ [see equation (5.16)]

$$v = \psi'(g) + \frac{\phi'(a)}{\phi''(a)}\frac{wl}{(i-g)^2} > \frac{\phi'(a)}{\phi''(a)}\frac{wl}{(i-g)^2}$$

By equation (5.19),

$$\partial \tilde{v}/\partial i < 0 \quad \text{at } \tilde{g}^{**}$$

(ii) By equation (5.19),

$$\partial \tilde{v}/\partial i > 0 \quad \text{if } v = 0 \quad \text{Q.E.D.}$$

Whether $g^{\#}$ increases or decreases as i increases is, therefore, ambiguous. Since $v^{\#}$ is greater than one because $\psi'(g) > 1$ for any $g > 0$ and may be closer to $\tilde{v}_{max}$ than to 0, it appears more likely that $\partial g^{\#}/\partial i < 0$ in view of corollary 5.2 (i), as is true in the case illustrated in Figure 5.5. We will assume this in the following. Then $g^{\#}$ is a function of i and w with $\partial g^{\#}/\partial i < 0$ and $\partial g^{\#}/\partial w < 0$.

In the case where the management chooses g in the manner predicted by proposition 5.2 or 5.3, the effect of i and w on the optimal rowth rate is more difficult to determine. We simply assume that the ffect of i or w is negative analogous to the case of the value-aximizing management. Since propositions 5.2 and 5.3 imply that e growth-maximizing management chooses g greater than the alue-maximizing management, it should be appropriate to write

$$g = G(i, w, z)$$

ith $\partial g/\partial i < 0$, $\partial g/\partial w < 0$, and $\partial g/\partial z > 0$, where z is the index of management preference toward growth. This is what we defined as quation (5.10) in the previous section.

.5 Why steady-state growth?

o far we have shown that if the management optimizes *restricting its hoice to constant g, l, and a*, then there exists a general equilibrium uch that i, w, g, and a stay constant over time. Hence a possibility emains that the management is not making its decision with full ationality. In other words, if the management is fully rational, it may ot pursue the policy of steady-state growth. This section will show at that at any steady-state general equilibrium the constancy of g, l, and a is in fact an optimal policy for the management. Thus once such an quilibrium is obtained, then every agent in the economy is content ith it.

First we prove this result for the case in which the management is a alue maximizer.

roposition 5.6. If the management maximizes the value of the firm ith respect to g, l, and a, given i, w, and ξ^e, then it is optimal to keep em constant over time at exactly the same level as already proved, rovided that ξ^e equals the value of a chosen by the management.

Proof: Management maximizes the following expression with respect to g, l, and a, given i, w, and ξ^e.

$$\int_0^\infty [F(K(t), L(t)) - w(t)N(t) - \psi(g(t))K(t) - \phi(a(t))L(t)]e^{-it}dt$$

$$= \int_0^\infty [F, (1, l(t)) - we^{\xi^e t}l(t)A(t)^{-1} - \psi(g(t)) - \phi(a(t))l(t)]$$
$$\times K(t)e^{-it}dt$$

subject to

$$\dot{K}(t) = g(t)K(t) \qquad (5.20)$$

$$\dot{A}(t) = a(t)A(t) \tag{5.2}$$

This is an optimal control problem and the correspondin current value Hamiltonian equation is defined as

$$H = [F(1, l) - we^{\xi t}lA^{-1} - \psi(g) - \phi(a)l]K + \lambda gK + \mu aA$$

The first-order condition is

$$\frac{\partial H}{\partial l} = [F_2(1, l) - we^{\xi t}A^{-1} - \phi(a)]K = 0 \tag{5.2}$$

$$\frac{\partial H}{\partial g} = -\psi'(g)K + \lambda K = 0 \tag{5.2}$$

$$\frac{\partial H}{\partial a} = -\phi'(a)lK + \mu A = 0 \tag{5.2}$$

$$i\lambda - \dot{\lambda} = \frac{\partial H}{\partial K} = F(1, l) - we^{\xi t}lA^{-1} - \psi(g) - \phi(a)l + \lambda g \tag{5.2}$$

$$i\mu - \dot{\mu} = \frac{\partial H}{\partial A} = we^{\xi t}lA^{-2}K + \mu a \tag{5.2}$$

and of course equations (5.20) and (5.21). We consider th following solution: (i) $l(t)$, $a(t)$, $g(t)$, and $\lambda(t)$ are constant an respectively, equal to l, a, g, and λ; (ii) $\mu(t) = \mu_0 \exp(g - a)$ Then equations (5.22) to (5.26) are rewritten as follow remembering that $A(0) = 1$:

$$F_2(1, l) - w \exp(\xi^e - a)t - \phi(a) = 0 \tag{5.22}$$

$$\lambda = \psi'(g) \tag{5.23}$$

$$\mu_0 = \phi'(a)lK_0 \tag{5.24}$$

$$(i - g)\lambda = F(1, l) - wl \exp(\xi^e - a)t - \psi(g) - \phi(a)l \tag{5.25}$$

$$(i - g)\mu_0 = wlK_0 \exp(\xi^e - a)t \tag{5.26}$$

Substituting $\xi^e = a$ and $v = [F(1, l) - wl - \psi(g) - \phi(a)l]$ $(i - g)$, we obtain the following equations after some substitu tions and rearrangements:

$$F_2(1, l) = w + \phi(a) \qquad \phi'(a) = w/(i - g) \qquad \psi'(g) = v$$

which are equivalent to the previous results.[13]   Q.E.D.

---

[13] Unfortunately, neither Mangasarian's nor Arrow's sufficiency conditio could be shown to be satisfied. Therefore we must leave this as an ope question. This is also true with respect to proposition 5.7.

or the growth-maximizing management, we investigate the constancy
l and a presuming that g is constant, because we derived the
anagement utility function in Chapter 2 assuming that g is constant.

roposition 5.7. If the management maximizes the value of the firm
ith respect to a and l, given $g(< i)$, i, w, and ξ^e, then it is optimal to
:ep them constant over time at exactly the same level as has been
roved, provided ξ^e equals the value of a chosen.

Proof: The problem is to maximize

$$\int_0^\infty [F(1, l(t)) - we^{\xi^t}l(t)A(t)^{-1} - \psi(g)$$

$$- \phi(a(t))l(t)]\exp(-(i - g)t)\, dt$$

with respect to $l(t)$ and $a(t)$, given g, i, w, and ξ^e, subject to
$\dot{A}(t) = a(t)A(t)$. The rest of the proof is exactly parallel to that
of proposition 5.6 and is left to the reader.   Q.E.D.

'hese two propositions imply that at any steady-state general equilib-
um, every management, whether a value maximizer or a growth
aximizer, is completely satisfied with it. Therefore the equilibrium
iscussed in section 5.3 is a *true* equilibrium in the sense that every
;ent in the economy, assuming that he is fully rational, is content
ith it and that all the markets are cleared.

.6.   Summary and concluding remarks

'his chapter presented two models of economic growth based on the
nalysis in Chapter 3 of the behavior of firms and on the saving-
vestment balancing condition proved in Chapter 4, first assuming
.at no firm undertakes research activity and then assuming that every
rm does. A comparative analysis was carried out with respect to each
odel to investigate the effects on the equilibrium of three parameters:
.e rate of increase of labor force n, the saving propensity of capitalists
, and the index of management preference toward growth z. It was
.own that the equilibrium growth rate is affected by all three
arameters if research activity is taken into account, but only by n if
ot.[14] Furthermore, it was shown that a higher z or s_c yields a higher

Interestingly, not every model that incorporates research activity has this
property. For instance, consider the production function of research
activity,

equilibrium growth rate, provided research activity is taken int account. This seems perfectly consistent with common sense. Fc instance, the argument has been made by many people that Japan hz achieved faster growth than other countries because of, among othe things, the higher propensity of its people to save and the aggressiv management of Japanese firms. (This will be discussed in more deta in Chapter 7.) In this regard, we say that our model offers a goo analytical framework for the international comparison of econom growth.

Theoretically, the contribution of our model may exist in that th microeconomic analysis of the firm is consistently combined with th macroeconomic analysis. This will be discussed further in the ne> chapter, comparing our model to four other well-known models c economic growth.

As for its implications, our model of economic growth with researc activity features the following properties:

Footnote 14 (*cont.*)

$$a = \dot{A}/A = Fr(L_r/L)$$

where L_r is the amount of labor employed for research activity and $L - I$ is the amount of labor employed for production activity. Such a functio was used by Uzawa (1965) in the context of optimal growth theory. Ther by following the same procedure as in section 3.5, one can show that if $\xi^e =$ a, the optimal rate of increase of labor productivity a is a function of $i -$ only and not of w. The general equilibrium condition that corresponds t equations (5.1), (5.5), (5.9), and (5.10), therefore, is

$$g = s_c i$$
$$g = G(i, w, z)$$
$$g = n + A(i - g)$$

From the first and the third equations, g^0 is uniquely determined so a to satisfy $g^0 = n + A((1 - s_c)g^0/s_c)$ and, consequently, g^0 depends on n an s_c but not on z. This suggests that when, as in this formulation, the cost an the benefit of research activity are both affected by the wage rate and as consequence the desired rate of technical progress is independent of th wage rate, the difference in management preference does not affect th equilibrium growth rate. Obviously, this result is crucially dependent on our balancing condition, $g = s_c i$, and if another condition such as the one fo a one-class economy in proposition 4.1 is assumed, then g^0 become dependent on z again. On the other hand, if no research activity is take into account, then g^0 is independent of z (and s_c) irrespective of th saving-investment balancing condition since an equilibrium requires $g^0 =$ n. This is an important difference between the two types of models.

1. Both output and capital grow at the same rate, which quite possibly is larger than the growth rate of labor force.
2. The growth rate of labor productivity equals the rate of increase of wage rate.
3. The capital-output ratio is constant but labor-output ratio (in physical units) steadily falls.
4. The rate of profit and the rate of interest may diverge but both are constant over time.
5. The share of profits and the share of wages in national income stay constant.

hese properties are evidently quite consistent with Kaldor's "stylized cts" (Kaldor 1961, p. 178) or Samuelson's "six basic trends of onomic development" (Samuelson, 1976, p. 740). This should courage the applicability of our model to the problem of modern onomic growth.

Without doubt, however, our model in this chapter is simplistic and any problems still remain to be analyzed. Some will be dealt with in arts IV and V. In Part IV the government is introduced into the odel to discuss the effects of taxation, government expenditure, and onetary policy on economic growth. In Part V we relax the assump-n of identical firms and assume that in addition to those corporations ready discussed – to which the entry is impossible and of which the anagement may not maximize the interest of shareholders – there are ose firms to which entry is free and of which the managers maximize e values of the firms.

Before we consider these analyses, however, it appears appropriate discuss the important question: "Why is it necessary to add a new eory to the existing theories of economic growth?" We will answer is question first from the theoretical viewpoint and, then, from the npirical viewpoint.

Appendix: The model with research activity: comparative analysis

otally differentiate the following three equations (suppressing the perscript 0):

$$g = s_c i$$

$$g = G(i, w, z)$$

$$g = n + A(w/(i - g))$$

'hen, we have in matrix notation (suppressing functional argu-ents):

$$
\begin{bmatrix}
1 & -s_c & 0 \\
1 & -G_1 & -G_2 \\
1 - \dfrac{wA'}{(i-g)^2} & \dfrac{wA'}{(i-g)^2} & \dfrac{-A'}{i-g}
\end{bmatrix}
\begin{bmatrix}
dg \\
di \\
dw
\end{bmatrix}
=
\begin{bmatrix}
ids_c \\
G_3 dz \\
dn
\end{bmatrix}
$$

Denote the determinant of this 3×3 matrix by Ω. Then,

$$
\Omega = \frac{G_1 A'}{i-g} + s_c G_2 + \frac{wG_2 A'(1-s_c)}{(i-g)^2} - \frac{s_c A'}{i-g} < 0
$$

because $G_1 < 0$, $G_2 < 0$, $G_3 > 0$, $A' > 0$, and $0 < s_c < 1$. By inverting the matrix, we get

$$
\begin{bmatrix}
dg \\
di \\
dw
\end{bmatrix}
= \Omega^{-1}
$$

$$
\times
\begin{bmatrix}
\dfrac{A'}{i-g}\left(G_1 + \dfrac{wG_2}{i-g}\right) & -\dfrac{s_c A'}{i-g} & s_c G_2 \\[2ex]
\dfrac{A'}{i-g} - G_2\left(1 - \dfrac{wA'}{(i-g)^2}\right) & -\dfrac{A'}{i-g} & G_2 \\[2ex]
\dfrac{wA'}{(i-g)^2} + G_2\left(1 - \dfrac{wA'}{(i-g)^2}\right) & -s_c - \dfrac{wA'(1-s_c)}{(i-g)^2} & s_c - G_1
\end{bmatrix}
\begin{bmatrix}
ids_c \\
G_3 d \\
dn
\end{bmatrix}
$$

The results in Table 5.2 are now immediate.

PART III

Why a new theory?

CHAPTER 6

Theoretical relevance:
growth models compared

he mechanism of the growth of a capitalist economy has already been
halyzed by many. In this short chapter we sketch some of the
ell-known models of economic growth and discuss what is new with
ir model and its raison d'être.

1 Models of economic growth

is usually said that the work of Harrod (1939) opened the door to
e modern theories of economic growth. This need not mean,
owever, that the analysis of the dynamic movement of a capitalist
onomy has not been previously made. Particularly, the names of
larx and Schumpeter cannot be forgotten as the great creators of
rnamic theories of capitalism. Marx regarded economic growth as the
ocess by which capitalists continue to accumulate their wealth by
xploiting workers, whereas Schumpeter regarded it as the process by
hich enterpreneurs engage in "creative destruction."

Since Harrod's work appeared many models of economic growth
ive been proposed. Among these growth models perhaps the most
ell-known controversy is the one between the two Cambridges. The
oclassical model – whose main advocates are in Cambridge, Massa-
usetts – envisions economic growth as the process such that, thanks
the invisible hand, investment of exactly the amount required to
istain full employment of all resources is always realized. The
eynesian model – mainly proposed by economists in Cambridge,
ngland – claims that the investment behavior of firms is the
termining force of the dynamic equilibrium of the economy and the
vel of investment is determined by, say, animal spirits.

Both neoclassical and Keynesian economists would agree, however,
iat technical progress is the major force of modern economic growth.
evertheless, it seems to have been one of the least comfortable
ibjects for economists, as discussed in section 5.1. What is the
echanism to produce technical progress and how to incorporate it in

a model of economic growth have never been analyzed convincing.
Kaldor (1957), for example, without giving a detailed explanati
(especially, of microeconomic aspects), assumed a functional relatio
ship between the increase in labor productivity and the accumulati
of capital per worker.

The following section attempts to describe the idea behind each
four models simply by a system of four equations and four variabl
These models are Marx's model,[1] the neoclassical model represent
by Solow's model (1956), the Keynesian model represented by Robi
son's model (1962), and Kaldor's model.[2,3] The four variables are t
wage rate w, the rate of profit p, the rate of interest i, and the grow
rate of capital g. Our aim in this analysis is to clarify what view of t
capitalist economy is behind each model and by what mechanism ea
model determines the equilibrium growth rate and the equilibriu
prices. To achieve this, we simplify each model as much as possib
and replace the assumptions in each model by a set of common on
except of course, the assumption we consider to be most important a
distinctive in each model. Therefore the reader is warned that t
models explained subsequently are based on my interpretation of wh
they seem to imply and may not necessarily be a faithful reformulati
of the original models.

[1] We totally disregard Marx's labor theory of value. This approach coincid
with Morishima's: "Marxian economics without the labor theory of value
in fact found to be as conceivable as Walrasian economics without utili
theory" (Morishima, 1973, p. 8).

[2] Of the theories discussed in the previous paragraphs, Schumpeter's w
omitted from our discussion, because his theory is rather stochastic and n
suitable for a mathematical deterministic formulation; by no means was
omitted because we consider it less important. Recent works by Nelson a
Winter (1974, 1977) attempt to depict the Schumpeterian process by mea
of computer simulation.

[3] We neglect many extended and sophisticated works performed since the
original models appeared. Examples are monetary growth models, mult
sectoral growth models, and vintage models. See Burmeister and Dob
(1970) and the literature cited therein. They were disregarded because
my opinion they only extended the original models without presenting ne
insights into the working of a capitalist economy. We also neglect optim
growth theories because our concern is with the positive analysis
economic growth rather than the normative one. A comparison of Marx'
the neoclassical, and Robinson's models has also been made by Marglin ar
Aoki (1973). Theirs are more sophisticated than ours, but the two a
essentially similar.

Section 6.3 compares these models to our model presented in chapter 5 and discusses why we believe the assumption of a corporate economy is fruitful.

To avoid tedious explanation, we will simplify the exposition as much as possible and either ignore technical details or relegate them to footnotes.

2   Four models: Marx, Solow, Robinson, and Kaldor

All these models ignore the role of corporate shares in the process of accumulation, either regarding firms as proprietorships (or partnerships) or assuming perfect arbitrage between real capital and financial assets. Hence the present value of a firm must always be equated to the value of its capital and, if as in these models the cost of investment is assumed not to exceed the value of the increment of capital caused by the investment, the rate of profit p must always equal the rate of interest i. (See section 4.1, particularly footnote 3.)

Let us assume that there exists a factor price frontier (FPF)[4], $w = w(p)$, with $w'(p) < 0$. This may be because there is a constant-returns-to-scale production function with perfect substitutability between labor and capital and each unit of every input receives the value of its marginal product,[5] or because there are multisectors and each sector has a fixed coefficient production function but the rate of profit is equated across sectors.[6] Or there may be no such thing as a production function but, nevertheless, there is some relationship between p and w, given the level of technology.[7] Whatever the reason, we assume that FPF exists, given the level of technology.

We now consider the balancing condition between saving and investment. Assume a two-class economy and a steady state as defined in section 4.2. Then Pasinetti's theorem holds; that is, $g = s_c p$. Or

This term is due to Samuelson (1962). Hicks (1965) called it "the wage equation."

See Burmeister and Dobell (1970, p. 14).

See Morishima (1973, p. 63). For the case of a simpler two sector see Allen (1967, p. 221).

As generally known, the most energetic advocate of this argument is Joan Robinson. See her famous 1953 paper or more recent 1975 paper. It does not seem, however, that she objects to FPF: "Technical conditions and the level of profits determine the level of money-prices relative to money-wage rates and so determine the level of real wages in terms of any basket of commodities" (Robinson, 1971, p. 47).

assume Kaldorian (Kaldor, 1956) saving behavior and that no savin̄
is made out of wages. This again leads to the condition, $g = s_c p$. In th
following we use this equation as the saving-investment balanciṅ
condition in any of the four models.[8]

Now we have a system of three equations:

$$p = i \tag{6.}$$

$$w = w(p), \qquad w'(p) < 0 \tag{6.}$$

$$g = s_c p \tag{6.}$$

But since we have four variables, p, i, w, and g, there must be
missing equation. Exactly here is what we consider to be the mo
important difference among the models. The rest of this sectio
discusses for each model what equation completes the system.

Let us begin with Marx's model. Marx's idea is that due to th
existence of what he called the reserve army of labor, capitalists explo

---

[8] This simplification, I am afraid, may obscure an important differen
between the neoclassical model and the Keynesian model. The neoclassica
as was shown by Samuelson and Modigliani (1966), would claim that
two-class economy is unstable and that the assumption of a one-cla
economy is more reasonable. Even under their assumption, however, it
possible to express the saving-investment balancing condition by a functio
that relates p to g: for (1) $g = S/K = sQ/K = sF(1, l)$, where the notation
as before, because of the saving-investment balancing condition; (
$p = F(1, l) - F_2(1, l)l$, where the right-hand side shows the margin
product of capital, because of the profit maximization behavior of firms; a
(3) by eliminating l from these two equations, one can obtain a relatio
between g and p such that $g = sf(p)$ with $f'(p) > 0$. Therefore, to subst
tute their condition by $g = s_c p$ hardly changes the character of the mode
except that s is replaced by s_c. It should be noted, however, that a mo
significant difference between the two models exists not in functional for
but in causality. In the neoclassical model, given g, l (namely, the techno
ogy to be used) is determined first and this in turn determines the fact
prices. In the Keynesian model, as shown by Pasinetti's theorem, given g,
is determined first, and then the technology is chosen given p so as
maximize profits. Nevertheless, this difference between the two seems
minor importance compared to the difference to be discussed later. For
similar view, see Stiglitz and Uzawa (1969, pp. 311–12). Marx's assump
tion on this problem is not necessarily clear but because he argues tha
workers receive only the subsistence wage rate, workers' saving rate must b
zero. Therefore it should be appropriate to use $g = s_c p$ as the condition i
Marx's model. See Morishima (1973, Part IV) for Marx's assumption o
saving behavior.

)rkers as much as possible and hence the wage rate w is depressed to
e subsistence level $\overline{w}$, which is supposedly given.[9] That is,

$$w = \overline{w} \tag{6.4}$$

nce w is thus determined, p is determined by FPF, and i is
termined at the same level. The level of saving is then determined at
$)K$, all of which is expended to accumulate real capital, for:
Accumulate, accumulate! That is Moses and the prophets!" (Marx,
'67, p. 595). However, in order to keep w from rising above $\overline{w}$, labor
mand must always be short of labor supply. It is for this reason that
Marx's model capitalism is supposed to be equipped with a
echanism that, whenever the rate of increase of labor demand
proaches that of labor supply, technical progress is induced to
duce the required amount of labor.[10] That is, using our previous
tation,

$$g \leq n + a(g) \tag{6.5}$$

here $a(g)$ is some function of g such that $a'(g) \geq 0$ for any g in the
propriate range.[11]
Solow's neoclassical model, on the contrary, presumes the full
nployment of labor, because "the real wage rate adjusts so that all
ailable labor is employed, and the marginal productivity equation
termines the wage rate which will actually rule" (Solow, 1956, p.
)). This of course comes from the belief behind the neoclassical
neral equilibrium theory that all prices in the economy adjust almost
stantaneously so that there is no excess demand in any market. If no

In Marx's own words, "the value of labour-power resolves itself into the
value of a definite quantity of the means of subsistence" (Marx, 1967, p.
172). The level of $\overline{w}$ would be dependent on "the climatic and other physical
conditions of his (worker's) country" (Marx, 1967, p. 171, my parentheses),
"the degree of civilization of a country" (Marx, 1967, p. 171), and probably
"the bargaining power of capitalists as a class and workers as a class"
(Robinson, 1966, p. 30), but "in a given country, at a given period, the
average quantity of the means of subsistence necessary for the labourer is
practically known" (Marx, 1967, p. 171).
"That is to say, the mechanism of capitalistic production so manages
matters that the absolute increase of capital is accompanied by no
corresponding rise in the general demand for labour" (Marx, 1967, p.
639). See also Robinson (1966, Chapter IV) and Sweezy (1942, Chapter
V).
Note that this could shift FPF over time.

technical progress is assumed,[12] therefore, the rates of increase of lab demand g and of labor supply n must be equated:

$$g = n \tag{6}$$

The prices are supposed to be so adjusted that just the amount saving required for the continuous full employment, nK, is made a invested in real capital. There is no such thing as an investme function, and it is assumed that investment always takes place by ju the amount saved.[13]

The major departure of the Keynesian model, particularly Robinson's model, lies exactly at this point, namely, how the level investment is determined. Robinson says that "investment in produ tive capital . . . is entirely governed by decisions of firms" (Robinso 1962, p. 36) and "whatever the rate of investment may be, the lev and the distribution of income must be such as to induce the firms a households, between them, to wish to carry out saving at an equ rate" (Robinson, 1962, p. 40), implying the reverse causality to t neoclassical model. Then, how is the level of investment by fir determined? It is for this purpose that she introduces the notion of t "animal spirits" function, which is "a function relating the desired r of growth of the stock of productive capital to the expected level profits" (Robinson, 1962, p. 38). Hence we have the followi equation:

$$g = g(p) \tag{6}$$

where $g'(p) > 0$ because "to sustain a higher rate of accumulati requires a higher level of profits, both because it offers more favou able odds in the gamble and because it makes finance more read available" (Robinson, 1962, p. 37). Then, equation (6.7) and t balancing condition (6.3) jointly determine the equilibrium values o and p. Obviously, this equilibrium growth rate must satisfy the sa

[12] The neoclassical growth model has never treated technical progress more than manna from heaven. Such exogenous technical progress, neutral, can be easily introduced into the model. See Allen (1967, Chap 13).

[13] Stiglitz and Uzawa (1969) say that "the government, through moneta and fiscal policy, takes action to ensure that the level of investm (required to sustain full employment) does in fact take place" (p. 311, parentheses). It seems to me more appropriate to say that this is becau the neoclassical has never taken into consideration the separation betwe ownership and management and between investment decision and savi decision.

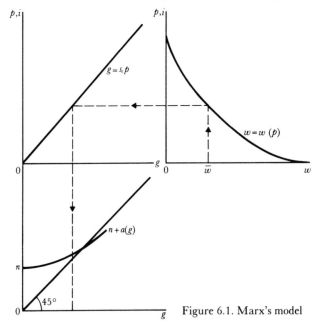

Figure 6.1. Marx's model

nstraint as in Marx's model with respect to the availability of labor.
ı this regard, she says that "when the urge to accumulate ('animal
ɔirits') is high relative to the growth of the labour force, technical
ɔrogress has a tendency to raise the 'natural' rate of growth to make
ɔom for it, so that near-enough steady growth, with near-enough full
ɔployment may be realized" (Robinson, 1963, p. 410, her paren-
ɩeses). Hence equation (6.5) again holds.

Kaldor (1957) completes his system by assuming what he called the
ɩechnical production function," which explains the rate of growth of
ɩbor productivity, $[d(Q/N)/dt]/(Q/N) \equiv \dot{Q}/Q - n$, as a function
ɔf the growth rate of capital per worker, $[d(K/N)/dt]/(K/N) \equiv$
$\dot{}/K - n$; that is, $\dot{Q}/Q - n = \chi(\dot{K}/K - n)$.[14] Specifically, he
ɩsumes that $\chi(0) > 0$, $\chi'(\dot{K}/K - n) > 0$ and $\chi''(\dot{K}/K - n) < 0$,
ɔcause "the more capital is increased, the more labour-saving techni-
ɩl improvements can be adopted, though there is likely to be some
ɩaximum beyond which the rate of growth in productivity could not
ɔ raised, however fast capital is being accumulated" (Kaldor, 1957,

Kaldor later modified this function along a vintage model: see Kaldor and
Mirrlees (1962).

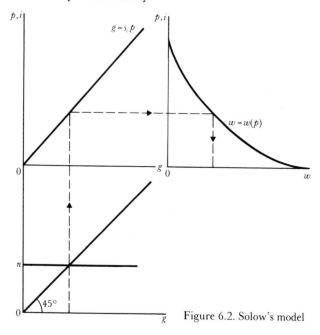

Figure 6.2. Solow's model

p. 596). At a steady state where $\dot{Q}/Q = \dot{K}/K = g$,[15] therefore,

$$g = \chi(g - n) + n \tag{6.}$$

Given n, equation (6.8) determines the equilibrium value of g and th
with equations (6.1) to (6.3), in turn, determines the prices and th
distribution of income.

The four models are now complete. Each model consists of fou
equations with four variables, g, p, i, and w, and possibly a
inequality. In spite of the alteration in only a single equation, the
four models reflect quite different views of a capitalist economy an
have quite different mechanisms to determine the equilibrium, a
illustrated in Figures 6.1 to 6.4. Arrows are used in the diagrams t
make the difference in causality clear.

6.3   The model of the growth of a corporate economy

It is my strong belief that no model can explain the modern econom
growth satisfactorily without introducing the idea of a corpora

[15] An investment function is introduced in Kaldor's model so that this stea
state is realized in the long run.

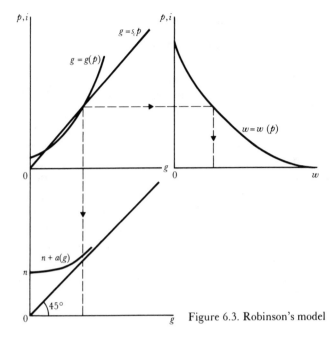

Figure 6.3. Robinson's model

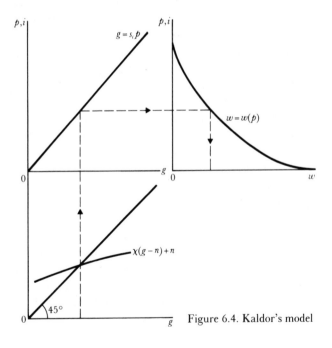

Figure 6.4. Kaldor's model

economy, where, as repeatedly argued, ownership and managemer are separated, the decisions to invest in real capital and to save an purchase financial assets such as corporate shares are separately mad entries to industries are not unlimited because of the highly sophisti cated skill required in management, and management possesse substantial discretionary power due to the imperfectness of the device such as takeovers to control it. Unless this fact is precisely grasped an formulated, a model of economic growth cannot take into consideratio the enormous role that firms – corporations – play in the process of modern economic growth. In this sense one may say that Marx's mode and Solow's neoclassical model may be appropriate in the econom where savers, wealth owners, and managers are identical, as in the er before corporations became the dominant form of firms, but not i modern economy. The Keynesians such as Robinson, on the othe hand, have been aware of the importance of the role that firms play i the process of economic growth. Nevertheless, the Keynesians als failed to incorporate the idea of a corporate economy; as a result thei models are not convincing. For example, Robinson's animal spirit function does not appear convincing in that although a higher rate of profit may mean greater incentive to investment as argued by Robin son, it also implies a higher rate of interest (because $p = i$) and hence larger cost of capital for firms, which should mean a smaller incentiv to investment. In fact, from our equation, $v = (p - \psi)/(i - g)$, whic holds whenever g, ψ, p, and i are constant over time (section 3.2), i should be obvious that $v = 1$ for any g if $g = \psi$ and $p = i$ for any g Hence under the assumptions of equality between the rate of profi and the rate of interest and the absence of the cost of adjusting the stoc of capital, the valuation ratio equals unity for any growth rate implying that there is no finite and unique optimal growth rate for firm whether it maximizes the valuation ratio or the growth rate. I other words, for an optimal growth rate to exist, v cannot be equal to for any g.

Then, how can v not always equal unity? It is here that ou assumption of a corporate economy, particularly of barriers for ordi nary shareholders to enter industries, proves to be so effective. Were i not for this assumption, the conclusion should be inevitable tha arbitrage between shares and real capital takes place whenever diverges from unity so that v is constrained to be unity for any growth rate. In addition, our theory has assumed that either p or ψ is function of g with a nontrivial second derivative so that v depends on such a manner that there exists a value g^{**} of g that maximizes v and $\partial v/\partial g < 0$ for any $g > g^{**}$, the relation having been called the v-g frontier. The optimal growth rate is then determined, whether the management is a value maximizer or a growth maximizer, depending on i and on factors such as w that determine p for any g. Accordingly, the optimal level of investment is determined as a function of the rate of interest and the wage rate. Of course this is nothing but the investment function, which supposedly plays a major role in the Keynesian system. That is, here we have provided a microeconomic rationale to the Keynesian model. At the same time, in our model all the markets are cleared in the general equilibrium and so the full employment of labor is always realized. In this sense the result is common with Solow's neoclassical model.[16] Interestingly, therefore, the assumed difference between the Keynesian and neoclassical models is mostly resolved in our framework of a corporate economy.

The analysis of research activity by firms does not appear fruitful either, unless the idea of a corporate economy is adopted, for if there were no optimal growth rate for the firm, how could one conceive of an optimal rate of technical progress? Moreover, if a firm invents a superior technology, this should immediately form a barrier to entry, unless new technology is assumed to be freely disseminated to any existing or potential rival, which means that the assumption of perfect competition with free entry is consistent with the phenomenon of technical progress only if no appropriability is assumed with respect to technical knowledge. But if the latter is true, then how can firms have any incentive to spend for research activity?[17] This again suggests that to analyze research activity one needs to assume the existence of barriers to entry as our model of a corporate economy does. Our model has assumed that firms can monopolize the benefits from their research activity and hence have an ample incentive to undertake research

---

This should save Robinson from her dubious argument on the realization of "near-enough full employment." In this respect, one should note that even Kaldor, supposedly a Keynesian, says that "it does not therefore seem unrealistic to assume that capitalist economies operate under full-employment conditions in all such periods when capital is accumulating and the national income is growing" (Kaldor, 1957, p. 595).

This explains why existing analyses of the role of inventive activity in economic growth assume a monopolist (Shell, 1973), independent inventors from whom every firm buys patents (Nordhaus, 1969a), or a government (Shell, 1967; Uzawa, 1965) as a sole producer of technical knowledge.

activity. We have, then, shown that the desired rate of increase of labor productivity is determined as a function of the growth rate and prices and have constructed a macroeconomic growth model based on this function. Our model thus embodies Marx's and Robinson's idea of the dependence of the macroeconomic rate of increase of labor supply in efficiency units on the desired rate of accumulation of capital, but with a microeconomic rationale that neither Marx nor Robinson provided.

In sum, the assumption of a corporate economy makes our model distinct from others. The introduction of this assumption opens up several possibilities that other models have failed to capture: Micro-economic analysis can be combined with macroeconomic analysis quite consistently, both the neoclassical and Keynesian ideas can be reconciled, Marx's and Robinson's idea of innovation to increase labor supply in efficiency units can be given a microeconomic rationale, and so forth. As a result of these features of our model, the equilibrium growth rate has been shown to be affected by factors such as management preference, which has been completely neglected by other models. This could be a powerful tool in analyzing international differences in the rate of economic growth; for instance, Japan's rapid economic growth may be explained more appropriately. This is the topic of the next chapter.

CHAPTER 7

Empirical relevance:
Japan's economic growth

Now that we have presented our basic model of economic growth and discussed its theoretical advantage over other models, it is only appropriate that we consider here its practical applicability. Our particular subject is the rapid growth of the Japanese economy in comparison with the economic growth of other countries, specifically the United States. The purpose of this study, however, is confined to an application of our model of economic growth and is not intended to be a comprehensive study of the mechanism behind Japan's economic growth.[1]

.1 The facts

"Miracle" is the word that has often been used to describe the unusually high rate of economic growth in post-World War II Japan. The comparison with other advanced countries may justify this use of the word. Denison and Chung (1976, p. 42) report that the annual growth rate of total national income[2] amounted to 8.81 percent in Japan (1953-71), more than double the figure, 4.00 percent, for the United States (1948-69). Even in West Germany (1950-62), which recorded the highest rate among the United States, Canada, and eight European countries investigated, it was 6.27 percent, less than three quarters of Japan's rate.

It is true that Japan's economic growth slowed down in the 1970s, particularly after the oil crisis of 1973. The annual rate of growth of

For the latter purpose, two collections of papers may be recommended to English-speaking readers: a special issue on postwar Japan, *The Developing Economies* (1970) and Patrick and Rosovsky, eds., *Asia's New Giant* (1976).

The rate quoted is what Denison and Chung (1976) called the standardized growth rate and has been adjusted for the difference among countries in deflation procedures, and so on. See Denison and Chung (1976, p. 40, Table 4-7) for the derivation of this standardized rate.

manufacturing output, for example, declined to 4.1 percent in 1973–7 from 12.7 percent of 1960–73. Still, however, it remained as the faste growing among major O.E.C.D. countries because of more or le similar decline in the rate in other countries. It declined from 4.8 to 1 percent in the United States, from 5.3 to 1.7 percent in West German and from 7.3 to 2.7 percent in France.[3] This suggests that Japan rapid economic growth was not a passing phenomenon. Nor is entirely attributable to the postwar reconstruction or to the catchu effect, namely, catching up to advanced countries with the help of the superior technologies and know-hows.

Let us now investigate the factors to account for this difference in th economic growth performance between Japan and other countrie particularly the United States. First, consider the rate of increase population or of employment. As mentioned in the previous chapte this is the only source of difference in the equilibrium growth rate i the naïve Solow model and is also one in our model. A look at the fac shows that this, however, can hardly be the cause of the larg difference in the growth rate. Japan's annual rate of populatio increase in the period was 1.1 percent,[4] which may be slightly larg than that for the United States, but evidently the difference is far le than what could be considered the major factor accounting for th difference in the growth rate of total national income. Employmen Denison and Chung (1976, pp. 55–6) report, increased in the sam period with the annual rate of 1.49 percent in Japan and 1.55 percer in the United States, surprisingly showing a faster increase in th United States than in Japan. This result is reversed once the change i age-sex composition and education is taken into account, for the rat then becomes 1.85 percent for Japan, larger than the 1.30 percent fc the United States. The difference (0.55 percent), however, is still fa less than 4.81 percent, the difference in the growth rate of income.

How about the propensity to save? For this we find a significar difference between Japan and the United States. The household savin ratio – net household saving as the percentage of household disposabl

---

[3] Organization for Economic Cooperation and Development, *Econom Surveys: United Kingdom* (Paris: Organization for Economic Cooperatio and Development, February 1980), p. 26.
[4] Denison and Chung (1976, p. 1).

ncome – was 22.0 in Japan, compared to 6.9 in the United States.[5,6] Thus it is consistent with the predicted positive effect of the saving propensity on economic growth. Strictly speaking, however, it is the saving rate of capitalists and not that of entire households that is supposed to play an important role in our model. Unfortunately, no data are available concerning the saving rate of capitalists and we can only make a rough estimate. In Japan the saving rate of wage earners and salaried employees was around 20 percent, only about 2 percent lower than that of entire households;[7] hence the saving rate of capitalists must be larger, but probably not much, than that of households. For the United States, it has been estimated that the saving propensity out of capital gains is 0.9 to 1.0; out of dividends, 0.5 to 0.7; and out of labor income, 0.02 to 0.05 (Arena, 1965 and Sato, 1971, as quoted in Moore, 1973, p. 537). Thus we may estimate that the saving rate of capitalists, to whom capital gains and dividends are the only income, is significantly larger than that of households in the United States. From these facts, it seems reasonable to assume that the difference in the saving rate of capitalists between Japan and the United States is not so large as that in the household saving ratio (or it may be that the United States has a larger saving rate of capitalists than Japan). Therefore, although the high saving propensity in Japan might be one of the reasons for the rapid economic growth, it unlikely is the only reason.

The remaining factor that is supposed to affect the equilibrium growth rate in our model is z, the index of management preference toward growth. This is exactly the factor that we consider to be the most important in explaining Japan's rapid economic growth. Thus our hypothesis is that Japan has achieved a higher rate of economic

Organization for Economic Cooperation and Development, *Economic Surveys: Japan* (Paris: Organization for Economic Cooperation and Development, July 1979). The quoted figure is the average of the ratios for each year between 1973 and 1977. In France the ratio was 17.0 and in Germany, 14.2, consistent with the ranking in terms of the rate of economic growth. However, the larger ratio, 25.0, in Italy than in Japan is inconsistent with Italy's lower growth rate than Japan, France, and Germany.

Why the personal saving rate was (and is) so large in Japan has been the subject of many studies. See Komiya (1966) and Mizoguchi (1970).

Japan, Office of Prime Minister, Bureau of Statistics, *Family Saving Survey 1978* (Tokyo: Printing Bureau of the Ministry of Finance, 1979).

growth than any other country because management preference of Japanese firms was (and probably still is) more inclined toward the growth of the firms than management preference in other countries. We will attempt to substantiate this hypothesis in the next section.

Before closing here, let us inquire whether the condition, $\xi = a$, has actually been satisfied as our model predicts. In Japan the rate of increase of real hourly earnings was about 6.3 percent in the period 1955–68, if deflated by the retail price index.[8] In the United States, it was about 2.4 percent in the period 1948–69.[9] Since $a = g - n$, the rate of increase of labor productivity was 6.96 (= 8.81 − 1.85) percent in Japan (1953–71), whereas it was 2.7 (= 4.00 − 1.30) percent in the United States (1948–69). Therefore, as the model predicts, the rate of increase of real wage rate was roughly equal to the rate of increase of labor productivity in both countries.

7.2   Management preference in Japan: more growth than market value

As shown in Chapter 2 and section 3.5, there are two factors that determine the shape of management preference; management preference per se, namely, the preference without regard to any external constraint, and the strength of external constraints such as the threat of takeovers. There are evidences that the environment surrounding the Japanese management is such that the preference for growth is enhanced in both aspects. Several of them are listed in the following.

7.2.1   Industrial organization

In Chapter 1 the industrial organizations of both Japan and the United States were discussed in detail. We found that in every aspect relevant to our definition of corporate economy – the dominance of the corporation (joint-stock company) as a form of business, the importance of large-scale corporations in economic activity, the diversification within them, the separation of ownership from control, and the motives for management – the two countries are quite alike. Without

---

[8] Kaneko (1970, p. 461). The rate was 9.7 percent if deflated by the wholesale price index.

[9] Calculated from the data in the U.S. Dept. of Labor, *Monthly Labor Review*. The rate was 3.4 percent if deflated by the wholesale price index.

further word, therefore, we conclude that the Japanese economy is a corporate economy in our sense as much as, if not more than, that of the United States.

7.2.2 Psychological factors

There seem to exist in Japan psychological factors that make pecuniary objects such as profits and market value less important and conspicuous objects such as growth and sales more important. One can see this from the following observation made by an American businessman, which is perhaps somewhat exaggerated but mostly accurate.[10]

> One of the prime motivations in Japanese life, face saving is very much in the mind of Japanese management. That is why maintenance of volume of sales becomes more important to managers than profit on sales. It is the volume of sales and the "size" of the enterprise that are emphasized, for these are quantitative and may be used to make the management's "face" bigger, while profit on sales will perhaps never been mentioned by managers. [Adams, 1969, p. 75.]

7.2.3 Employment system

The one practice in the Japanese economy that is the most distinctive from the American or European practices and has been the object of intellectual curiosity by many foreigners is Japan's employment system. Therefore it is natural to ask how this employment system affects the economic behavior. The most prominent features of Japan's employment system are perhaps lifetime permanent employment and the seniority wage system, which apply not only to blue-collar workers but also to white-collar workers. The former refers to the fact that usually an employee is hired by a firm directly from school and stays at the same firm until the age of compulsory retirement. The latter refers to the system of wage payment, whereby earnings are related mostly to length of service with the firm. How this system operates and what its consequences are have been discussed by many and will not be covered here.[11] Instead, we will confine our analysis to the effect of this system

---

[10] According to Caves and Uekusa (1976, p. 7), "the pursuit of profit, like the activity of selling, has never been held in high esteem in Japan." This agrees with Adams.
[11] See, for instance, Galenson (1976).

on management choice between growth and market value. There are both economic and noneconomic (psychological or sociological) reasons to speculate that Japan's employment system has contributed to a preference inclined more toward growth on the side of management.

Abegglen (1973)[12] argued that Japan's employment system has a consequence that the faster a firm grows, the lower its average labor cost is. He reached this conclusion for two reasons. First,

> the company that is growing rapidly . . . is hiring large numbers of personnel directly from school. This addition of young workers directly from school to the work force lowers the average age of the force of the successful and growing company or industry. Thereby the average cost of labor for the company or industry is reduced, . . . (Abegglen, 1973, p. 31)

for under the seniority wage system the lower the age of the worker the smaller the compensation he receives.[13] Second,

> when the choice of company is a career choice, and essentially irrevocable, a man is likely to be thoughtful indeed in deciding which company he will join. . . . To the extent that he is perceptive and careful in his decision, he will seek to join a firm and an industry that has the widest choice of the best men in its recruiting, the process again reinforcing the successful firm and working against the interests of the less successful firm, . . . [Abegglen, 1973, p. 32]

where the successful firm is more likely to mean the faster growing firm rather than the firm with larger profits because growth is more conspicuous than profits and because potential recruits are most concerned with whether they will be in a big company and in a decent position when they become senior members of the firm. These two facts thus imply that the faster the firm grows, the lower its average labor cost is and the more likely new employees are of good quality. Therefore even a value-maximizing management would choose a growth rate larger than the rate that should have maximized the value were it not for this employment system. Although, analytically, this

---

[12] This is the revised version of his *The Japanese Factory,* published in 1958, which earned quite a popularity both in the United States and in Japan. Inevitably, the book has been the target of several criticisms. See, for example, Cole (1971, 1972), although Cole does not deny the quoted part of Abegglen's thesis.

[13] See also Chao (1968).

may mean that we should make the wage rate dependent on the growth rate and maximize the value rather than choose a growth rate larger than the value-maximizing rate under the constancy of the wage rate, the result should not be much different between the two analyses.

The second consequence of Japan's employment system is more psychological and sociological. As a result of lifetime employment, workers in a firm are more likely to identify the interest of the firm with theirs and, even if they do not agree with a given goal of the firm, they would rather stay in the firm and attempt to influence the goal than to quit. In this regard, the situation perfectly coincides with Galbraith's description of the motivation of the technostructure: "so it can be reasonably concluded that identification – the voluntary exchange of one's goals for the preferable ones of organization – and adaptation – the association with organization in the hope of influencing its goals to accord more closely with one's own – are strong motivating forces in the technostructure and become increasingly so in the inner circles" (Galbraith, 1967, p. 162). Such technostructure, as we have already discussed (section 1.6), seeks more than anything else the opportunities for promotions and appointments and the resulting expansion of itself. Of course this expansion can be attained only through the growth – in the volume of sales, capital, and employees – of the firm.

The creation of new openings for promotions as the advantage of rapid growth is particularly important in Japanese firms. Because of lifetime employment and the practice of internal promotion, an employee is supposed to be promoted to a higher rank as he gets older. Hence if unable to be promoted to a decent post, he is quite likely to lose *face,* which is the least bearable pain to the worker under the Japanese system of value judgment, as witnessed by Adams (see the quotation in the previous subsection). The boss will also lose face by not being able to offer him a decent post. Needless to say, the faster the firm grows, the more openings it can create and, therefore, the less likely this uncomfortable situation occurs. In this regard, too, the employment system in Japan tends to foster the pursuit of growth at the sacrifice of the value of the firms.

The immobility of workers and the practice of internal promotion is common even in the United States. In fact, it is more common than is usually thought. According to a study by one of the world's largest executive recruiters, Korn/Ferry International, quoted in *Newsweek*

(June 18, 1979, p. 50), it was found in a survey of 3,600 senior-level executives (excluding presidents) working at several hundred of the nation's largest companies that "the average senior vice president has worked for the same company for nearly twenty years." Still, however, there should be no doubt that in the United States top managements are more often recruited from outside the companies than is the case in Japan. The consequence of the practice of outside recruitment is just the reverse of the consequence of internal promotion previously discussed and is twofold. First, executives are tempted to prove themselves as able and competent in a short period so that they are offered jobs with more responsibilities and more compensations before their present tenures expire. (Academic jobs are no exception!). Inevitably, they seek short-run achievements, most usually short-run profits, and not growth which may be justly evaluated only after, say, ten years. Secondly, employees in lower ranks find their opportunities for promotion narrowed and try to obtain better paying jobs outside their present companies to maximize their lifetime incomes. As a result, identification and adaptation of the interests of employees to those of their companies, to use Galbraith's terms, occur rarely and the pressure for faster growth from lower rank employees to the top management is weaker. In both respects, therefore, we expect management preference toward growth to be weaker in countries such as the United States, characterized by relatively more frequent recruitment of top officers from outside, than in countries such as Japan, characterized almost exclusively by internal promotion.

7.2.4   Takeovers

It probably goes without saying that Japan's employment system makes takeovers by outsiders extremely difficult. Because Japanese workers regard the firm they work for as a solid and rather autonomous organization of which they are members and because they identify its goals with theirs, they will furiously reject any invasion by outside raiders. This apparently raises the cost, the time, and the risk of a takeover and inevitably reduces the profitability of a takeover Perhaps this explains why takeovers have been so rare in Japan Although the rare occurrence of takeovers in Japan may be partly attributable to the fact that takeover bids (tender offers) had not been legal for years, they have still been quite infrequent in Japan even after 1971 when takeover bids were legalized. Therefore it seems more

easonable to attribute the rarity of takeovers to the employment
;ystem rather than to the legal factor.[14]

7.2.5 Business groupings

\nother unique feature of the Japanese economy is the existence of
)usiness groupings, such as Mitsubishi, Mitsui, and Sumitomo. Busi-
1ess groupings are not necessarily easy to define or to characterize
)ecause, unlike conglomerates in the United States, firms in any
;rouping are not tied by majority shareholding. I once defined a
)usiness grouping by the following three characteristics: (1) it is a
;roup of a number of firms and is diversified as a whole; (2) any
nember of the group is independently making its decision but once a
:onflict arises between member firms, the group as a whole mediates
(not necessarily successfully) between them; and (3) any information is
,oluntarily exchanged within the group (Odagiri, 1975, p. 145). How
;uch groupings act, what the actual groupings are like, and what effect
hey have on the national economy would require an entire book to
answer and thus will not be discussed here.[15] Odagiri (1975) argued

[14] The first and perhaps only T.O.B. after its legalization was made in 1972
by Bendix Corporation of the United States against the Jidosha Kiki
Company. It was said, however, that this T.O.B. was made under the
agreement of the management of Jidosha Kiki. This incident shows that in
Japan the agreement of the victim is quite important for a successful
takeover. It should also be noted that mergers under the peaceful agreement of both sides are as common in Japan as in the United States.

[15] For English-speaking readers, Hadley (1970) gives an excellent account of
business groupings. See particularly its Chapter 11. *Business Week* (1975),
which dealt with one of the most prominent groupings, *Sumitomo*, may be
a more readable introduction to this subject. Caves and Uekusa (1976) also
has a chapter on it. A comment on the terminology may be in order. A
grouping is usually called *kigyo-shudan* in Japan, which literally means
nothing but a group of firms. The words, *zaibatsu* and *keiretsu* have also
been used to describe grouping. However, *zaibatsu* is the word for a group
of firms completely controlled by the parent company that existed in
prewar Japan but is quite different from the present-day *kigyo-shudan*,
even though most of the latter are the descendants of the former. *Keiretsu*,
on the other hand, is more often used to describe a group that has a central
firm that usually controls other firms in the group through shareholdings
or bank loans. Toyota group is an example of it, with Toyota Motor
Company controlling miscellaneous firms such as producers of auto parts.
It is therefore inappropriate to use the word *zaibatsu* or *keiretsu* in place of
kigyo-shudan. Since "a group of firms" may sound too general, we
followed Hadley's terminology, "a business grouping."

that a firm belongs to a business grouping because it has the effect of shifting its v-g frontier upward and reducing its $\bar{v}$, the minimum valuation ratio to prevent a takeover, owing to the exchange of information within the grouping, preferential trading among the member firms, joint ventures among the member firms, and the mutual shareholding. He empirically confirmed this hypothesis by comparing the values of the valuation ratio and the growth rate between member firms, namely, those firms belonging to the Mitsui, Mitsubishi, or Sumitomo group, and comparable nonmember firms, namely, those firms not belonging to any of these groups but comparable to the member firms in terms of size and industrial classification. His findings were that there is little difference in the average valuation ratio between the two types of firms but that the average growth rate of the member firms was found to exceed that of the nonmember firms in most of the tests performed, although the difference was not statistically significant in most instances (Odagiri, 1974, 1975).[16] It may be concluded, therefore, that the business groupings have the effect of encouraging management preference toward growth.

All the previous evidences suggest that the peculiar features of Japan's economy encourage the management to pursue faster growth. More precisely, it is expected that Japan's management chooses a higher growth rate and a lower market value of the firm than its American counterpart if both are subject to the same v-g frontier. In terms of our notation, this of course means that z has been (and probably still is) larger in Japan than in the United States.

7.3   Application of the model and some qualifications

The foregoing analysis suggests that the Japanese economy is characterized by about the same n, a somewhat larger s_c, and a definitely larger z, compared to the U.S. economy. If our model of economic growth with research activity is an accurate description of both the Japanese and U.S. economies, then we should expect a higher growth

---

[16] Caves and Uekusa (1976, pp. 72–83), to analyze the effect of business groupings on the performance of the member firms empirically, regressed the rate of profit to several variables including a dummy variable that separates member firms from nonmember firms. However, it is the growth rate that should be treated as the dependent variable as Odagiri's result shows. It is no wonder, therefore, that the relation turned out insignificant.

ate of national income in Japan than in the United States. The rate of
ncrease of labor productivity should also be larger in Japan. These
redictions are perfectly consistent with actual findings. This consis-
2ncy, to emphasize again, is only obtained when research activity and
1e resulting technical progress are explicitly taken into account under
1e framework of a corporate economy. Robinson may explain this by
1ying that the animal spirit of Japan's management was stronger
1an that of the United States, but it may be a mere tautology as our
riticism in Chapter 6 revealed.

It should be pointed out, however, that several factors neglected so
1r in this study may have been affecting the process of Japan's
conomic growth as well. We now discuss some of them.

.3.1   Importation of technology

t has been argued often that Japan could enjoy the rapid increase in
roductivity because of the advanced technology imported from the
Jnited States and other countries. However, as Peck (1976, p. 532)
uts it, "the usual emphasis on importing technology tends to obscure
1e fact that the Japanese economy is research intensive." That is, even
1ough Japan could borrow ready-made technology, it still had to
pend a considerable amount of resources to adapt such imported
2chnology. Now suppose that due to the importation the marginal cost
f increasing the rate of increase of labor productivity, $\phi'(a)$, is smaller.
'hen, this increases the level of a given i, w, and g (see equation (5.9)),
·hich implies an upward shift of the LL curve in Figure 5.1; hence the
quilibrium growth rate is larger, the equilibrium wage rate is lower,
1e equilibrium rate of interest is higher, and the equilibrium rate of
2chnical progress is larger. This we find to be consistent with Japan's
xperience.

.3.2   Labor supply

·nother factor that has often been mentioned as contributing to
apan's economic growth is the flexibility of the labor supply. It is not
1at substantial unemployment existed nor that the rate of increase of
·opulation was high, although some researchers have referred to the
·igh birthrate immediately after World War II as a factor responsible
·r increasing labor supply.[17] In fact, unemployment in the true sense

' See Ohkawa and Rosovsky (1965, p. 84) and Galenson (1976, p. 590).

of the word has never been a serious problem in Japan since th Korean War boom of 1950–51. More importantly, however, th flexibility in labor supply was provided through the shift of worke from the agricultural sector and the low productivity manufacturin sector to the more advanced manufacturing sector, as well as the shi of self-employed workers to wage earners and salaried employees.[18] A a result, the labor market was not very tight, despite the high rate increase of labor demand in the high productivity manufacturin sector. This was especially true in the early stage of the postwa economic growth, which probably explains why the wage rate ha been lower in Japan than in the United States, in spite of ou prediction that $\partial w^0 / \partial z > 0$ (see Table 5.2).

7.3.3 The role of government

The role of government may well have been very important in th process of Japan's economic growth. As Ackley (1976, p. 24 observed, "the primary objective of Japanese economic policy wa rapid growth of output and real income. The basic concern was . . . n with the full realization of potential output, but with the faste possible growth of potential and then of actual output." To this en three types of policy appear to have been effective: (1) maintainin artificially low rates of interest to stimulate private investment an rationing funds to deal with the inevitable excess demand in financi markets,[19] (2) giving definite goals and predictions to both public an private sectors by means of successive economic planning,[20] and (3 avoiding "excessive" competition and protecting against foreign invad ers by means of "administrative guidance" by the Ministry of Interna tional Trade and Industry (MITI).[21] Assessment of these policies

---

[18] See Kaneko (1970, pp. 452–61) and Galenson (1976, pp. 589–93).

[19] See Kawaguchi (1970) and Wallich and Wallich (1976). For all th policy, Japan's rate of interest has been somewhat larger than that of th United States. In the period 1956–68 the interest rate on bank loans large firms in Japan was 6 to 8 percent (Kawaguchi, 1970, p. 405 whereas the interest rate on corporate Aaa bonds in the United States wa 3 to 6 percent (Duesenberry, 1972, p. 30). This suggests that were it not fc the low interest rate policy the equilibrium rate of interest in Japan woul have been much higher than that in the United States, coinciding with ou prediction that $\partial i^0 / \partial z > 0$.

[20] See Miyazaki (1970).

[21] See Caves and Uekusa (1976, pp. 53–6).

either an easy task nor the main purpose of the present study. In addition, our analytical tool is inadequate for this purpose because the model we have discussed so far neglects the role of government. Perhaps all we can say is that these policies, by enhancing the optimistic expectation on the side of management and reducing uncertainty and risk concerning the future and also the threat of invasion by outsiders, contributed to the pursuit of faster growth by the management.

4   Summary and concluding remarks

We have shown in this chapter that Japan's unusually rapid economic growth after World War II can be explained quite consistently with our model of economic growth as a result of the pursuit of growth by the management among other things, although some caution and qualifications are in order. We have also argued that such an explanation is not possible if the conventional theories of economic growth are to be adopted. Ironically, although not surprisingly, our viewpoint has been totally neglected in most academic literature, whereas it has not been uncommon in nonacademic publications.

Needless to say, the empirical relevance of the present theory of economic growth is not confined to Japan and the United States but is applicable to any capitalist economy possessing those characteristics of a corporate economy as defined in this book. As an example we can think of the contrast between West Germany and the United Kingdom. In many respects such as the extent of interfirm mobility of workers and of internal promotion, as opposed to outside recruitment, the grouping of firms, and the frequency of takeovers, Germany appears more akin to Japan whereas the United Kingdom appears more akin to the United States. German managements, therefore, may be said to be more growth oriented than those in the United Kingdom and the United States. This conjecture perfectly agrees with the following observation by Vogl (1973, p. 95, my parentheses added): "the only reason why such a rigid system (of hierarchy and promotion) has not produced major problems is that most German companies have been expanding at such a rapid pace over the last two decades, that it has been no problem to promote people on to better salary levels and give them more impressive titles at a swift pace." This of course means that we should assign a large value of z to Germany and a smaller value to the United Kingdom or the United States, and with our theory we should expect faster economic growth in Germany than in th United Kingdom or the United States, which surely is quite consisten with the fact.

Finally, it is noted that the causes of Japan's rapid economic growt as discussed in this chapter are markedly different from the conven tional (liberal, neoclassical, or whatever) wisdom. Conventionally, has been thought that to achieve a better allocation of resources an faster economic growth (although that the first does not imply th second has been frequently overlooked) (1) labor mobility should k maximized so that an efficient allocation of labor across industries an firms is realized, (2) owner control of firms should be maintained so a not to permit "wasteful" discretionary behavior of the managemen (3) capital markets should be frictionless so that a firm run by "poor management is taken over by someone with "better" manageria ability, and (4) grouping firms and holding shares mutually amon firms should be prohibited or at least restricted to prevent th concentration of economic power in a few hands. These, we have bee taught, are necessary to achieve a Pareto-optimal allocation c resources in an economy, and this thesis has been supposed to be tru even in dynamic contexts, namely, in the course of economic growth.

In view of our analysis in this chapter, however, every one of these likely to lower the choice by management of the rate of growth of th firm and, as a consequence, the rate of economic growth of the countr That is, even though these conventional policies may be effective i attaining a higher *level* of income, as the fundamental theorem c welfare economics teaches, they are not only ineffective but may we be harmful in attaining a higher *rate of increase* of income.

This is quite antineoclassical. It should surprise and perplex thos who have been accustomed to teach economics courses based on th superiority of competitive, mobile, and frictionless markets and th doctrine of "the invisible hand." It presents a serious dilemma in term of policymaking: For a better resource allocation in a static sense an less concentration of economic power, a set of policies are recom mended; for faster economic growth, a set of almost opposite policie may be recommended. Furthermore, how a policy affects an econom is probably not universal. For instance, making takeovers costly ma contribute to a higher degree of management preference towar growth and, consequently, more rapid economic growth in countrie such as Japan but may well result in an inefficient management (i.e strictly inside the v-g frontier) with excess capacity and excess labor i

untries with limited competition and weaker vocational ethics.[22] To
proceed further to give specific policy recommendations on these
matters, therefore, requires a detailed inquiry into the business environment of the economy in its broadest sense, including historical,
sociological, and psychological aspects.

It is noted that, in several aspects not discussed here, the Japanese economy
may be competitive – possibly, more competitive than the U.S. economy.
Competition at product markets and intrafirm competition among
employees are the examples. This fact will be elaborated elsewhere,
however.

PART IV

Fiscal and monetary policy

CHAPTER 8

Fiscal policy in a moneyless economy

1 Introduction

We will now discuss the policy implications of our theory of growth of corporate economy. That is, we ask what a government can do to achieve faster economic growth in an economy with barriers to enter the corporate sector and the separation of ownership from control. More specifically, should the government increase government expenditure over time? How should it be financed – through taxation or new issue of money? If taxation, what is the combination of corporate and personal taxes that is least harmful to a growing economy? What are the implications of these alternative policies to inflation? Does inflation contribute to economic growth by stimulating investment or is it harmful?

No one will doubt the importance of these questions. Economic growth is one of the most important and perhaps most conspicuous achievements of a country, and there is hardly a day when the government, journalists, businessmen or economists do not talk about the growth rate of national income. Economic growth, as a consequence, has been of high priority among policy goals for most countries, not only for Japan and West Germany, where their completely destroyed production equipment needed urgent restoration after World War II but also for other capitalist economies as well as socialist economies. Several policies have been undertaken in many countries toward this goal: tax credit to investment; government investment to increase production such as building plants and, more indirectly, building infrastructures to help production activity of the private sector; governmental support of research activity; and so on. Without doubt, analyzing the effectiveness of these policies toward economic growth is an important task of economists.

Our analysis so far has been confined to an economy without government. We will now incorporate governmental activity in our model in order to address ourselves to these policy questions. First, in

this chapter we introduce the government but still confine our analy
to an economy where corporate shares are the only type of financi
assets and there is neither money nor bonds. In this econom
therefore, government revenue comes only from taxation. Second,
Chapter 9, we add a money market into the model to allow for the ca
where the government issues new money to pay for its expenditure.

Other than these modifications, the model maintains the san
characteristics as before: There are a fixed and finite number
identical firms; individuals in the noncorporate sector do not ha
sufficient managerial ability to enter the corporate sector; the manag
ment utility depends on the growth of the firm as well as on the mark
value; there are two classes in the noncorporate sector – workers ar
capitalists – who are both rational in the sense defined in Chapter
and the only technical progress is Harrod-neutral. We will confine o
analysis again to that of the steady state. This may limit the applicabi
ity of our results because many actual government policies refle
short-run economic and political considerations that fluctuate ov
time. We intend, however, to analyze the long-run effects of a stab
policy, namely, the asymptotic tendency of the economy when polici
are held constant. I believe that such a steady-state analysis
economic policy is more useful than it may appear at first becau
every policymaker is concerned with the long-run effects of his policie
This is particularly so because long-range economic planning is no
popular even among countries with a free-enterprise economic systen

The following section presents the model of the firm, section 8.
discusses the macroequilibrium condition, and section 8.4, the gener
equilibrium of this economy. Finally, its implications to econom
policy are considered in section 8.5.

8.2   The model of the firm

Suppose that the government levies a corporate profit tax to firn
applying a tax rate t_p to profits P gross of capital cost. Total corpora
tax is hence $t_p P = t_p(Q - wN - \phi(a)L)$, maintaining all oth
assumptions and notation in our earlier analysis, and the net cash flo
of the firm at time t is $(1 - t_p)[Q(t) - w(t)N(t) - \phi(a(t))L(t)]$
$\psi(g(t))K(t)$. This profit tax scheme, we should note, has a neutr
effect on corporate financial policy because it is levied on profits gro
of capital cost. That is, whether a firm finances its investment throug
retention or new share issue (new bond issue or borrowing is neglecte

this chapter as in Part II), the cost of investment is not tax deductible.

To take into account the contribution of government expenditure to the economy, let us assume that government expenditure affects production. That is, the government provides public services such as police, fire fighting, public transportation, education, and pollution control and public goods such as roads, bridges, and ports, and these services and goods make production activity by the private sector easier and less costly. We will for this reason rewrite the production function $Q = F(K, L, E)$, where E denotes government expenditure. It is assumed that $F_3 > 0$, $F_{33} < 0$, and F is homogeneous of degree one with respect to all three arguments, meaning that doubling the amounts of both capital and labor (in efficiency units) doubles output if and only if government expenditure is doubled at the same time. In addition, two assumptions are implicit in this formulation. First, E is assumed independent of the wage rate, implying that the government purchases goods but does not employ labor. Second, in the sense that E is the expenditure during a given time period, say, a year, and not the accumulated value, it is not investment.

Using this production function, we write the present value of net cash flow for a firm as

$$\int_0^\infty \{(1 - t_p)[F(K(t), L(t), E(t)) - w(t)N(t)$$
$$- \phi(a(t))L(t)] - \psi(g(t))K(t)\}e^{-it}dt$$

Let us now assume that the management considers only a steady state where, as before, $g(t) \equiv \dot{K}(t)/K(t)$ is constant and equal to g, $a(t) \equiv \dot{A}(t)/A(t) = \dot{L}(t)/L(t) - \dot{N}(t)/N(t)$ is constant and equal to a, $(t)/K(t)$ is constant and equal to l, and $w(t)$ is expected to grow at a constant rate ξ^e. This restriction on the optimization behavior of the management is again justified by the fact that such a policy is in fact optimal in a general equilibrium, the proof of which is a straightforward extension of propositions 5.6 and 5.7. As for the government policy, a steady state requires that tax rates are constant. In view of the government budget constraint, this implies that government expenditure E also grows at rate g in a steady state,[1] implying that $E(t)/K(t)$ stays constant over time. This constant we denote by e.

See equation (8.6) in the next section. In a steady state P, Y_w, and Y_c all grow at rate g, as does E.

The present value of the net cash flow, after being divided by t[?] initial amount of capital K_0, is now simplified as

$$\int_0^\infty \{(1 - t_{\mathrm{p}})[F(1, l, e) - wl \exp((\xi^e - a)t) - \phi(a)l]$$

$$- \psi(g)\} \exp(-(i - g)t)$$

because $F(K, L, E) = KF(1, l, e)$ by the assumption of line[?] homogeneity. As in section 3.5, we first maximize this expression wi[?] respect to l and a. The first-order condition is satisfied if l^* and [?] satisfy

$$\frac{F_2(1, l^*, e)}{i - g} = \frac{w}{i - g - \xi^e + a^*} + \frac{\phi(a^*)}{i - g} \tag{8.}$$

$$\frac{w}{(i - g - \xi^e + a^*)^2} = \frac{\phi'(a^*)}{i - g} \tag{8.}$$

A comparison with equations (3.16) and (3.17) immediately revea[?] that the first-order condition for the optimal values l^* and a^* is n[?] affected by the introduction of the corporate tax and the only differen[?] is that the marginal product of labor now depends on governme[?] expenditure per capital e. Therefore both l^* and a^* are solved functions of w, $i - g$, ξ^e, and e.

Let us now evaluate the value of the firm per K_0 at these optim[?] values and denote it by v.

$$v = \int_0^\infty \{(1 - t_{\mathrm{p}})[F(1, l^*, e) - wl^* \exp((\xi^e - a^*)t) - \phi(a^*)l^*]$$

$$- \psi(g)\} \exp(-(i - g)t)$$

$$= \frac{(1 - t_{\mathrm{p}})[F(1, l^*, e) - \phi(a^*)l^*] - \psi(g)}{i - g}$$

$$- \frac{(1 - t_{\mathrm{p}})wl^*}{i - g - \xi^e + a^*} \tag{8.}$$

Since l^* and a^* are determined as functions of w, $i - g$, ξ^e, and e, [?] depends on g, w, i, ξ^e, e, and t_{p}, where

$$\frac{\partial v}{\partial e} = \frac{(1 - t_{\mathrm{p}})F_3(1, l^*, e)}{i - g} > 0$$

and

$$\frac{\partial v}{\partial t_{\mathrm{p}}} = -\frac{F(1, l^*, e) - \phi(a^*)l^*}{i - g} + \frac{wl^*}{i - g - \xi^e + a^*} < 0$$

as long as profits are positive. Hence the v-g frontier shifts upwa[?]

ownward) as $e(t_p)$ increases. Consequently, the optimal growth rate be determined by the management in the manner discussed in hapter 2 depends on e and t_p, as well as on w, i, and ξ^e.

3   The macroequilibrium

'e now turn to the noncorporate sector. Following Chapter 5, we sume that there are two classes – workers and capitalists – and both e rational. Denote by t_w and t_c personal income tax rates applied to orkers and capitalists, respectively. Needless to say, the case where ere is a single tax rate applied to every individual is only a special se where $t_w = t_c$. It is assumed that these rates are applied to the tire incomes, without differentiating between dividends and capital ins. Income taxes are, therefore, $t_w Y_w$ for workers and $t_c Y_c$ for pitalists. Because saving rates will be applied to after-tax incomes, e have

$$S_w = s_w(1 - t_w)Y_w = s_w(1 - t_w)(W + D_w + G_w) \tag{8.4}$$

$$S_c = s_c(1 - t_c)Y_c = s_c(1 - t_c)(D_c + G_c) \tag{8.5}$$

The stock market is in equilibrium if $S = \dot{V}$ [see equation (4.8)]. nd if $S = \dot{V}$, the goods market is also in equilibrium because of the 'alras law. The proof of this law is left to the reader for it is sentially the same as that in section 4.2, except that the budget nstraint of the government must now be taken into account. This is

$$t_p P + t_w Y_w + t_c Y_c = E \tag{8.6}$$

The macroequilibrium condition for the two markets is derived in e manner parallel to the proof of proposition 4.4. First, note that at a eady state the wealth owned by each class, V_w and V_c, must grow at a mmon rate; otherwise, the relative share changes over time. This quires that

$$\frac{S_w}{S_c} = \frac{\dot{V}_w}{\dot{V}_c} = \frac{V_w}{V_c} = \frac{D_w + G_w}{D_c + G_c} \tag{8.7}$$

he first equality holds because shares are the only means of holding ealth available to the noncorporate sector, and the last equality holds ecause returns are proportional to the amount of share ownership. By mbining equations (8.4), (8.5), and (8.7), we have

$$S = S_w + S_c$$

$$= \frac{D_w + G_w}{D_c + G_c} \cdot S_c + S_c$$

$$= s_c(1 - t_c)(D + G) \tag{8.}$$

provided that $s_c(1 - t_c) > s_w(1 - t_w)$,[2] because $D_w + D_c = D$ a
$G_w + G_c = G$. We now combine this equation with the equilibriu
condition, $\dot{V} = S$, and the definition of the rate of interest, i
$(D + G)/V$, to get

$$\dot{V} = s_c(1 - t_c)iV$$

At a steady state where $v \equiv V/K$ is constant, $\dot{V}/V = g$. Hence t
goods and stock markets are in equilibrium if and only if

$$g = s_c(1 - t_c)i \tag{8.}$$

This equation demonstrates that the properties of our *generaliz*
Pasinetti theorem (proposition 4.4) is intact even when taxes a
introduced into the model; in particular, workers' saving rate still do
not affect the equilibrium. Surprisingly, equation (8.9) also shows th
the tax rate for workers does not affect the equilibrium either. In fa
equation (8.8) implies that an increase in the tax rate for capitalis
reduces total saving, but an increase in the tax rate for workers do
not. This irrelevance of workers' tax rate occurs because an increase
the tax rate for workers reduces workers' saving and, in the long ru
workers' share of wealth, implying an increase in capitalists' share
wealth and hence an increase in returns for capitalists, which increas
capitalists' saving by exactly the amount needed to offset the decrea
in workers' saving. The only difference in the equilibrium condition
a result of the introduction of taxes is that the appropriate saving ra
of capitalists must now be adjusted for taxes; that is, $s_c(1 - t_c)$ instea
of s_c. The rate of interest must equal the growth rate divided by th
adjusted saving rate of capitalists in an equilibrium.

8.4   The model of economic growth

As before, the following two conditions must be satisfied at a
steady-state equilibrium: $\xi^e = \xi$, because the management expectatio

---

[2] By multiplying both sides of equation (8.7) with $s_c(D_c + G_c)$ and substitu
ing equations (8.4) and (8.5), we have $s_w(1 - t_w) (W + D_w + G_w)$
$s_c(1 - t_c)(D_w + G_w)$. Since $W > 0$, it must be that $s_w(1 - t_w) < s_c(1 - t_c)$

ust be fulfilled; and $\xi = a$, because otherwise, the value of the
arginal product of labor eventually deviates from the wage rate.
bstituting these into equation (8.2), we have (suppressing asterisks
r optimal values)

$$a = A\left(\frac{w}{i - g}\right) \tag{8.10}$$

kewise, we can obtain the locus of the growth rate optimal for the
rporate sector against different values of parameters in the manner
veloped in section 5.4. The only difference here is that the v-g
ontier now depends on e (in a positive fashion) and t_p (in a negative
shion), in addition to the variables that appeared before, i, w, and z.
herefore, with a straightforward extension of the previous analysis,
have[3]

$$g = G(i, w, z, e, t_p) \tag{8.11}$$

ith $G_1 < 0$, $G_2 < 0$, $G_3 > 0$, $G_4 > 0$, and $G_5 < 0$.
The model of economic growth is now summarized by the following
ree equations:

$$g = s_c(1 - t_c)i \tag{8.9}$$

$$g = G(i, w, z, e, t_p) \tag{8.11}$$

$$g = n + A(w/(i - g)) \tag{8.12}$$

here equation (8.9) depicts the preceding equilibrium condition for
e goods and stock markets; equation (8.11), the optimization behav-
r of the corporate sector; and equation (8.12), the equilibrium
ndition for the labor market. This model is identical to the model in
ction 5.3, except for the addition of three parameters, e, t_p, and t_c.
hus we can again define the LL curve [by substituting equation (8.9)
to equation (8.12)] and the GG curve [by substituting equation (8.9)
to equation (8.11)] on the (w, g) plane to analyze the equilibrium
d to conduct a comparative analysis. The result is summarized in
able 8.1. Because this is a simple extension of the analysis in section
3, we omit the proof.

We have used the same notation G for the function but, obviously, the
functional form here is different from that in Chapter 5 because of the
addition of e and t_p as the arguments.

Table 8.1. *The sign of the effect of parameters on equilibrium values*

Equilibrium values	Parameters					
	s_c	n	z	e	t_p	t_w
g^0	+	+	+	+	−	0
i^0	?	+	+	+	−	0
w^0	?	−	+	+	−	0
a^0	+	−	+	+	−	0

8.5   Policy implications

Needless to say, the policy variables of the government are governme
expenditure per capital, e, and tax rates, t_p, t_w, and t_c. The obviou
question, therefore, is how the government should determine the
values if it wants to raise the growth rate of national income and t
growth rate of labor productivity. According to Table 8.1, the answ
to this question is that the government should increase e and decrease
and t_c. This must be reasonable. The more public goods and servic
that are available, the less costly the production is and hence the mo
investment firms will make. On the other hand, an increase
corporate tax decreases the value of the firm and the contribution
investment to the value of the firm, thus reducing the incentive
invest. An increase in personal tax to capitalists reduces their dispo
able income and hence total saving to be used for capital formation.

An odd result of the model is that the income tax rate to workers
affects neither the equilibrium growth rate nor the equilibrium price
We have already discussed why this is the case. In terms of polic
implications, this suggests that if faster growth is the only polic
objective, the government should levy taxes to workers as much a
possible to finance large government expenditure, maintaining low ta
rates for the corporate sector and capitalists. Needless to say, such
policy must be unpopular among workers, and political consideration
including the threat of revolution by the working class, would preve
the adoption of this policy.

It may be more plausible, therefore, to assume that t_w and t_c must l
equal, namely, personal tax rate must be common to every individua
In this case, the government is faced with a trade-off. To stimula
investment and faster growth, the government wants to maintain
large government expenditure-capital ratio e. This, however, requir

ge government expenditure and inevitably a large amount of taxes.
the government chooses corporate taxes for this purpose, it will cool
wn the incentive of the corporate sector to invest. If it chooses
rsonal income taxes, the amount of saving will be reduced and the
te of interest raised, which again hurts investment. Therefore the
vernment is faced with a trade-off between the positive effect of
vernment expenditure on growth and the negative effect of taxes on
owth.

Economic policy in a monetary economy

9.1   Introduction

This chapter presents a model of the growth of a corporate econom
with a money market in order to discuss the effects of monetary poli
on economic growth. Once money is introduced into the model, incom
has to be redefined so as to include capital gains due to the change
money prices. In addition, the decision making in the noncorpora
sector must be analyzed as to not only how much to save but also ho
to allocate wealth between money and corporate shares (bonds are sti
ignored). We will approach these problems in the following manne
Let us take goods as the standard of value, namely, *numéraire*, an
define p_m as the price of money in terms of goods. Then, capital gai
(measured in terms of goods) obtained from holding money are $\dot{p}$
multiplied by the quantity of moneyholdings. We define compreher
sive income as income including these capital gains from moneyhold
ings as well as from wages and returns to share ownership. Similarl
we define comprehensive profit as profit including the capital gai
from holding money as well as from the profit defined earlier, namel
sales revenue minus production costs, except the cost of capital.

The first assumption to be made is that the government levie
personal income tax and corporate profit tax based on, respectively, th
comprehensive income and the comprehensive profit thus define
Specifically, the amount of tax one has to pay is determined at h
comprehensive income (or profit if this is a firm), multiplied by th
appropriate tax rate. In other words, there is no differential ta
treatment among categories of income and this has to be true not onl
between dividends and capital gains from share ownership but als
between capital gains due to the fluctuation of the purchasing power
money and other income sources such as wages. This tax system ma
be called ideal in that it leaves the relative contribution of each incom
source to total income unchanged. Our second assumption pertains t
the saving behavior of the noncorporate sector. We assume that eac

178

ndividual determines how much to save by applying his propensity to
save to his after-tax comprehensive income. This may imply that every
individual recognizes all income, including capital gains, as income
and then divides this comprehensive income between consumption and
saving, the rule for this division being summarized by the saving rate
which is assumed constant. In other words, individuals are assumed
rational where rationality now requires not only the indifference
between dividends and capital gains from share ownership, as in
Chapter 4, but also the indifference between an increase in the value of
moneyholding due to deflation and an increase by the same amount in
other income sources such as wages. In short, people are supposed to
be free of money illusion.

Because two types of assets, shares and money, are now available to
the noncorporate sector, workers and capitalists have to allocate their
savings between the two alternative assets so as to achieve an optimal
portfolio. We assume that one's demand for money is determined as a
proportion of his comprehensive income and that the ratio of this
desired stock of money to the comprehensive income (this ratio we
denote by β) is dependent on the rate of appreciation of the value of
money, namely, the rate of deflation $\pi(\equiv \dot{p}_m/p_m)$, positively and on
the rate of return to the alternative asset i negatively. This variation of
β with the expected capital gains or losses from holding money one
may say is a form of speculative effect: Our formulation thus has a
similarity to the quantity theory of money but takes into account the
Keynesian liquidity-preference theory at the same time. The demand
for money by the corporate sector is similarly determined. That is, it is
assumed that the corporate sector's demand for money is given as a
proportion of its comprehensive profit and that this proportion
(denoted by α) depends on π positively and on i negatively. It should be
noted here that the comprehensive income (or profit) to be multiplied
by β (or α) in order to compute for the desired stock of money is gross
before taxes, because money is needed not only to pay against the
purchase of goods, labor, and shares but also to pay taxes.

The following sections present a model of economic growth based on
these assumptions. The details of these assumptions are not very
important, however. One may assume differently and proceed similarly to the analysis in the following sections. For instance, one may
assume that taxes are levied on income net of capital gains from
moneyholdings, that individuals disregard capital gains from money-

holdings in making consumption decisions, and/or that the demand f₁
money is proportional to after-tax comprehensive income rather tha
before-tax. Such variations do not change the basic characteristics
the model although they naturally modify the equations.

It should be noted, however, that one assumption, namely, th
constancy of α and β for constant i and π, does play an important rol
To see why, first note that the real value of total money in the econom
is p_m times the quantity of money in the economy M and

$$\frac{d(p_m M)/dt}{p_m M} = \frac{\dot{p}_m}{p_m} + \frac{\dot{M}}{M} = \pi + \mu$$

where μ denotes the rate of increase of the money supply. Since in
steady state i stays constant and income and profit grow at a comm₀
rate g, the demand for money also grows at rate g as long as π
constant, for α and β are then constant by assumption. At equilibriu₁
where demand and supply of money are equal, therefore, it must ʰ
that $g = \pi + \mu$ with constant g and μ, making π constant. Hence ther
is a steady-state equilibrium such that g, π, μ, i, α, and β are a₁
constant and $g = \pi + \mu$.

As readers may have already noticed, this is a world of the quantit
theory of money. The quantity equation of exchange says that th
quantity of money times income velocity of money equals the price ₀
goods times the quantity of goods or, stated differently, the quantity ₀
money M times the velocity times the price of money in terms of goo₀
p_m equals real national income. Hence if M grows at rate μ, th
velocity is constant, p_m increases at rate π, and real national incom
grows at rate g, then it must be that $\mu + \pi = g$. An importa₁
implication here is that the rate of deflation π (or the rate of inflatio₁
$-\pi$) in a steady state is immediately determined once the governme₁
chooses μ, provided g is given. If $\mu = g$, then there is neither deflatic
nor inflation; if $\mu > g$, then there is inflation; and if $\mu < g$, then there
deflation. Even though the story is not this simple because a change i
μ affects g as we will presently see, limitations in the applicabili₁
toward a prescription for real-world inflation may be undeniable. Th
may not surprise anyone because the inflation that we are faced wit
in recent years has been more of a short-run phenomenon than that ₀
a steady state where all expectations are fulfilled, there is no mone
illusion, and every ratio stays constant.

One should not conclude, however, that an analysis of a steady sta₁
in a monetary economy is of no use. On the contrary, it can give a

insight into the role money plays in a long-run growth path and what would be the mixture of fiscal and monetary policies in achieving a desired long-run tendency of an economy. Such an analysis surely adds to a better understanding of our economy and to a better long-range economic planning.

The structure of this chapter is identical to that of Chapter 8. The following section deals with the microeconomic model of the firm; section 9.3, the macroequilibrium condition; section 9.4, the model of economic growth; and the final section, policy implications of the model.

9.2   The model of the firm

Denote by M_p the holdings of money by the corporate sector. In terms of goods the moneyholdings are worth $p_m M_p$. Comprehensive profit P^c is now defined as $Q - wN - \phi(a)L + \dot{p}_m M_p$ because $\dot{p}_m M_p$ is the capital gains (or capital losses if $\dot{p}_m$ is negative) that the corporate sector receives from holding money. Because we have assumed that in order to determine the amount of corporate tax the tax rate t_p is to be multiplied by P^c, the after-tax profit equals $(1 - t_p)[Q - wN - \phi(a)L + \dot{p}_m M_p]$. The firm allocates this after-tax profit among three purposes: to pay out dividends, to retain in order to reinvest in physical capital, and to increase the value of moneyholdings. Assuming the production function, $Q = F(K, L, E)$, as before, we now have the following budget constraint for the firm:

$$(1 - t_p)P^c = (1 - t_p)[F(K, L, E) - wN - \phi(a)L + \dot{p}_m M_p]$$
$$= D + R + d(p_m M_p)/dt \tag{9.1}$$

where R denotes the retention solely for the purpose of reinvesting in physical capital and not for increasing the moneyholdings. To finance investment, the firm uses this retention and/or sells new shares. Hence, as before,

$$I = R + q\dot{N} \tag{9.2}$$

The net cash flow of the firm, namely, the returns that belong to the current shareholders, is the after-tax profit minus the costs of investing in physical capital and of increasing the moneyholdings, that is $(1 - t_p)P^c - I - d(p_m M_p)/dt$. Hence, the value of the firm, namely, the present value of the net cash flow of the firm, equals

$$\int_0^\infty [(1 - t_p)P^c - I - d(p_m M_p)/dt]e^{-it}\, dt$$

$$= \int_0^\infty \{(1 - t_p)[F(K, L, E) - wN - \phi(a)L + \dot{p}_m M_p]$$

$$- I - d(p_m M_p)/dt\}e^{-it}\, dt \quad (9.3)$$

The demand for money by the firm is a constant proportion of P^c a was assumed in the previous section:

$$p_m M_p = \alpha P^c$$

where

$$\alpha = \alpha(i, \pi) \quad \text{with } \alpha_1(i, \pi) < 0 \quad \text{and} \quad \alpha_2(i, \pi) > 0 \quad (9.4)$$

Let us assume, again, that the firm is considering only a steady-stat path, for which the rationale is given in the manner similar to th analysis in section 5.5. A steady state now requires, however, not onl the constancy of $g, i, l, a, \xi^e, e,$ and t_p but also the constancy of π. Ther utilizing equation (9.4),

$$\dot{p}_m M_p = \pi p_m M_p = \pi \alpha P^c$$

$$\frac{d(p_m M_p)/dt}{p_m M_p} = \frac{d(\alpha P^c)/dt}{\alpha P^c} = g$$

because p_m grows at rate π, P^c grows at rate g, and α is constant at steady state. By substituting these into the definition of P^c, we have

$$P^c = Q - wN - \phi(a)L + \pi \alpha P^c$$

or

$$P^c = \frac{Q - wN - \phi(a)L}{1 - \alpha \pi} \quad (9.5)$$

Equation (9.3) can now be rewritten as

$$\int_0^\infty [(1 - t_p)P^c - I - \alpha g P^c]e^{-it}\, dt$$

$$= \int_0^\infty \left\{ \frac{1 - t_p - \alpha g}{1 - \alpha \pi} [F(K, L, E) - wN - \phi(a)L] - I \right\} e^{-it}\, d$$

By substituting $L/K = l$, $K = K_0 e^{gt}$, and so on, we have the followin expression for the present value of the net cash flow per initial capi tal K_0:

$$\int_0^\infty \left\{ \frac{1 - t_p - \alpha g}{1 - \alpha \pi} [F(1, l, e) - wl \exp ((\xi^e - a)t) - \phi(a)l] - \psi(g) \right\}$$
$$\exp (-(i - g)t) \, dt \quad (9.6)$$

As before, the firm maximizes this expression first with respect to l and a for a given value of g. By differentiating equation (9.6) with respect to l and a, one will easily find that the first-order condition for this maximization problem is exactly the same as before (equations 8.1) and (8.2)]. Moneyholding does not affect the optimality condition because l and a appear only in the bracket of equation (9.6) and the quational form of this part is identical to that of the previous chapter. Hence the optimal values of l and a are again determined as functions of w, $i - g$, ξ^e, and e. Define v, as before, by the value of the firm per K_0 evaluated at the optimal values of l and a (asterisks for l and a to denote the optimality are suppressed):

$$v = \int_0^\infty \left\{ \frac{1 - t_p - \alpha g}{1 - \alpha \pi} [F(1, l, e) \right.$$
$$\left. - wl \exp ((\xi^e - a)t) - \phi(a)l] - \psi(g) \right\} \exp (-(i - g)t) \, dt$$
$$= \frac{1 - t_p - \alpha g}{1 - \alpha \pi} \frac{F(1, l, e) - \phi(a)l}{i - g}$$
$$- \frac{1 - t_p - \alpha g}{1 - \alpha \pi} \frac{wl}{i - g - \xi^e + a} - \frac{\psi(g)}{i - g} \quad (9.7)$$

The right-hand side depends not only on g, w, i, ξ^e, e, and t_p as was the case in Chapter 8 but also on α and π. Immediately we can see that if α is kept constant then v depends negatively on w, i, ξ^e, and t_p and positively on e and π, provided $g > (1 - t_p)\pi$. Also, *ceteris paribus*, a larger α implies a smaller v under the same condition. The reasons for these results are not difficult to detect. A large α means that the firm has to allocate more of its comprehensive profit to the increase in moneyholdings to maintain the desired money-profit ratio, which implies a smaller net cash flow and v. A larger π for a given g, on the contrary, means an increase in capital gains from moneyholdings and hence an increase in v. The reasons for the effects of other variables are exactly as before.

Once the fact that α depends on i and π is taken into account, however, the effects of i and π on v are no longer unambiguous, because a larger i implies a smaller α and, consequently, a larger v in addition to the negative effect previously mentioned, whereas a large π implies a larger α and a smaller v in addition to its positive effect.

The optimal growth rate will be determined by the management so as to maximize its intertemporal utility, subject to equation (9.7) in the manner developed in Chapter 2. This will depend on w, i, ξ^e, e, t and π.

9.3   The macroequilibrium

The comprehensive incomes of workers and capitalists are defined as

$$Y_w^c = W + D_w + G_w + \dot{p}_m M_w$$

$$Y_c^c = D_c + G_c + \dot{p}_m M_c \tag{9.8}$$

where M_w and M_c denote moneyholdings by workers and capitalists respectively. Personal income taxes are levied on these comprehensive incomes and the after-tax comprehensive incomes are divided into consumption and saving; thus $S_w = s_w(1 - t_w)Y_w^c$ and $S_c = s_c(1 - t_c)Y_c^c$. These are then divided into the demand for money and the demand for shares (both in terms of flow), where, as was assumed in section 9.1, the desired stock of money is a constant proportion of comprehensive income; hence

$$\dot{p}_m M_w = \beta_w Y_w^c$$

$$\dot{p}_m M_c = \beta_c Y_c^c \tag{9.9}$$

where β_w and β_c are both dependent on i and π with the effect of i being negative and that of π being positive. The demand for shares is then determined as the residual of the saving after an adjustment is made to maintain the desired stock of money. For capitalists, therefore, the desired increment in the value of shares, $\dot{V}_c$, is $S_c - d(\dot{p}_m M_c)/dt$. At steady state this can be rewritten as follows, using equations (9.8) and (9.9).

$$\dot{V}_c = s_c(1 - t_c)Y_c^c - g\beta_c Y_c^c$$

$$= \frac{[s_c(1 - t_c) - g\beta_c](D_c + G_c)}{(1 - \pi\beta_c)} \tag{9.10}$$

The latter equality holds because from equation (9.8) we have, by substituting $\dot{p}_m M_c = \pi \dot{p}_m M_c = \pi\beta_c Y_c^c$,

$$Y_c^c = (D_c + G_c)/(1 - \pi\beta_c) \tag{9.11}$$

The stock market is in equilibrium if and only if the total increase in the value of shares, $\dot{V}$, equals the sum of the desired increases by workers, $\dot{V}_w$, and by capitalists, $\dot{V}_c$. In a steady state, however, $\dot{V}_w/\dot{V}_c = V_w/V_c = (D_w + G_w)/(D_c + G_c)$ for the reason that, I believe, is by now familiar to the reader (see equation (8.7)). Using this, we rewrite the equilibrium condition.

$$\dot{V} = \dot{V}_w + \dot{V}_c$$
$$= \left(\frac{D_w + G_w}{D_c + G_c}\right)\dot{V}_c + \dot{V}_c$$
$$= \left(\frac{D + G}{D_c + G_c}\right)\dot{V}_c \tag{9.12}$$

Substitute equation (9.10) into this equation to get

$$\dot{V} = \frac{[s_c(1 - t_c) - g\beta_c](D + G)}{(1 - \pi\beta_c)} \tag{9.13}$$

By definition of the rate of return i, $D + G = iV$. Also, at a steady state $\dot{V}/V = g$. Substituting, we finally obtain the equilibrium condition.

$$g = \frac{[s_c(1 - t_c) - g\beta_c]i}{(1 - \pi\beta_c)}$$

or

$$g = \frac{s_c(1 - t_c)i}{(1 - \pi\beta_c + i\beta_c)} \tag{9.14}$$

This is a more complicated condition than before (cf. equation (8.9)). Especially, g is no longer proportional to i. Yet the effect of i on g is positive because

$$\frac{\partial g}{\partial i} = \frac{1}{(1 - \pi\beta_c + i\beta_c)^2}\left[s_c(1 - t_c)(1 - \pi\beta_c) - s_c(1 - t_c)i(i - \pi)\frac{\partial\beta_c}{\partial i}\right]$$

is positive as long as $i - \pi$ (the money rate of interest) is nonnegative, since $\partial\beta_c/\partial i < 0$, $t_c < 1$, $\beta_c < 1$, and $\pi < 1$ (unless the deflation rate is more than 100 percent!). In other words, a higher growth rate induces a larger demand for funds and raises the rate of interest, and this fact remains true whether or not a money market is incorporated. Again, the effect on g of s_c is positive and that of t_c is negative.

Equation (9.14) provides another interesting result: The equilibrium condition depends on s_c, t_c, and β_c but not on s_w, t_w, or β_w! This a remarkable result. Even when both money and stock markets a explicitly taken into consideration and taxes are introduced, the fa still remains that the long-run equilibrium condition in a two-cla economy does not depend on any decision of workers or any paramet pertinent exclusively to workers. In other words, the Pasinetti par dox, if one follows the terminology by Samuelson and Modiglia (1966), cannot be resolved by an introduction of shares, money, an taxes.[1] This will demonstrate how robust the Pasinetti paradox This result occurs, again, due to the long-run adjustment of tl distribution of wealth among the two classes; that is, even thoug workers' decision affects the amount of their saving, this is offset by increase or decrease in capitalists' saving due to the change in the sha of capitalists' wealth.

9.4   The model of economic growth

The model consists of the following seven equations:

$$g = \frac{s_c(1 - t_c)i}{(1 - \pi\beta_c + i\beta_c)}$$ (9.1

where $\beta_c = \beta_c\,(i, \pi)$

$$g = g(i, w, \xi^e, z, e, t_p, \pi)$$ (9.1

$$a = a(w, i - g, \xi^e, e)$$ (9.1

$$g = n + a$$ (9.1

$$\xi = \xi^e$$ (9.1

$$\xi = a$$ (9.1

$$g = \mu + \pi$$ (9.2

Equation (9.14) is the equilibrium condition for the stock mark derived in the previous section; equations (9.15) and (9.16) come fro our analysis in section 9.2 on how the desired rates of growth and technical progress are determined through the optimization behavi of the management of the corporate sector; equation (9.17) is tl

[1] Ramanathan (1976), like ours, has shown that the Pasinetti paradox st holds in a monetary growth model. His analysis is based on somewh different assumptions from those here and does not take shares and tax into account.

ady-state equilibrium condition for the labor market; equation
.18) requires the fulfillment of management expectations; equation
.19) states that the value of marginal product of labor and the
arginal cost of labor must grow at a common rate; and equation
.20) is the steady-state equilibrium condition for the money market
cause the supply of money increases at rate $\pi + \mu$, whereas the
mand for money increases at rate g since α, β_w, and β_c must be
nstant at a steady state.

Again, we substitute equations (9.18) and (9.19) into equation
.16) to get $a = A(w/(i - g))$ and then substitute this into equation
.17):

$$g = n + A(w/(i - g)) \tag{9.21}$$

ext, we substitute equation (9.16), (9.18), (9.19), and (9.20) into
quation (9.15) to get

$$g = G(i, w, z, e, t_p, \mu) \tag{9.22}$$

'e assume the signs of the partial derivatives as follows:

$$\frac{\partial g}{\partial i} < 0, \quad \frac{\partial g}{\partial w} < 0, \quad \frac{\partial g}{\partial z} > 0, \quad \frac{\partial g}{\partial e} > 0, \quad \frac{\partial g}{\partial t_p} < 0, \quad \text{and} \quad \frac{\partial g}{\partial \mu} < 0$$

mong these, the effects of t_p, e, z, and w should be obvious. An
crease in t_p reduces after-tax profit and the values of the firm. This
ifts the v-g frontier downward and will reduce the desired growth
te. An increase in e increases the productivity and shifts the frontier
ward. An increase in z will let the management choose a larger
owth rate. An increase in the wage rate increases labor cost and
ifts the frontier downward. Unfortunately, the effect of i is not
ambiguous. On the one hand, a larger i means a larger discount rate
d thus shifts the v-g frontier downward. On the other hand, a larger
implies a smaller α. If α is smaller, then the firm can allocate its
ofit less to the increase in the value of moneyholdings and more to
vidend payment and retention as long as the rate of deflation π is less
an the rate of increase of the real value of money stock g, for if $g > \pi$
en capital gains from money, $\pi p_m M_p$, are not large enough to pay
r the desired increase in the value of the stock of money, $g p_m M_p$.
his, in turn, will increase the net cash flow of the firm available to its
rrent shareholders and shift the frontier upward. Hence the effects
i on the frontier are two and conflicting. For now assume that the
rmer effect (i.e., the negative direct effect) is stronger. Finally, let us

consider the effect of μ. Given g, a larger μ implies a smaller π sin$\pi = g - \mu$. On the one hand, a smaller π implies smaller capital gain and smaller v. On the other hand, a smaller π implies a smaller α and a larger v by the same reason as in the effect of a change in i. The two effects are thus conflicting. We again assume for now that the former effect is stronger and, therefore, the overall effect of μ to g negative. These assumptions on the effects of i and μ will be satisfied α is relatively insensitive to a change in i or π.

Finally, we substitute equation (9.20) into equation (9.14) to get

$$g = \frac{s_c(1 - t_c)i}{[1 + (i + \mu - g)\beta_c]} \qquad (9.2$$

By totally differentiating this equation and making necessary rearrangements, we have

$$-[1 - g\beta_c + (i + \mu - g)\beta_c + (i + \mu - g)g(\partial\beta_c/\partial\pi)]\,dg$$
$$+[s_c(1 - t_c) - g\beta_c - (i + \mu - g)g(\partial\beta_c/\partial i)]\,di$$
$$+[-g\beta_c + g(i + \mu - g)(\partial\beta_c/\partial\pi)]\,d\mu$$
$$+(1 - t_c)i\,ds_c - s_c i\,dt_c = 0 \qquad (9.2$$

The coefficient for dg is negative as long as the money rate of interest $i + \mu - g = i - \pi$, is nonnegative because $g < 1$ (unless we have 10 percent growth!), $\beta_c < 1$, and $\partial\beta_c/\partial\pi > 0$. The coefficient for di positive if $i - \pi \geq 0$ because by substituting equation (9.14) the first two terms can be rewritten as $s_c(1 - t_c)(1 - \pi\beta_c)/(1 - \pi\beta_c + i\beta_c$ which is positive, and $\partial\beta_c/\partial i < 0$. The sign of the coefficient for $d\mu$ ambiguous because the first term is negative but the second term positive. That is, on the one hand, a faster increase in the supply of money, given g, decreases π and capital gains from moneyholding resulting in less saving but, on the other hand, the smaller π decrease β_c and increases the share of corporate shares in the portfolio of capitalists' wealth. The following discussion deals with the case when β_c is insensitive to π and hence the first effect of μ outweighs the second. Needless to say, the coefficients for ds_c and dt_c are positive and negative, respectively. Summing up, we rewrite equation (9.23) in the following manner:

$$i = f(g, s_c, t_c, \mu) \qquad (9.25$$

where $f_1 > 0, f_2 < 0, f_3 > 0$, and $f_4 > 0$.

We now have the three equations (9.21), (9.22), and (9.25) to solv

r the equilibrium values of g, i, and w. Let us follow the procedure
sed in previous chapters and derive the GG and LL curves. First,
substitute equation (9.25) into equation (9.22) to get

$$g = G(f(g, s_c, t_c, \mu), w, z, e, t_p, \mu)$$

view of the signs of the partial derivatives of the functions, G and f,
e can rewrite this equation as

$$g = \tilde{G}(w, s_c, z, e, t_p, t_c, \mu) \tag{9.26}$$

here $\tilde{G}_1 < 0$, $\tilde{G}_2 > 0$, $\tilde{G}_3 > 0$, $\tilde{G}_4 > 0$, $\tilde{G}_5 < 0$, $\tilde{G}_6 < 0$, and $\tilde{G}_7 < 0$. In
e (w, g) plane this is depicted by a downward-sloping curve, which
e again call the GG curve.

Second, substitute equation (9.25) into equation (9.21) to get

$$g = n + A\left(\frac{w}{f(g, s_c, t_c, \mu) - g}\right)$$

hich we can rewrite as

$$g = \tilde{L}(w, s_c, n, t_c, \mu) \tag{9.27}$$

here $\tilde{L}_1 > 0$, $\tilde{L}_2 > 0$, $\tilde{L}_3 > 0$, $\tilde{L}_4 < 0$, and $\tilde{L}_5 < 0$, provided $f_1 > 1$.
his last condition is satisfied if the coefficient (without negative sign)
dg in equation (9.24) is larger than that of di; that is, if

$$1 - g\beta_c + (i + \mu - g)\beta_c + (i + \mu - g)g(\partial\beta_c/\partial\pi) - s_c(1 - t_c)$$
$$+ g\beta_c + (i + \mu - g)g(\partial\beta_c/\partial i)$$
$$= 1 - s_c(1 - t_c) + (i + \mu - g)\beta_c + (i + \mu - g)g\left(\frac{\partial\beta_c}{\partial\pi} + \frac{\partial\beta_c}{\partial i}\right)$$

positive. Since $s_c(1 - t_c) < 1$ and $i + \mu - g = i - \pi$ (the money rate
interest) is usually nonnegative, the equation is positive unless
$\partial\beta_c/\partial\pi) + (\partial\beta_c/\partial i)$ is negative and outweighs the first two positive
rms. However, an increase in both i and π by 1 percent seems most
kely to affect β_c only slightly, if at all, since it leaves the difference in
e returns between the two assets – shares and money – unchanged.
resumably, therefore, $(\partial\beta_c/\partial\pi) + (\partial\beta_c/\partial i)$ is very small in absolute
alue and the condition that $f_1 > 1$ is satisfied. Consequently, equation
).27) can be depicted by an upward-sloping curve in the (w, g) plane,
hich we again call the LL curve.

The two curves on the (w, g) plane are now used to analyze the
fects of exogenous variables: s_c, n, z, e, t_p, t_w, t_c, and μ. The effects on

Table 9.1. *The sign of the effect of parameters on equilibrium values*

Equilibrium values	Parameters						
	s_c	n	z	e	t_p	t_w	t_c
g^0	+	+	+	+	—	0	—
i^0	?	+	+	+	—	0	?
w^0	?	—	+	+	—	0	?
a^0	+	—	+	+	—	0	—
π^0	+	+	+	+	—	0	—

g^0 and w^0 are analyzed simply by inquiring how the two curves shift
the value of a parameter changes. The effect on i^0 is then analyzed
looking at equation (9.25) and the effect on a^0 is analyzed usin
equation (9.17). Finally, the effect on π^0 immediately follows sin
$\pi^0 = g^0 - \mu$. The result, without proof, is summarized in Table 9.1.

9.5   Policy implications and concluding remarks

A comparison of this table with Tables 5.1 and 8.1 yields tw
observations. First, the effects of three parameters exogenous to t
government, s_c, n, and z, are unchanged even when the governme
levies taxes, purchases goods, and issues money. Second, the effects
four fiscal policy variables, e, t_p, t_w, and t_c, stay the same whether
not the government issues money. Consequently, our discussions
the implications of three exogenous parameters (section 5.6 and Pa
III) and of fiscal policy (section 8.5) remain intact.

The policy variable newly introduced in this chapter is μ, the rate
increase of money supply. The preceding result shows that an increa
in μ affects the growth rates of both national income and lab
productivity adversely. An intuitive explanation follows. An increa
in μ induces less deflation (or more inflation) and less capital gains (
more capital losses). This will, on the one hand, reduce the saving
the economy (both corporate and noncorporate sectors) and reduce t
supply of funds. On the other hand, it will decrease the optimal grow
rate for the management by reducing the comprehensive profit and t
value of the firm, indicating that the demand for funds also decreas
The shifts of both demand and supply curves to the left, of cour
result in a smaller equilibrium amount of fund, that is, less investme
but an ambiguous change in the rate of interest. The incentive

earch and development also decreases because the target rate of
⸱wth of production has decreased.

In terms of monetary policy, therefore, our analysis so far suggests
⸱t increases in money supply should be restricted as much as possible
aster growth is desired.[2] Some readers, however, may question this
⸱ult because it is rather contradictory to the Keynesian thesis that
⸱netary expansion lowers the rate of interest and hence stimulates
⸱estment – although this thesis is basically on the short-run effect
d whether it is still true in a steady state where everything is
⸱rectly foreseen and no short-run disturbance occurs is not obvious.
Recall that to obtain the result in Table 9.1, α and β_c were assumed
⸱ensitive to the rate of return on shares, i, and that on money, π. This
⸱plies that the demand for money is primarily dependent on income
d profits and that little room is left for portfolio choices between the
⸱o financial assets; in other words, money is held primarily out of the
⸱ed for transactions and not out of speculative purposes. In this sense
⸱e may say that the model was more of the quantity theory (in its
⸱rrower sense) than of the liquidity-preference theory.

It should be of interest, therefore, to investigate a more Keynesian
⸱uation where liquidity preference plays a significant role in the
⸱mand for money. That is, consider a case where α and β_c are
⸱sitive to both i and π. Then, in equation (9.22), the signs of the
⸱rtial derivatives with respect to i and μ become more difficult to
⸱ermine. An increase in i shifts the v-g frontier downward as before
⸱t at the same time shifts it upward because of the decrease in α and
⸱ the cost of holding money. It seems reasonable to assume that the
⸱mer direct effect is strong enough to be still dominant; then, $G_1 \equiv$
⸱$/\partial i < 0$. Both increase in μ and the resulting decrease in π decrease
⸱pital gains from moneyholdings and thus v but at the same time
⸱rease v because of the decrease in α and in the cost of holding
⸱ney. Here let us assume that, contrary to the previous section, the
⸱ond portfolio effect dominates; that is, $G_6 \equiv \partial g / \partial \mu > 0$.

Now turn to equation (9.25). Here again, we have conflicting

⸱Note that our model assumes that transactions are carried out without any
⸱riction even if the quantity of money is very small and that economic
⸱rowth is not hampered even if the quantity of money is decreasing. One
⸱nay criticize this on the ground that some growth of M should be desirable
⸱o secure frictionless transactions. After all, even Friedman (1968) proposed
⸱ to 5 percent increase in M and not a constant amount of M!

effects. Both an increase in μ and the resulting decrease in π decrea
capitalists' capital gains and, consequently, their demand for shar
but at the same time decrease β_c, making more of their saving invest
in shares than money. Again, contrary to section 9.4, we assume th
the second portfolio effect dominates; that is, $f_4 \equiv \partial i/\partial \mu < 0$. Then v
find that, in equation (9.26), $\tilde{G}_7 = (G_1 f_4 + G_6)/(1 - G_1 f_1) > 0$ an
in equation (9.27), $\tilde{L}_5 = (\partial a/\partial i) f_4 /[1 - (f_1 - 1)(\partial a/\partial i)] > 0$, sin
$\partial a/\partial i = -wA'/(i - g) < 0$ and $f_1 > 1$, both contrary to the previo
analysis. This means that an increase in μ now shifts GG and L
curves upward, yielding of course a greater g^0 and an ambiguo
change in w^0. The effect on i^0 is ambiguous because, on the one han
an increase in μ itself decreases i but, on the other hand, the resulti
increase in g^0 increases i. If the latter repercussion effect (through t
change in g^0) is not so strong as to cancel out the former direct effect
lower i^0 results.

These results are exactly what one would expect as a long-r
version of the Keynesian theory on monetary policy. That is, we ha
shown that if the elasticities of money demand with respect to the ra
of return to alternative financial assets are sufficiently large as t
Keynesian liquidity-preference theory presumes, then we have t
Keynesian result even in a steady state to the effect that an increase
the rate of increase of money supply reduces the rate of interest a
stimulates investment, resulting in a higher rate of economic grow
Whether we should adopt an expansionary or restrictive moneta
policy to foster economic growth in a steady state, therefore, cannot
determined a priori without knowledge of how large the elasticities
money demand are.

As mentioned in section 9.1, our model (however large the elasti
ties are) resembles the quantity theory of money in the followi
(broader) sense: As long as i and μ are constant, income velocity
money is constant. This agrees with Friedman's definition of
quantity theorist:

> The quantity theorist accepts the empirical hypothesis that t
> demand for money is highly stable. . . . For the stability he expects
> in the functional relation between the quantity of money demand
> and the variables that determine it . . . The quantity theorist not or
> regards the demand function for money as stable; he also regards it
> playing a vital role in determining variables that he regards as
> great importance for the analysis of the economy as a whole, such
> the level of money income or of prices. [Friedman, 1956, p. 16]

Moreover, the constancy of income velocity of money in a steady state predicted in our model is consistent with Friedman's observation that "there is an extraordinary empirical stability and regularity to such magnitudes as income velocity that cannot but impress any one who works extensively with monetary data" (Friedman, 1956, p. 21).

We disagree with Friedman, however, in terms of the effectiveness monetary policy in controlling real variables. In our model a change the rate of increase of money supply changes not only the rate of inflation but also the rates of increase of real income, of capital, of labor productivity, and so forth. This sharply disagrees with the following statement by Friedman: "It (the monetary authority) cannot use its control over nominal quantities to peg a real quantity – the real rate of interest, the rate of unemployment, the level of real national income, the real quantity of money, the rate of growth of real national income, or the rate of growth of the real quantity of money" (Friedman, 1968, p. 11, my parentheses).

As a prescription to reduce the rate of inflation $(-\pi)$, the usefulness our analysis may be limited because of its concentration on a steady state, as well as of its neglect of other financial assets such as short-term and long-term bonds and of labor unions. Because most problems in real-world inflation arise from a short-run transition where expectations are not fulfilled and an adjustment to a long-run equilibrium is under way, our result, admittedly, may not be quite applicable to seek solutions to actual inflation. Supposedly, therefore, an analysis of how individuals and firms behave in a transitional period and how a short-run instantaneous equilibrium is reached is indispensable to a more fruitful discussion on inflation. Obviously, such a nonsteady-state analysis requires the discussion of extremely difficult questions that we have avoided in this book: What is the decision rule of growth-maximizing management in a nonsteady-growth path? How are the rate of increase of labor productivity a and the rate of increase of wage rate ξ related in a transition period? How the management expectation of ξ and π formed? How is the distribution of wealth between the two classes determined in the short run? How do individuals formulate expectations of ξ and π? And how they behave based on these expectations? And so on.

To answer these questions is a very difficult task and beyond the scope of the present study; however, the need for extending our study along this line is unquestionable.

PART V

Toward a dynamic theory of a multisector economy

The managerial sector versus the neoclassical sector

0.1 Introduction

ll foregoing analyses have assumed a homogeneous corporate sector; that is, the economy has been assumed to consist of a single type of rm – big corporations in which control is separated from ownership nd the management of which requires highly specialized skills. No ntry into the corporate sector has been assumed possible. This escription of firms, I believe, applies well to major companies in dvanced economies. It is also true, however, that there are numerous ny firms: farmers, "Ma-and-Pa" stores, automobile service stations, aundries, pizza restaurants, physicians, and so on. The capital equirement to establish this type of firm may be within the reach of aany, if not most, of the people. Likewise, its management may not equire the highly advanced skill and complex organization that are eeded in big corporations. Of course it requires some entrepreneurial alent and a venturesome spirit to start even a tiny firm; however, it aay be oversimplified to argue that no one will, when substantial rofits are expected. These facts suggest that it is perhaps more easonable to assume that those smaller firms with easy entry exist in n economy, in addition to the big corporations we have discussed so ar. This final chapter considers the question of whether the results in arlier chapters have to be modified when this coexistence of different ypes of firms is taken into account.

To facilitate the analysis, we take the simplest case and separate the conomy into two sectors, each of which consists of homogeneous firms. n one sector we have big corporations and in the other, smaller firms. 'he crucial difference between the two, we assume, is that entry from he noncorporate sector is impossible into the former even if the value f the firm (the present value of its net cash flow) exceeds the value of he capital, whereas entry is made into the latter in the same situation. 'his should force the value of the smaller firm equal to the value of the apital in equilibrium; that is, its valuation ratio should be unity. The valuation ratio for big corporations, however, may deviate from unit as in earlier chapters.

For lack of better terminology, let us call the sector with big corporations to which entry is impossible, *the managerial sector;* and the sector with small firms to which entry is free, *the neoclassic sector.* This latter terminology is used because these firms mostly conform to the assumptions of the orthodox neoclassical theory of the firm, as we will discuss in the next section.

Many readers may have already noticed the similarity between our argument and Galbraith's in his *Economics and the Public Purpose* (1973; 1975a), as evidenced by the following quotation:

> It follows that the economic system cannot usefully be dealt with as single unit. Ideally it should be considered as a continuum – procession of organizations extending in the United States from the simplest surviving family farm at the one extreme to American Telephone and Telegraph and General Motors at the other, and similarly from peasant to Volkswagen in other industrial countries But classification, even though it involves arbitrary lines, is the first step toward clarity. Little is lost and much is clarified by dividing business organization between two classes, those that deploy the full range of the instruments of power – over prices, costs, suppliers consumers, the community and the government – and those that do not. [Galbraith, 1975a, pp. 9–10]

Galbraith's position appears similar to ours because he regards the economy, be it the United States or Japan or wherever, as a conglomeration of firms with diverse size and power. In addition, we take the same stand as Galbraith in that, at least as a first approximation dividing these diverse firms into two categories is the most useful approach to analyze such an economy.

One should not overlook an important difference between Galbraith's argument and ours, however, which is mainly due to the different analytical methods and scopes employed by the two. Ours is theoretical analysis and in order to construct a rigorous mathematical model of the firm and the economy, we have ignored many aspects of big corporations, such as influence over consumers through advertising, oligopolistic interdependence, lobbying in Congress, and bargaining between management and labor unions. These were all discussed by Galbraith who was most concerned with the unequal distribution of power in its broadest sense between the two sectors (or systems, in his words) of an economy. Therefore we use "the managerial sector" and the neoclassical sector" to describe the two sectors instead of Galbraith's "the planning system" and "the market system." Although some readers may find our approach too austere, it is a necessary first step toward constructing a theoretically rigorous model of an economy with diverse sectors. As will be described next, several difficult problems arise even under this simplified situation. Still, however, we will show an interesting result from this simplified model.

Specific assumptions of the model are discussed in the following section. The equilibrium of the stock market is discussed in section 10.3 and the behavior of the firms is considered in section 10.4. The model of economic growth based on these assumptions and analyses is presented in the final section, with some concluding remarks.

10.2 Assumptions

As we have assumed, the basic difference between the managerial sector and the neoclassical sector (respectively denoted by subscripts m and n for any variable) is that entry is impossible into the former but is free into the latter. This should force v_n to unity; otherwise, people will find an opportunity to make extra money by entering (or leaving from) the sector. On the other hand, v_m may deviate from unity as before because, even if v_m exceeds unity and people find entry into the managerial sector profitable, they cannot do so for lack of the required managerial skill. An immediate consequence of this assumption is that the management of the neoclassical firm necessarily maximizes the market value of the firm and the valuation ratio. Otherwise, because the maximum potential valuation ratio is always unity due to free entry, the valuation ratio of this firm must be less than one and the owner will decide to exit in pursuit of better returns from other assets.[1] On the other hand, because we still assume that a takeover of a managerial firm is not without cost, the management of a managerial firm can pursue goals other than the valuation ratio, and the objective function discussed in Chapter 2 is still valid as long as our discussion in Chapter 1 is the true description of the motive of the management.[2]

Since v_n is always unity, capital gains always equal retained profits

---

Individuals are still assumed to be rational in the sense defined in Chapter 4 and to maximize their wealth.
This should explain why we call the sector "managerial."

in a steady state for the shares issued by a neoclassical firm.[3] Th
suggests that its share is, so to speak, a veil, as assumed by the orthodo
neoclassical theory, which does not play any role in determinin
equilibrium. Without loss of generality, therefore, we assume th
neoclassical firms do not issue shares.

Individuals in the noncorporate sector have three sources of incom
wages received by offering labor, returns from the shares of commo
stock issued by the managerial sector, and profits earned from ownin
neoclassical firms. In the following, we confine our analysis to
two-class economy where workers may save but their means of holdin
wealth is limited to shares, whereas capitalists may elect to ow
neoclassical firms besides shares. This is a simplification but we thin
reasonable, because owning and controlling a neoclassical firm usuall
requires full-time work which would prevent the owner from bein
employed by another firm.

Our next assumption pertains to the Penrose curve (see section 3.4
We assume that the cost of investment is determined according to th
Penrose curve for managerial firms but not for neoclassical firm
Instead, because neoclassical firms are usually small, they are assume
capable of increasing their stock of capital without adjustment cos
hence $I_n = \dot{K}_n$, or by dividing both sides by K_n, $\psi_n = g_n$.[4] Then, becaus
$v_n = (p_n - \psi_n)/(i - g_n) = (p_n - g_n)/(i - g_n)$, $v_n = 1$ implies $p_n =$
that is, the rate of profit for a neoclassical firm must equal the rate o
interest. This again conforms to the orthodox [pre-Uzawa (1969)
neoclassical theory.

Products are assumed different between the two sectors. This w
assume because, in most countries, big corporations dominate suc
industries as heavy industries, utilities, and communications, wherea
smaller firms prevail in other industries such as agriculture, retail, an
services [Galbraith (1973) raises arts as another example].[5] This list o
industries for each sector also suggests that most products of thos
industries dominated by big corporations are oriented toward bot
consumption and investment purposes, whereas those industrie
composed of smaller firms are mostly consumer oriented. Taking thi

---

[3] See equation (4.12): If $v_n = 1$ and if $g_n = \psi_n$ as we will soon assume, the
$G_n = r_n P_n$.
[4] The following discussion can easily be extended to the more general cas
where $\psi_n = \psi_n(g_n)$.
[5] See, for instance, Scherer (1970, p. 40).

nto account, we assume that investment goods are produced only by he managerial sector; that is, the two sectors produce different goods nd the managerial sector's product is used for the purpose of both nvestment and consumption, whereas the neoclassical sector's product s used only for the purpose of consumption.

Confining our analysis to a steady state, we now require, in addition o the previous properties of a steady state, a constant ratio of output etween the two sectors; hence both Q_m and Q_n must grow at a ommon rate. Because investment grows at the same rate, consumption f each of the two products must grow at the same rate as well. A teady state also requires the constancy of the relative price between he two products. These two factors together require that at a constant elative price with increasing income, consumers choose to allocate heir income into the two products at a constant proportion. This hoice would be rational if and only if their utility function is omothetic;[6] this we will assume.

As in Part II, we consider a closed economy without the government. The labor market is competitive and the wage rate is not differentiated etween the two sectors. The stock market (for the shares issued by the nanagerial sector) is perfect in the usual sense except that transaction osts are incurred in takeovers. Thus the Modigliani–Miller theorem s again satisfied.

Our final assumption pertains to the treatment of research activity y firms and the resulting technical progress. Let us maintain our ssumption that any technical progress is Harrod-neutral. In view of he vast R & D expenditures by big corporations noted in section 5.1, loubtlessly, research activity by managerial firms has to be incorpoated into our model; hence the assumption on research activity in ection 3.5 is maintained for the managerial sector. What about eoclassical firms? There is ample evidence that only a tiny fraction of mall companies expend for R & D and that even if they do, they only pend a small amount. In the United States, "in 1958 there were pproximately 283,000 manufacturing firms with fewer than 1,000 mployees. A formal R & D effort was maintained by somewhat etween 3 and 20 percent of those firms. . . . Thus, nearly all very arge manufacturing firms engage in some formal R & D, while only a

---

A utility function is homothetic if and only if any Engel curve is a ray through the origin, that is, if and only if the marginal rate of substitution stays constant whenever goods are consumed in constant proportion.

small fraction of the smallest companies do" (Scherer, 1970, p. 359).
More recent evidence shows that "companies with employment of les
than 5,000 numbered over 10,000, or 95 percent of R & D-performin₉
companies, but they accounted for just 10 percent of the industria
performance."[8] Similarly, in Japan in 1977, among 176,422 compa
nies investigated, 171,331 companies (93 percent of the total
employed less than 300 and only 9,580 companies among them – ₐ
mere 5.6 percent of them – did engage in research activity, and their R
& D expenditure accounted for only 10 percent of the total.[9]

In view of these facts, it appears acceptable simply to assume tha
neoclassical firms do not undertake research activity at all. Th₍
question, then, is: Is there any technical progress in the neoclassica
sector? Here seems to rest one of the most difficult problems i₁
analyzing an economy with more than one sector.

Suppose that there is no technical progress, namely, no increase i₁
labor productivity, in the neoclassical sector, but there is technica
progress at rate a in the managerial sector due to the research activit₉
undertaken. Then it must be that $\dot{Q}_n/Q_n = \dot{L}_n/L_n = \dot{N}_n/N_n$ in a stead₉
state where the labor–capital ratio (in efficiency units) stays constant
and at the same time $\dot{Q}_m/Q_m = \dot{L}_m/L_m = \dot{N}_m/N_m + a > \dot{N}_m/N_m.$
From these equations it follows that if the ratio of outputs is to sta₉
constant between the two sectors, employment has to be increased at ₐ
faster rate in the neoclassical sector than in the managerial sector, an₀
eventually almost all workers have to be employed in the neoclassica₁
sector; whereas if the ratio of the amounts of labor is to stay constan₊
between the two sectors, output has to increase at a faster rate in th₍
managerial sector than in the neoclassical sector, and eventually almos₊
all the output in the economy must come from the managerial sector.

---

[7] Chapter 15 of Scherer's book as well as Kamien and Schwartz (1975)
surveys the literature on the so-called Schumpeter hypothesis, namely, the
hypothesis that a larger and/or more monopolistic firm makes R & D
efforts more intensely. Much evidence suggests that large firms are much
more active in R & D than small firms are, as discussed in the text, but i₁
these large firms are further divided, it is not the largest firms, but the
moderately large firms that are most active. We should also note, however,
that not all existing studies agree with this conclusion.

[8] U.S. National Science Foundation, *Research and Development in Industry
1974* (Washington, D.C.: U.S. Government Printing Office, 1976), p. 6.

[9] Japan, Office of the Prime Minister, Bureau of Statistics, *Report on the
Survey of Research and Development, 1977* (Tokyo: Nihon Tokei Kyokai,
1978), p. 68, Table 2.

In short, a steady state cannot be sustained in this economy! The argument is not affected even if the rate of technical progress is not zero in the neoclassical sector unless it happens to equal a. This consideration leads us to conclude that to facilitate a steady-state analysis of a two-sector economy, one must assume that even if neoclassical firms do not pay for research activity they enjoy perfect spillover of the technical progress generated through research activity in the managerial sector. This is an uncomfortable assumption, especially if we recall the assumption made in section 3.5 that among managerial firms new technology can neither be bought nor stolen from others. Nevertheless, in the following analysis, we will maintain the preceding assumption.

These considerations may suggest the limitation of restricting the analysis to a steady state. We know that to analyze the long-run nature of the movement of a macroeconomy, a steady-state analysis could be powerful, as exemplified in our explaining all of Kaldor's (1961) stylized facts (see section 5.6). Unfortunately, however, an analysis of the relation between multiple production sectors or, in other words, of industrial structure seems to require more unless one entirely neglects technical progress. In fact, the disparity of the rates of increase of labor productivity among industries and among firms, and the resulting shift of industrial structure, must be one of the greatest concerns to economists and policymakers today. These problems are hard to discuss without considering scientific progress, governmental policy, world trade, and the change in taste. Leaving these problems to the future, our analysis here will concentrate on the steady-state macro-economic equilibrium and the interaction between the two sectors under the previous assumptions.

10.3 The stock market

In this model there are four markets: labor, stock, goods produced by the managerial sector, and goods produced by the neoclassical sector. We will first prove the Walras law for this economy. As a preparation, let us look at budget constraints. Workers receive wages and returns from their share ownership and allocate them to consumption and increasing share ownership; hence

$$Y_w = W_m + W_n + D_w + G_w$$
$$= C_{wm} + C_{wn} + \dot{V}_w \tag{10.1}$$

where $W_m(W_n)$ denotes wages received from the managerial (neoclassical) sector and $C_{wm}(C_{wn})$ denotes workers' consumption of managerial (neoclassical) sector's product. Other notation should need no explanation.

Capitalists receive not only returns from their share ownership but also profits from the neoclassical sector, P_n. They allocate this income between consumption, increasing share ownership, and increasing their ownership in the neoclassical sector. Because this last item must equal the investment in the neoclassical sector I_n, we have

$$Y_c = D_c + G_c + P_n$$
$$= C_{cm} + C_{cn} + \dot{V}_c + I_n \tag{10.2}$$

The managerial sector faces the same budget constraint as in section 4.3:

$$I_m = q\dot{N} + rP_m \tag{10.3}$$

where subscript m is suppressed for q (stock price), N (the number of outstanding shares) and r (retention rate), because these are relevant only for the managerial sector.

The following two equations define profits:

$$P_m = Q_m - wN_m - \phi(a)L_m$$
$$P_n = xQ_n - wN_n \tag{10.4}$$

where x denotes the price of the neoclassical sector's product in terms of the managerial sector's product, and $N_m(N_n)$ denotes man-hours of labor employed by the managerial (neoclassical) sector.

The equilibrium condition for the stock market is

$$\dot{V} = \dot{V}_w + \dot{V}_c$$

By substituting equations (10.1) and (10.2), we obtain

$$\dot{V} = W_m + W_n + D + G + P_n - C_m - C_n - I_n \tag{10.5}$$

where $D = D_w + D_c$, $C_m = C_{wm} + C_{cm}$, and so on. At the same time, by the definition of V, $\dot{V} = \dot{q}N + q\dot{N}$, which after substituting equation (10.3) is rewritten as $\dot{V} = \dot{q}N + I_m - rP_m$. By combining this equation with equation (10.5), rearranging, and using $G = \dot{q}N$ (equation (4.7)) and $D + rP_m = P_m$ (equation (4.6)), we obtain

$$C_m + C_n + I_m + I_n = W_m + W_n + P_m + P_n$$

Or substituting equation (10.4) and rearranging, we have

$$(Q_m - C_m - I_m - I_n - \phi(a)L_m)$$
$$+ (xQ_n - C_n) + (W_m + W_n - wN_m - wN_n) = 0 \tag{10.6}$$

The first parentheses vanish if the market for the managerial sector's product is in equilibrium, the second vanish if the market for the neoclassical sector's product is in equilibrium, and the third vanish if the labor market is in equilibrium. The equation, therefore, states that if the stock market is in equilibrium, then one of the three markets is necessarily in equilibrium whenever the other two are in equilibrium. This verifies the Walras law.

We now investigate the equilibrium of the stock market. Again, we assume constant saving rates, s_w and s_c, for workers and capitalists, respectively. Then, workers' saving will equal their income defined in equation (10.1), multiplied by s_w, and this is used up to increase their shareholdings because there is no alternative means of wealth ownership available to them; hence

$$\dot{V}_w = s_w (W_m + W_n + D_w + G_w) \tag{10.7}$$

Capitalists, on the other hand, can allocate some of their saving to increase their ownership in the neoclassical sector. The increment in their share ownership is thus the difference between their saving and their investment in the neoclassical sector:

$$\dot{V}_c = s_c(D_c + G_c + P_n) - I_n \tag{10.8}$$

The stock market is in equilibrium if and only if $\dot{V} = \dot{V}_w + \dot{V}_c$ or, by substituting equations (10.7) and (10.8), if and only if

$$\dot{V} = s_w(W_m + W_n + D_w + G_w) + s_c(D_c + G_c + P_n) - I_n \tag{10.9}$$

Again, however, a steady state requires a constant distribution of wealth between the two classes; hence V_w and $V_c + K_n$ must grow at a common rate, where K_n denotes total capital in the neoclassical sector and $\dot{K}_n = I_n$:

$$\frac{\dot{V}_w}{V_w} = \frac{\dot{V}_c + \dot{K}_n}{V_c + K_n} = \frac{\dot{V}_c + I_n}{V_c + K_n} \tag{10.10}$$

At the same time, note that $D_w + G_w = iV_w$, $D_c + G_c = iV_c$, and $P_n = iK_n$. The first two equations are immediate from the definition of the rate of interest. The last equation holds because the rate of profit in the neoclassical sector always equals the rate of interest by our assumption of free entry into the sector. Substitute these equations into equation (10.10), divide both sides by i, and substitute equations (10.7) and (10.8) to get

$$\frac{s_w(W_m + W_n + D_w + G_w)}{D_w + G_w} = \frac{s_c(D_c + G_c + P_n)}{D_c + G_c + P_n}$$

By multiplying both sides by $D_w + G_w$, we get

$$s_w(W_m + W_n + D_w + G_w) = s_c(D_w + G_w) \qquad (10.11$$

Note that this is identical to equation (4.21) in our proof of proposition 4.3. Surprisingly, an addition of a neoclassical sector to the managerial sector does not alter the requirement for a steady state.

The steady-state equilibrium condition for the stock market is now easy to obtain. Substituting equation (10.11) into equation (10.9) and using $D_w + D_c = D$, and so on, we obtain

$$\dot{V} = s_c(D + G) + s_c P_n - I_n$$

A steady state requires that $\dot{V} = v\dot{K}_m = vgK_m$ and $I_n = \dot{K}_n = gK_n$ because both K_m and K_n must grow at a common rate in a steady-state growth path. Also $D + G = iV = ivK_m$ by the definition of i, and $P_n = iK_n$ due to free entry. Using these, we rewrite the previous equation as

$$vgK_m = s_c ivK_m + s_c iK_n - gK_n$$

or

$$(g - s_c i)(vK_m + K_n) = 0$$

But since $vK_m > 0$ and $K_n > 0$, it must be that

$$g = s_c i \qquad (10.12$$

One will immediately notice that this equation is exactly identical to the condition we obtained as proposition 4.3. This is a surprising result: The condition (the generalized Pasinetti theorem) holds for the introduction of two sectors, managerial and neoclassical! This again demonstrates the robustness of the Pasinetti theorem. We showed in Part IV that the independence of macroequilibrium from workers' behavior is not affected by the introduction of taxes and money. We have now shown that it is also not affected by the addition of a nonshare-issuing sector.

10.4   The firms

Before proceeding to the discussion of general equilibrium, we should analyze the behavior of the firms. First, consider a managerial firm. At time t, it produces its output according to the production function $Q_m = F_m(K_m(t), L_m(t))$, sells it at unitary price, employs labor and pays $w(t)N_m(t)$, invests $I_m(t) = \psi(g(t))K_m(t)$, and spends $\phi(a(t))L_m(t)$ to achieve the desired increase in labor productivity $a(t)$. The present value of the net cash flow is

$$\int_0^\infty [F_m(K_m(t), L_m(t)) - w(t)N_m(t) - \psi(g(t))K_m(t) - \phi(a(t))L_m(t)]e^{-it}\, dt$$

At a steady state, $\dot{K}_m(t)/K_m(t) = g$, $L_m(t)/K_m(t) = l_m$, $\dot{A}_m(t)/A_m(t) =$ a, where $A_m(t) = L_m(t)/N_m(t)$, and $\dot{w}(t)/w(t) = \xi^e$, for any t, with constant g, a, l_m, and ξ^e. At a steady state, therefore, the present value per initial capital is

$$\int_0^\infty [F_m(1, l_m) - wl_m \exp((\xi^e - a)t)$$
$$- \psi(g) - \phi(a)l_m] \exp(-(i - g)t)\, dt \quad (10.13)$$

It is seen immediately that this equation is identical to equation (3.16), except for the addition of subscript m. The optimal values of l_m and a are, therefore, determined identically to those in section 3.5, as is the v-g frontier, indicating that the behavior of the managerial sector is not affected by the addition of the neoclassical sector.

A neoclassical firm produces according to $Q_n = F_n(K_n(t), L_n(t))$, sells it at price $x(t)$, employs $N_n(t)$ units of labor and pays $w(t)N_n(t)$, and invests $I_n(t)$ which is equal to $\dot{K}_n(t) = g(t)K_n(t)$. By assumption, however, they need not expend for research activity, even though $L_n(t)/N_n(t) = A_n(t)$ grows at rate $a(t)$ which is given to the firm. The present value of the net cash flow is

$$\int_0^\infty [x(t)F_n(K_n(t), L_n(t)) - w(t)N_n(t) - \dot{K}_n(t)]e^{-it}\, dt$$

At a steady state where $L_n(t)/K_n(t) = l_n$, $\dot{K}_n(t)/K_n(t) = g$, $x(t) = x$, $\dot{A}_n(t)/A_n(t) = a$, and $\dot{w}(t)/w(t) = \xi^e$, for any t, and l_n, g, a, ξ^e, and x are constant, the present value per its initial capital is

$$\int_0^\infty [xF_n(1, l_n) - wl_n \exp((\xi^e - a)t) - g]\exp(-(i - g)t)\, dt \quad (10.14)$$

The firm maximizes this expression with respect to l_n and g given w, i, x, ξ^e, and a.[10] Therefore the optimal values of l_n and g depend on w, i, x, ξ^e, and a, which give employment and investment functions over time for the neoclassical sector.

Instead of seeking these functions, however, we concentrate our analysis on a steady-state general equilibrium path as in Chapter 5. In

---

[10] Again, one may maximize equation (10.14) with respect to l_n to obtain the v-g frontier and then determine the optimal growth rate. Since the firm maximizes v_n, however, simple maximization of equation (10.14) with respect to l_n and g is sufficient.

such a path we know that the expected rate of wage increase ξ^e must equal its actual rate ξ, which, in turn, must equal the rate of increase of labor productivity a to maintain equilibrium in the labor market. Hence along any steady-state general equilibrium path, the valuation ratio v_n is written as follows, after substituting l_n with its optimal value.

$$
\begin{aligned}
v_n &= \int_0^\infty [xF_n(1, l_n^*) - wl_n^* - g] \exp(-(i - g)t)\, dt \\
&= \frac{xF_n(1, l_n^*) - wl_n^* - g}{i - g}
\end{aligned}
\tag{10.15}
$$

where l_n^* denotes the optimal labor-capital ratio and depends on w and x along a steady-state general equilibrium path.[11]

Because free entry requires a unitary valuation ratio for the sector, it must be that $v_n = 1$, or in view of equation (10.15),

$$
xF_n(1, l_n^*) - wl_n^* = i
\tag{10.16}
$$

which is an equation that determines one of w, i, and x, given the other two. In other words, once w, i, and x are determined so as to satisfy equation (10.16), v_n is unity irrespective of the growth rate and the choice of the growth rate by the firm is irrelevant. This conforms to the orthodox neoclassical theory where the optimal size of the firm is indeterminate due to the horizontal long-run average cost curve.

10.5   The model of economic growth

Because the behavior of the managerial sector has been proved to be unaffected by the introduction of the neoclassical sector into the model, we have, as before,

$$
a = a(w, i - g, \xi^e)
\tag{10.17}
$$

$$
g = g(i, w, \xi^e, z)
\tag{10.18}
$$

where z, again, denotes the index of management preference (of the managerial sector) toward growth. The stock market has been proved

---

[11] This is true because if $\xi^e = a$, l_n^* is the l_n that satisfies the following first-order condition:

$$
x\partial F_n(1, l_n)/\partial l_n = w
$$

This of course states that the value of the marginal product of labor must equal the wage rate.

to be in equilibrium if and only if

$$g = s_c i \tag{10.12}$$

The labor market is in equilibrium over time only if

$$g = n + a \tag{10.19}$$

In addition, a steady-state general equilibrium requires that

$$\xi^e = \xi = a \tag{10.20}$$

for the reason discussed in section 5.3.

These six equations constitute a system for six unknowns; w, i, g, a, ξ, and ξ^e. In comparing the six equations, (10.1), (10.4), (10.5), (10.6), (10.7), and (10.8) with those in section 5.3, one immediately notes that the two systems of equations are identical. The equilibrium values of these variables are determined, therefore, in exactly the same manner as in section 5.3 and, accordingly, the comparative analysis yields exactly the same result (see Table 5.2). This is remarkable: The result we obtained by analyzing a model of a single sector stands without any modification for a two-sector economy!

Does the neoclassical sector play a role, then, in this model? The answer is: No and yes. The neoclassical sector plays no role at all in determining the equilibrium values of the growth rate, the rate of interest, the wage rate, the rate of technical progress, and the rate of wage increase. However, it does play a role in determining the only remaining variable, the relative price x. The equilibrium relative price is determined, given i^0 and w^0 (superscript 0 is used for equilibrium values), according to equation (10.16), the requirement that the valuation ratio of the neoclassical sector is unity so that there is no further entry (or exit) into the sector. This is the only role the sector plays in this model of economic growth.

Summing up, we have constructed a simple model of economic growth for an economy consisting of not only the managerial sector but also of the neoclassical sector. Entry into the managerial sector was assumed impossible but entry into the neoclassical sector was assumed free. The two sectors were assumed to produce different goods with only the product of the managerial sector demanded for the purpose of invest-ment. The managerial sector was assumed to be able to generate technical progress through research activity, which fully benefits the neoclassical sector. Under these and other assumptions, we showed that the result obtained in section 5.3 stands without any modification.

The role of the neoclassical sector was confined to determining the relative price between the products of the two sectors.

The result is rather astonishing but strongly supports our discussion in previous chapters. We attempted to grasp the dynamics of modern advanced economies by viewing them as consisting of many, but a limited number of, big corporations, which are similar. We noted the importance that management preference of these big corporations has in determining the speed of economic growth, which was shown to explain very well the observed difference in the growth rate between the United States and Japan. Now, according to the result in this final chapter, our arguments do not lose any validity, even considering the coexistence of small firms with free entry and big corporations. This greatly enhances the applicability of our analysis and of the conclusion that management preference is one of the most important factors in determining the speed and property of a country's economic growth.

Another very interesting implication of the result pertains to the relative power of the two sectors: The equilibrium values of all the economic variables are determined solely as a consequence of the behavior of the managerial sector, whereas the neoclassical sector can only take these values as given. The one exception is the relative price that is determined through arbitrage by capitalists so that owning neoclassical firms is indifferent to holding the shares of managerial firms. In other words, the neoclassical sector has no power to affect the rate of economic growth or any other variable except the relative price which is determined so as to deprive the sector of any extra profit.

This conclusion, let us emphasize, was obtained from a simple, perhaps too simple, model without considering the government, trade unions, or advertising. Yet how similar it is to the conclusion reached by Galbraith who discussed all of them: "The planning system seeks to exercise control over its economic development, and . . . it succeeds. The market system manifests the same desire, is much more visible in its effort and is much less successful. The one system dominates its environment; the other remains generally subordinate to it" (Galbraith, 1975a, pp. 49–50).

Bibliography

Abegglen, James C. (1973). *Management and Worker: The Japanese Solution*. Tokyo & New York: Sophia University in cooperation with Kodansha International.

Ackley, Gardner with the collaboration of Ishi, Hiromitsu. (1976). "Fiscal, Monetary, and Related Policies," in *Asia's New Giant: How the Japanese Economy Works*, eds. H. Patrick and H. Rosovsky. Washington, D.C.: The Brookings Institution, pp. 153–248.

Adams, T. F. M. (1969). "Through Western Eyes," in *The World of Japanese Business*. eds. T. F. M. Adams and N. Kobayashi. Tokyo & Palo Alto: Kodansha International, pp. 13–225.

Alberts, William W. (1966). "The Profitability of Growth by Mergers," in *The Corporate Merger*, eds. W. W. Alberts and J. E. Segall. Chicago: University of Chicago Press. pp. 235–87.

Allen, R. G. D. (1967). *Macro-Economic Theory: A Mathematical Treatment*. London: Macmillan.

Arena, John J. (1965). "Postwar Stock Market Changes and Consumer Spending," *Review of Economics and Statistics* 47(4): 379–91.

Arrow, Kenneth J. (1962a). "The Economic Implications of Learning by Doing," *Review of Economic Studies* 29(3): 155–73.

(1962b). "Economic Welfare and the Allocation of Resources for Invention," in National Bureau of Economic Research, *The Rate and Direction of Inventive Activity: Economic and Social Factors*. Princeton, N.J.: Princeton University Press. pp. 609–25.

Baba, Masao. (1974). *Han-dokusen no Keizaigaku* (Economics of Anti-monopoly). In Japanese. Tokyo: Chikuma Shobo.

Baumol, William J. (1959). *Business Behavior, Value and Growth*. New York: Macmillan.

Berle, Adolf A. and Means, Gardiner C. (1932; 1967). *The Modern Corporation and Private Property*. New York: Macmillan; revised ed., New York: Harcourt Brace Jovanovich.

Blair, John M. (1972). *Economic Concentration: Structure, Behavior and Public Policy*. New York: Harcourt Brace Jovanovich.

Brechling, Frank. (1975). *Investment and Employment Decisions*. Manchester: Manchester University Press.

Bronfenbrenner, Martin. (1970). "Japan's Galbraithian Economy," in *Capitalism Today*, eds. D. Bell and I. Kristol. New York: Basic Books.

Burmeister, Edwin and Dobell, A. Rodney. (1970). *Mathematical Theories of Economic Growth*. New York: Macmillan.

Business Week. (1975). "Sumitomo: How the "Keiretsu" Pulls Together to Keep Japan Strong" (2374): 42–8.

211

Cary, William. (1969). "Corporate Devices Used to Insulate Management from Attack," *Antitrust Law Journal* 39(1): 318–24.

Caves, Richard E. and Uekusa, Masu. (1976). *Industrial Organization in Japan.* Washington, D.C.: The Brookings Institution.

Chao, Kang. (1968). "Labor Institutions in Japan and Her Economic Growth," *Journal of Asian Studies* 28(1): 5–17.

Charnes, A. and Cooper, W. W. (1959). "Chance-Constrained Programming," *Management Science* 6(1): 73–9.

Cole, Robert E. (1971). *Japanese Blue Collar: The Changing Tradition.* Berkeley: University of California Press.

    (1972). "Permanent Employment in Japan: Facts and Fantasies," *Industrial and Labor Relations Review* 26(1): 615–30.

Cyert, Richard M. and March, James G. (1963). *A Behavioral Theory of the Firm.* Englewood Cliffs, N.J.: Prentice-Hall.

Denison, Edward F. and Chung, William K. (1976). *How Japan's Economy Grew So Fast: The Sources of Postwar Expansion.* Washington, D.C.: The Brookings Institution.

The Developing Economies. (1970). *Special Issue: Postwar Japan, Part III. Aspects of Japan's Postwar Economic Development* 8(4). Tokyo: Institute of Developing Economies.

Duesenberry, James S. (1972). *Money and Credit: Impact and Control.* 3rd ed. Englewood Cliffs, N.J.: Prentice-Hall.

Foley, Duncan K. and Sidrauski, Miguel. (1971). *Monetary and Fiscal Policy in a Growing Economy.* New York: Macmillan.

Friedman, Milton. (1956). "The Quantity Theory of Money – A Restatement," in *Studies in the Quantity Theory of Money,* ed. M. Friedman. Chicago: University of Chicago Press, pp. 3–21.

    (1968). "The Role of Monetary Policy," *American Economic Review* 58(1): 1–17.

Futatsugi, Yusaku. (1976). *Gendai Nihon no Kigyo Shudan: Daikigyo-Bunseki o Mezashite* (Business Groupings in Modern Japan: Toward an Analysis of Big Corporations). In Japanese. Tokyo: Toyo Keizai Shimposha.

Galbraith, John K. (1967; 1972). *The New Industrial State.* Boston: Houghton Mifflin; New York: Mentor Book.

    (1973; 1975a). *Economics and the Public Purpose.* Boston: Houghton Mifflin; New York: Signet Books.

    (1975b; 1976). *Money: Whence It Came, Where It Went.* Boston: Houghton Mifflin; New York: Bantam Books.

Galenson, Walter with the collaboration of Odaka, Konosuke. (1976). "The Japanese Labor Market," in *Asia's New Giant: How the Japanese Economy Works,* eds. H. Patrick and H. Rosovsky. Washington, D.C.: The Brookings Institution, pp. 587–672.

Gordon, Robert A. (1945; 1961). *Business Leadership in the Large Corporation.* Washington, D.C.: The Brookings Institution; revised ed. with a new preface, Berkeley: University of California Press.

Hadley, Eleanor M. (1970). *Antitrust in Japan.* Princeton, N.J.: Princeton University Press.

Harrod, Roy F. (1939). "An Essay in Dynamic Theory," *Economic Journal* 49(193): 14–33.

Hayes, Samuel L., III and Taussig, Russell A. (1967). "Tactics of Cash Takeover Bids," *Harvard Business Review* 45(2): 135–48.

Hicks, John. (1965). *Capital and Growth*. London: Oxford University Press.

Hirose, Yuichi. (1963). *Kabushiki Gaisha Shihai no Kozo* (Structure of Corporate Management). In Japanese. Tokyo: Nihon Hyoron Shinsha.

Jensen, Michael C. and Meckling, William H. (1976). "Theory of the Firm: Managerial Behavior, Agency Costs and Ownership Structure," *Journal of Financial Economics* 3(4): 305–60.

aldor, Nicholas. (1956). "Alternative Theories of Distribution," *Review of Economic Studies* 23(2): 83–100.

(1957; 1960). "A Model of Economic Growth," *Economic Journal* 67(268): 591–624; reprinted in Kaldor, *Essays on Economic Stability and Growth*. London: Gerald Duckworth, pp. 259–300.

(1961). "Capital Accumulation and Economic Growth," in *The Theory of Capital*, eds. F. A. Lutz and D. C. Hague. London: Macmillan. pp. 177–222.

(1966)."Marginal Productivity and the Macroeconomic Theories of Distribution: Comment on Samuelson and Modigliani," *Review of Economic Studies* 33(4): 309–19.

and Mirrlees, James A. (1962). "A New Model of Economic Growth," *Review of Economic Studies* 29(3): 174–92.

Kamien, Morton I. and Schwartz, Nancy L. (1969). "Induced Factor Augmenting Technical Progress from a Micro-economic Viewpoint," *Econometrica* 37(4): 668–84.

and Schwartz, Nancy L. (1971). "Limit Pricing and Uncertain Entry," *Econometrica* 39(3): 44–54.

and Schwartz, Nancy L. (1972). "Uncertain Entry and Excess Capacity," *American Economic Review* 62(5): 918–27.

and Schwartz, Nancy L. (1975). "Market Structure and Innovation: A Survey," *Journal of Economic Literature* 13(1): 1–37.

Kaneko, Yoshio. (1970). "Employment and Wages," *The Developing Economies* 8(4): 445–74.

Kawaguchi, Hiroshi. (1970). " 'Over-Loan' and the Investment Behavior of Firms," *The Developing Economies* 8(4): 386–406.

Kennedy, Charles. (1964). "Induced Bias in Innovation and the Theory of Distribution," *Economic Journal* 74(295): 541–47.

Keynes, John M. (1936). *The General Theory of Employment, Interest and Money*. London: Macmillan.

Komiya, Ryutaro. (1966). "The Supply of Personal Savings," in *Postwar Economic Growth in Japan*, ed. R. Komiya. Translated from Japanese by Robert S. Ozaki. Berkeley: University of California Press, pp. 157–86.

Larner, Robert J. (1966). "Ownership and Control in the 200 Largest Non-financial Corporations, 1929 and 1963," *American Economic Review* 56(4): 777–87.

Lewellen, Wilbur. (1969). "Management and Ownership in the Large Firm," *Journal of Finance* 24(2): 229–322.

and Huntsman, Blaine. (1970). "Managerial Pay and Corporate Performance," *American Economic Review* 60(4): 710–20.

Lucas, Robert E., Jr. (1967). "Tests of a Capital-Theoretic Model of Technological Change," *Review of Economic Studies* 34(2): 175–89.

McGuire, Joseph W., Chiu, John S. Y., and Elbing, Alvar O. (1962). "Executive Incomes, Sales and Profits," *American Economic Review* 52(4): 753–61.

Manne, Henry G. (1965). "Mergers and the Market for Corporate Control," *Journal of Political Economy* 73(2): 110–20.

Mansfield, Edwin. (1968). *Technological Change*. New York: W. W. Norton.

Marglin, Stephen and Aoki, Masahiko. (1973). "Shihon-shugi no Mittsu no Moderu" (Notes on Three Models of a Capitalist Economy). In Japanese. In *Radical Economics*, ed. M. Aoki. Tokyo: Chuo Koron Sha, pp. 47–70.

Marris, Robin. (1964). *The Economic Theory of "Managerial" Capitalism*. London: Macmillan.

(1971a). "An Introduction to Theories of Corporate Growth," in *The Corporate Economy*, eds. R. Marris and A. Wood. Cambridge: Harvard University Press, pp. 1–36.

(1971b). "Some New Results on Growth and Profitability," in *The Corporate Economy*, eds. R. Marris and A. Wood. Cambridge: Harvard University Press, pp. 422–7.

(1972a). "Review of *The Ownership Income of Management* by W. G. Lewellen," *Journal of Economic Literature* 10(1): 491–3.

(1972b). "Why Economics Needs a Theory of the Firm," *Economic Journal* 82(325s): 321–52.

Marx, Karl. (1967). *Capital*, Vol. 1. New York: International Publishers.

Masson, Robert T. (1971). "Executive Motivations, Earnings, and Consequent Equity Performance," *Journal of Political Economy* 79(6): 1279–92.

Matthews, R. C. O. (1973). "The Contribution of Science and Technology to Economic Development," in *Science and Technology in Economic Growth*, ed. B. R. Williams. London: Macmillan, pp. 1–31.

Miller, Merton H. and Modigliani, Franco. (1961). "Dividend Policy, Growth, and the Valuation of Shares," *Journal of Business* 34(4): 411–33.

Miyazaki, Isamu. (1970). "Economic Planning in Postwar Japan," *The Developing Economies* 8(4): 369–85.

Miyazaki, Yoshikazu. (1972). *Kasen* (Oligopoly). In Japanese. Tokyo: Iwanami Shoten.

(1976). *Sengo Nihon no Kigyo Shudan* (Business Groupings in Postwar Japan). In Japanese. Tokyo: Nihon Keizai Shinbun Sha.

Mizoguchi, Toshiyuki. (1970). "High Personal Saving Rate and Changes in the Consumption Pattern in Postwar Japan," *The Developing Economies* 8(4): 407–26.

Modigliani, Franco and Miller, Merton H. (1958). "The Cost of Capital, Corporation Finance and the Theory of Investment," *American Economic Review* 68(3): 261–97.

Moore, Basil J. (1973). "Some Macroeconomic Consequences of Corporate Equities," *Canadian Journal of Economics* 6(4): 529–44.

(1975). "Equities, Capital Gains, and the Role of Finance in Accumulation," *American Economic Review* 65(5): 872–86.

Morishima, Michio. (1973). *Marx's Economics: A Dual Theory of Value and Growth*. Cambridge: Cambridge University Press.

Mueller, Dennis C. (1969). "A Theory of Conglomerate Mergers," *Quarterly Journal of Economics* 83(4): 643–59.

Nelson, Richard R., Peck, Merton J., and Kalachek, Edward D. (1967). *Technology, Economic Growth and Public Policy*. Washington, D.C.: The Brookings Institution.

and Winter, Sidney G. (1974). "Neoclassical vs. Evolutionary Theories of Economic Growth: Critique and Prospectus," *Economic Journal* 84(336): 886–905.

and Winter, Sidney G. (1977). "Simulation of Schumpeterian Competition," *American Economic Review* 67(1): 271–6.

Nerlove, Marc and Arrow, Kenneth J. (1962). "Optimal Advertising Policy under Dynamic Conditions," *Economica* 29(114): 129–42.

Nishiyama, Tadanori. (1975). *Gendai Kigyo no Shihai Kozo* (The Structure of Control in Modern Corporations). In Japanese. Tokyo: Yuhikaku.

Noda, Kazuo. (1966). "Postwar Japanese Executives," in *Postwar Economic Growth in Japan*, ed. Ryutaro Komiya. Translated from Japanese by Robert S. Ozaki. Berkeley: University of California Press, pp. 229–46.

Nordhaus, William D. (1969a). "An Economic Theory of Technological Change," *American Economic Review* 59(2): 18–28.

   (1969b). *Invention, Growth, and Welfare: A Theoretical Treatment of Technological Change*. Cambridge: M.I.T. Press.

Odagiri, Hiroyuki. (1974). "Kigyo no Choki Seicho-ritsu ni Ataeru Shudanka no Koka ni Tsuite" (The Grouping of Firms: Its Effect on Their Long-run Growth Rates). In Japanese with English summary. *Osaka Economic Papers* 24(1–2): 89–96.

   (1975). "Kigyo-shudan no Riron: Kigyo-kodo no Kanten kara" (A Theory of the Grouping of Firms). In Japanese. *Economic Studies Quarterly* 26(2): 144–54.

   (1977). *A Theory of Growth in a Corporate Economy*. Ph.D. dissertation, Northwestern University.

Ohkawa, Kazushi and Rosovsky, Henry. (1965). "A Century of Japanese Economic Growth," in *The State and Economic Enterprise in Japan*, ed. William W. Lockwood. Princeton, N.J.: Princeton University Press, 47–92.

Pasinetti, Luigi L. (1962). "Rate of Profit and Income Distribution in Relation to the Rate of Economic Growth," *Review of Economic Studies* 29(4): 184–96.

Patrick, Hugh and Rosovsky, Henry (eds.) (1976). *Asia's New Giant: How the Japanese Economy Works*. Washington, D.C.: The Brookings Institution.

Peck, Merton J. with the collaboration of Tamura, Shuji. (1976). "Technology," in *Asia's New Giant: How the Japanese Economy Works*, eds. H. Patrick and H. Rosovsky. Washington, D.C.: The Brookings Institution, pp. 525–86.

Penrose, Edith T. (1959). *The Theory of the Growth of the Firm*. Oxford: Basil Blackwell.

Phelps, Edmund S. (1966). "Models of Technical Progress and the Golden Rule of Research," *Review of Economic Studies* 33(2): 133–45.

Radner, Roy. (1975). "A Behavioral Model of Cost Reduction," *Bell Journal of Economics* 6(1): 196–215.

Ramanathan, R. (1976). "The Pasinetti Paradox in a Two-Class Monetary Growth Model," *Journal of Monetary Economics* 2(3): 389–97.

Reid, Samuel R. (1976). *The New Industrial Order: Concentration, Regulation, and Public Policy*. New York: McGraw-Hill.

Roberts, David R. (1956). "A General Theory of Executive Compensation Based on Statistically Tested Propositions," *Quarterly Journal of Economics* 70(2): 270–94.

Robinson, Joan. (1953). "The Production Function and the Theory of Capital," *Review of Economic Studies* 21(2): 81–106.

   (1962). *Essays in the Theory of Economic Growth*. London: Macmillan.

   (1963). "Findlay's Robinsonian Model of Accumulation: A Comment," *Economica* 30(120): 408–11.

   (1966). *An Essay on Marxian Economics*. 2nd ed. London: Macmillan.

216   Bibliography

(1971). *Economic Heresies: Some Old-Fashioned Questions in Economic Theory.* New York: Basic Books.

(1975). "The Unimportance of Reswitching," *Quarterly Journal of Economics* 89(1): 32–9.

Ruff, Larry E. (1969). "Research and Technological Progress in a Cournot Economy," *Journal of Economic Theory* 1(4): 397–415.

Samuelson, Paul A. (1962). "Parable and Realism in Capital Theory: The Surrogate Production Function," *Review of Economic Studies* 29(3): 193–206.

(1965). "A Theory of Induced Innovation along Kennedy-Weisäcker Lines," *Review of Economics and Statistics* 47(4): 345–56.

(1976). *Economics.* 10th ed. New York: McGraw-Hill.

and Modigliani, Franco. (1966). "The Pasinetti Paradox in Neoclassical and More General Models," *Review of Economic Studies* 33(4): 269–301.

Sato, Kazuo. (1971). "A Theory of the Saving Function," Discussion Paper, No. 166. State University of New York at Buffalo.

Scherer, Frederick M. (1970). *Industrial Market Structure and Economic Performance.* Chicago: Rand McNally.

Schumpeter, Joseph A. (1934). *The Theory of Economic Development: An Inquiry into Profits, Capital, Credit, Interest, and the Business Cycle.* (Translated by Redvers Opie from *Theorie der Wirtschaftlichen Entwicklung,* 2nd ed. 1926.) Cambridge: Harvard University Press.

Scitovsky, Tibor. (1976). *The Joyless Economy: An Inquiry into Human Satisfaction and Consumer Dissatisfaction.* London: Oxford University Press.

Shell, Karl. (1966). "Toward a Theory of Inventive Activity and Capital Accumulation," *American Economic Review* 56(2): 62–8.

(1967). "A Model of Inventive Activity and Capital Accumulation," in *Essays on the Theory of Optimal Economic Growth,* ed. K. Shell. Cambridge: M.I.T. Press, pp. 67–85.

(1973). "Inventive Activity, Industrial Organization and Economic Growth," in *Models of Economic Growth,* eds. James A. Mirrlees and N. H. Stern. New York: Halsted Press, pp. 77–96.

Simon, Herbert A. (1955). "A Behavioral Model of Rational Choice," *Quarterly Journal of Economics* 69(1): 99–118.

(1957). "The Compensation of Executives," *Sociometry* 20(1): 32–5.

Smiley, Robert. (1976). "Tender Offers, Transactions Costs and the Theory of the Firm," *Review of Economics and Statistics* 58(1): 22–32.

Smyth, David J., Boyes, William J., and Peseau, Dennis E. (1975). *Size, Growth, Profits and Executive Compensation in the Large Corporation: A Study of the 500 Largest United Kingdom and United States Industrial Corporations.* London: Macmillan.

Solow, Robert M. (1956). "A Contribution to the Theory of Economic Growth," *Quarterly Journal of Economics* 70(1): 65–94.

Stiglitz, Joseph E. (1969). "A Re-examination of the Modigliani-Miller Theorem," *American Economic Review* 59(5): 784–93.

(1972). "Some Aspects of the Pure Theory of Corporate Finance: Bankruptcies and Take-overs," *Bell Journal of Economics and Management Science* 3(2): 458–82.

and Uzawa, Hirofumi. (1969). "Introduction to Cambridge Growth and Distribution Theory," in *Readings in the Modern Theory of Economic Growth,* eds. J. Stiglitz and H. Uzawa. Cambridge: M.I.T. Press, pp. 309–13.

Sweezy, Paul M. (1942). *The Theory of Capitalist Development.* New York: Monthly Review Press.

Uzawa, Hirofumi. (1961). "Neutral Inventions and the Stability of Growth Equilibrium," *Review of Economic Studies* 28(2): 117–24.

(1965). "Optimum Technical Change in an Aggregative Model of Economic Growth," *International Economic Review* 6(1): 18–31.

(1969). "Time Preference and the Penrose Effect in a Two-Class Model of Economic Growth," *Journal of Political Economy* 77(4): 628–52, Part II.

Vogl, Frank. (1973). *German Business after the Economic Miracle.* London: Macmillan.

Wallich, Henry C. and Wallich, Mable I. (1976). "Banking and Finance," in *Asia's New Giant: How the Japanese Economy Works,* eds. H. Patrick and H. Rosovsky. Washington, D.C.: The Brookings Institution, pp. 249–316.

Williamson, John H. (1966; 1970). "Profit, Growth and Sales Maximization," *Economica* 33(129): 1–16; reprinted in *Readings in the Economics of Industrial Organization,* ed. D. Needham. New York: Holt, Rinehart and Winston, pp. 48–62.

Williamson, Oliver E. (1963). "Managerial Discretion and Business Behavior," *American Economic Review* 53(6): 1032–57.

Winter, Sidney G. (1971). "Satisficing, Selection and the Innovating Remnant," *Quarterly Journal of Economics* 85(2): 237–61.

Yaari, Menahem E. (1965). "Uncertain Lifetime, Life Insurance, and the Theory of the Consumer," *Review of Economic Studies* 32(2): 137–50.

Yarrow, G. K. (1976). "On the Predictions of Managerial Theories of the Firm," *Journal of Industrial Economics* 24(4): 267–79.

Index

Abegglen, J. C., 156
adjustment cost, 75, 96
animal spirits function, 144, 148
Arrow, K. J., 7, 81n, 111

Baumol, W. J., 2, 43
Berle, A. A., 26–8, 31–2
Boyes, W. J., 34–5

capital gains
    from moneyholdings, 178, 181, 184
    from shareholdings, 96
Caves, R. E., 37, 155n, 160n
chance-constrained programming, 55–6
Charnes, A., 55
Chiu, J. S. Y., 32–5
concentration, 21, 66–7
Cooper, W. W., 55
corporate economy, 2–4, 89–90, 146,
    148–50, 163
corporation, 3, 17
    see also firm

diversification, 24–5, 74

economic growth model
    Keynesian, 139–40, 144, 148–50
    neoclassical, 139–40, 143, 148–50
Elbing, A. O., 32–5
executive compensation, 31–7
    Simon's model, 32, 40, 61–2

factor price frontier, 141
firm
    behavioral or satisficing model, 43
    managerial theory, 2, 43–4
    neoclassical theory, 4
Friedman, M., 192–3

Galbraith, J. K., 6, 39–44, 157, 198–9,
    210
Germany, 151–2, 163
GG curve, 118–20, 175, 189
Gordon, R. A., 44
government expenditure, 169, 171, 176–
    7, 190

Harrod-Domar knife-edge problem,
    101, 109
Hayes, S. L., 65
hazard rate, 56–7, 78, 128
Hirose, Y., 28
Houghton, H., 24
Huntsman, B., 33–6

inflation, 180, 193

Japan
    administrative guidance, 162
    business grouping, 28–30, 159–60
    economic growth, 151–2
    economic planning, 162
    employment system, 155–8
    industrial organization, 154–5
    low-interest policy, 162
    management preference, 153–4, 160,
        164
    saving, 152–3
    takeover, 158–9
    technology importation, 161
    zaibatsu, 28, 159

Kaldor, N., 108n, 135, 140, 142, 145
Kamien, M. I., 56–8, 80n

Larner, R. J., 27–8
Lewellen, W., 33–6
liquidity-preference, 179, 191–2
LL curve, 118–20, 175, 189

219

McGuire, J. W., 32–5
management, 39
  control, 25–31
  utility, 57–64, 68, 78, 83, 125–7
management preference
  index of, 78-9, 83, 115–16, 120–1,
    131, 210
  in Japan, 153–4, 160, 164
Manne, H. G., 44n
Marris, R., 2, 33n, 36–7, 43–7, 55, 61,
    66, 71–4, 76n, 84, 108n, 112, 125n,
    128n
Marx, K., 139–40, 142–3, 148, 150
Masson, R. T., 35–7
Means, G. C., 26–8, 31–2
Miller, M. H., 71
  see also Modigliani-Miller theorem
Miyazaki, Y., 28–30
Modigliani, F., 71, 109n
Modigliani-Miller theorem, 52, 98, 103,
    107, 201
Moore, B. J., 91–2, 101, 108n
Mueller, D. C., 49

Nishiyama, T., 31
Nordhaus, W. D., 113

Odagiri, H., 49, 159–60

Pasinetti, L. L., 91–2, 106, 109, 141,
    174, 186, 206
Penrose curve (or effect), 75–6, 84, 96,
    125n, 200
Peseau, D. E., 34–5
portfolio choice, 179, 191
production function, 72, 80, 141, 171
promotion, 40–1, 157–8

quantity theory of money, 179–80,
    191–3

research and development, 4, 7, 80, 111–
    13, 120–1, 127, 133–4, 149–50,
    201–3

Roberts, D. R., 31–3
Robinson, J., 144, 148, 150, 161

Samuelson, P. A., 17, 109n, 111, 135
Schumpeter, J. A., 112, 139–40, 202n
Schwartz, N. L., 56–8, 80n
Scitovsky, T., 38
Shell, K., 80n, 113
Simon, H. A., 32, 43, 61
Smiley, R., 65
Smith, A., 15
Smyth, D. J., 34–5
Solow, R. M., 143, 148–9
steady state, 7, 72, 81, 93, 119, 131–3,
    170–1, 180, 193, 201–3
Stiglitz, J. E., 52, 103n
stock option, 35–6

takeover, 44–5, 48
  bid, 49–51, 158
  transaction cost, 48–50, 65, 78–9,
    126–8
Taussig, R. A., 65
tax, 169–70, 173–4, 176–9, 181, 184,
    190
technical progress, 139, 143, 145
  see also research and development
technostructure, 39–41, 157

Uekusa, M., 37, 155n, 160n
United Kingdom, 163
Uzawa, H., 75–8, 80, 84, 94, 113, 121

v-g frontier, 45–7, 68–9, 73, 75–7, 83,
    121–5, 149, 172, 183, 207
valuation ratio, 44–6, 96, 128, 148, 199
  minimum, 44–5, 47, 52–3

Walras law, 95–6, 173, 203–5
Williamson, J. H., 45n, 47n, 66
Williamson, O. E., 2, 43–4

Yarrow, G. K., 45n, 47n, 66